# Shaking Heaven and Earth

# Shaking Heaven and Earth

*Essays in Honor of Walter Brueggemann and Charles B. Cousar*

EDITED BY

Christine Roy Yoder

Kathleen M. O'Connor

E. Elizabeth Johnson

Stanley P. Saunders

WESTMINSTER JOHN KNOX PRESS
LOUISVILLE • KENTUCKY

*Book design by Sharon Adams*
*Cover design by Mark Abrams*

*First edition*
Published by Westminster John Knox Press
Louisville, Kentucky

This book is printed on acid-free paper that meets the American National Standards Institute Z39.48 standard. ♾

PRINTED IN THE UNITED STATES OF AMERICA

05 06 07 08 09 10 11 12 13 14—10 9 8 7 6 5 4 3 2 1

**Library of Congress Cataloging-in-Publication Data**

Shaking heaven and earth : essays in honor of Walter Brueggemann and Charles B. Cousar / edited by Christine Roy Yoder . . . [et al.].
p. cm.
Includes bibliographical references and index.
ISBN 0-664-22777-5 (alk. paper)
1. Church and the world—Biblical teaching—Congresses. 2. Bible—Criticism, interpretation, etc.—Congresses. I. Brueggemann, Walter. II. Cousar, Charles B. III. Yoder, Christine Elizabeth, 1968–

BR115.W6S42 2005
230—dc22 2005042245

# Contents

# Contributors

**Beverly Roberts Gaventa**
Helen H. P. Manson Professor of New Testament Literature and Exegesis
Princeton Theological Seminary, Princeton, New Jersey

**E. Elizabeth Johnson**
J. Davison Philips Professor of New Testament
Columbia Theological Seminary, Decatur, Georgia

**Leander E. Keck**
Winkley Professor Emeritus of Biblical Theology
The Divinity School, Yale University, New Haven, Connecticut

**J. Louis Martyn**
Edward Robinson Professor Emeritus of Biblical Theology
Union Theological Seminary, New York, New York

**Patrick D. Miller**
Charles T. Haley Professor of Old Testament Theology
Princeton Theological Seminary, Princeton, New Jersey

**Carol A. Newsom**
Professor of Old Testament
Candler School of Theology, Emory University, Atlanta, Georgia

**Kathleen M. O'Connor**
William Marcellus McPheeters Professor of Old Testament
Columbia Theological Seminary, Decatur, Georgia

**David L. Petersen**
Professor of Old Testament
Candler School of Theology, Emory University, Atlanta, Georgia

**Stanley P. Saunders**
Associate Professor of New Testament
Columbia Theological Seminary, Decatur, Georgia

**Louis Stulman**
Professor of Religious Studies
The University of Findlay, Findlay, Ohio

**Christine Roy Yoder**
Associate Professor of Old Testament Language, Literature, and Exegesis
Columbia Theological Seminary, Decatur, Georgia

# Preface

Walter Brueggemann and Charlie Cousar announced their respective retirements and then together led the Columbia Theological Seminary community in worship at its opening Convocation on September 11, 2002. The world on that bright autumn day was shaking with

> grief over the events of the previous year and dread that they might recur,
> anxiety about warfare in Afghanistan and impending war in Iraq,
> apprehension over the sturdiness of traditional moral values,
> doubt about wavering economic indicators,
> anger at intransigent injustice and persistent poverty across the earth,
> fear for the future of the so-called mainline church in North America, and
> nearly universal urgency to protect individual and national security.

Although the world has been shaking, of course, for much longer than since September 11, 2002—or 2001—the trembling seems more palpable in recent days. Charlie Cousar preached that September morning from Matthew's story about the conspiracy to foil Jesus' resurrection. The chief priests and Pharisees go to Pilate and say,

> "Therefore command the tomb to be made secure until the third day; otherwise his disciples may go and steal him away, and tell the people, 'He has been raised from the dead,' and the last deception would be worse than the first." Pilate said to them, "You have a guard of soldiers; go, make it as secure as you know how." (Matt. 27:64–65)[1]

The quests for security in the midst of cosmic shaking, said Cousar, are prompted not so much by the fear of death as the fear of life. "The resurrection, by opening up the past as it does—with its unresolved relationships and awareness of failures—always arouses in us the fear of living."[2] The gospel of Christ crucified and raised, while it can calm fear and offers the security of God's own love, also *un*settles and *de*stabilizes the world by judging the old order and invading it with the new. No amount of human or homeland security is able to protect against the transforming power of the God who creates out of nothing, who rescues sinners, and who raises the dead.

This capacity to bring the Bible, the church, and the world into confrontation and conversation has characterized the careers of Charlie Cousar and Walter Brueggemann in the church, the classroom, and the academy for an aggregate of eighty-some years. Any tribute to them must attend to the clash of worlds provoked by the proclamation of the Word of God that they have taught us to look for, to recognize, and to welcome. Columbia Theological Seminary therefore designed its 2003 Colloquium to hear from interpreters of Scripture whose work Brueggemann and Cousar have influenced. Over two hundred conversation partners—friends, colleagues, and students past and present—gathered in April 2003 for the discussion that has resulted in this book. The Colloquium, titled "Shaking Heaven and Earth: Bible, Church, and the Changing Global Order," took its inspiration from the vision in Haggai of God's shaking the entire universe in order to make the restored Temple even more glorious than the one that had been destroyed.

> For thus says the LORD of hosts: Once again, in a little while, I will shake the heavens and the earth and the sea and the dry land; and I will shake all the nations, so that the treasure of all nations shall come, and I will fill this house with splendor, says the LORD of hosts. The silver is mine, and the gold is mine, says the LORD of hosts. The latter splendor of this house shall be greater than the former, says the LORD of hosts; and in this place I will give prosperity, says the LORD of hosts. (Hag. 2:6–9)

Anticipation of similarly cataclysmic redemption brings the same text to the mind of an early Christian writer who looks at a world shaking under the impact of the unthinkable, the destruction of the Second Temple. The writer of Hebrews says,

> At that time [God's] voice shook the earth; but now he has promised, "Yet once more I will shake not only the earth but also the heaven." This phrase, "Yet once more," indicates the removal of what is shaken—that is, created things—so that what cannot be shaken may remain. (Heb. 12:26–29)

Haggai's listeners think that they are responsible to recreate the glory of God's house after its destruction by the Babylonians. The prophet insists instead that God will restore the Temple. God shakes the prevailing world order so as to rebuild it. The writer of Hebrews claims that the word of God's redemption rattles not only the earthly Temple destroyed by the Romans but heaven itself to unveil the gospel that is firm and solid and trustworthy. These texts—and others like them—provided the lenses through which the conversation honoring Cousar and Brueggemann sought to interpret the global shaking of our time. These essays seek to understand and address the fears evoked by the present shaking of families and domestic morality, by global political upheaval, by assaults against political and economic empires, and by international struggles for cultural supremacy.

Walter Brueggemann and Charlie Cousar have told us repeatedly to watch for the ways God's Word shakes the earth; they have assured us that God's realm is unshakable; and they call us to respond to the shaking of God's Word and the unshakability of God's realm with worship, with reverence, and with thanksgiving. In celebration of that wisdom, and for their countless other gifts to us of collegiality and friendship, we offer this book to them with deep love and gratitude.

Christine Roy Yoder
Kathleen M. O'Connor
E. Elizabeth Johnson
Stanley P. Saunders

*Decatur, Georgia*
*The Day of Atonement, 2004*

## NOTES

1. Cousar's translation. "Make It as Secure as You Know How: Matthew 27:55–28:10," *Journal for Preachers* 26, no. 3 (2003):16–19, reprinted in this volume, 1–7.
2. Ibid., 18.

1

# Make It as Secure as You Know How

*Charles B. Cousar*

On a warm day in mid-November of 2001 a number of us from the seminary—faculty and students—were traveling to Denver to a meeting of the Society of Biblical Literature and the American Academy of Religion. In the airport in Atlanta, we passed through the security checks and made our way to our various gates of departure. Only when we were settled in, awaiting the call of our flights, did we hear the announcement that for some reason we were to vacate the airport. Toting our carry-on luggage, we walked back through the airport, up the escalators, through all the security checkpoints, initially at least, not knowing exactly the reason for the evacuation. Thousands of passengers, plus pilots, flight attendants, and other employees were herded outside the airport to wait for about four hours (and with no access to restrooms). As you can imagine, we were not happy campers.

As we later discovered, a University of Georgia football fan, once having cleared security, had tried to go back and pick up his child's lost toy, and in doing so had run up a down escalator. His actions set the nervous security personnel aflutter. All of our flights were cancelled, leaving us with the uncertainty of when we would ever get to Denver.

Of course since last September the issue of heightened security has become a national one. We have *all* had our experiences with security checks at the airport. The airlines probably own more pairs of nail clippers than anyone else in human history. We now have a new department of homeland security, and

A Sermon on Matthew 27:55–28:10, preached at Opening Convocation, Columbia Theological Seminary, September 11, 2002. Charles B. Cousar, "Make It as Secure as You Know How: Matthew 27:55–28:10," *Journal for Preachers* 26/3 (2003):16–19. Used with permission. *Journal for Preachers*, P.O.B. 520, Decatur, GA, 30031.

a member of the president's cabinet recently made the suggestion that rather than being neighborly we should keep a close eye out on our neighbors and report any suspicious activity we encounter. At the major Fourth of July celebrations last summer, planes from air force units circled overhead to reassure us that all was well.

Of course we have known about security measures for a long time. Many of us live in homes where we punch in the codes when we leave and when we return. Even here at the seminary we need to know the right combinations to enter buildings at night and on the weekends.

On that November afternoon last fall as Professor Kathleen O'Connor and I were standing outside the Atlanta airport, trying to be as cheerful as we could (she succeeding, as you could imagine, much better than I), I remember overhearing another passenger whom I did not know comment about the problem of security. He predicted that we would experience a number of false alarms in the future and give up many of our civil rights. "After 9/11 we are going to have to get used to security checks, even when they are frivolous. It is the only way to be safe, and we have got to make our country as secure as we can."

Somehow this passenger's words began to ring a bell in my mind. When had I heard that phrase before—"make it as secure as we can"? It was at the burial of Jesus. In Matthew's account, Joseph of Arimathea, a wealthy disciple, had claimed the body of Jesus from Pilate following the crucifixion, had placed it in a tomb, and had rolled a huge stone against the door of the tomb—a very generous thing to do, protecting the body from dogs and other wild animals.

Word had gotten out that Jesus had predicted that he would be raised on the third day. And so the religious leaders went to Pilate and petitioned him to make the tomb even more secure. "Otherwise his disciples may go and take away this imposter," they said, "and then tell the people that he has been raised from the dead. That will leave us in a worse mess than ever."

Pilate, who often speaks in the gospel narratives with an ironical twist, sneered at the religious leaders, "You have a guard of soldiers; go, make the tomb as secure as you know how." "Make it as secure as you possibly can." And we, in our preoccupation with national security, begin to squirm a bit, and our hair stands on end.

But the religious leaders did make the tomb secure. They sealed the stone and set a guard of soldiers to keep watch. The apocryphal Gospel of Peter goes to great detail in telling how the soldiers sealed the stone with seven seals. Then they pitched a tent before the tomb and settled in to prevent any tampering or deception.

Here's the picture: a dead body laid in a tomb carved out of rock, a huge stone covering the entrance to the tomb, the stone sealed up tight, and outside a squad of soldiers keeping watch. Sounds like pretty good homeland security to me!

Let's not be too hard on these religious leaders. They had worked to engineer this crucifixion. They had jockeyed back and forth between the high priest and the Roman governor. And they naturally wanted to keep things as they were—Jesus dead and the disciples scattered and fearful. That's the meaning of security—protection of what we have, protection against loss and risk; keeping things normal; not messing with our minds or our pocketbooks; not exposing us to change and the new. It's quite simple; we want to feel safe. After all, we've got things worked out pretty well. Why *not* take realistic precautions to keep things in place, to maintain the status quo?

What happened the next morning shattered such security forever. The two Marys, who had faithfully stuck by Jesus throughout the ordeal of his crucifixion, devastated by grief and despair, came to the tomb. They came to grieve the loss of their dear friend. Instead, they felt the earth tremble under their feet as they experienced God's rule erupting with volcanic force. They saw a strange messenger of God, a surreal figure, standing in the tomb, all dressed in white. The huge stone, carefully sealed, was rolled back, and the soldiers set to guard the tomb were so stunned by the sight that they were helpless and afraid, no more than corpses themselves. The body of Jesus was gone. So much for homeland security!

The women had come to see a tomb, to pay their respects to a deceased friend, to grieve the loss of one they loved; instead they met this messenger of God, who declared that Jesus had risen and would meet them in Galilee. Security left in shambles; protection gone; safe no longer; exposed in a way that they can hardly understand; open to all sorts of threats and dangers.

As we begin a new school year in a time of national and international insecurity, we do well to learn from these faithful women about what life is like after the shattering of a security—out there in a world of risk, of collapse, and now of a heightened uncertainty about the economy. Three features of their experience with the resurrection are significant. The first thing is *fear*. The same Greek word used for the fright of the soldiers, who are so stunned by the events as to be rendered helpless, is used for the women as well. No doubt about their fright at what they had seen and experienced. Their natural, normal world was disrupted. They had come to a quiet garden to meditate and to grieve; instead they had experienced an earthquake. What were they to think? This new and incalculable life had broken into their lives. It is not the fear of dying that engulfs them. If anything, it is the fear of life here and now, the scariness of the moment, the uncertainty of what living in the days ahead will be like.

Stuart McWilliam, who taught here for many years, used to tell of Robert Louis Stevenson's having received a letter from a rather pompous missionary. Stevenson was critically ill, and the missionary wanted to come and talk to him "as a man in danger of dying." Stevenson replied with his characteristic humor that the missionary should visit him as "a man in danger of living. I am a very sick man, but suppose I get better! Any fool can die, as a matter of fact, all do. I'm going to need much more help if I go on living." The resurrection, by opening up the past as it does—with its unresolved relationships and awareness of failures—always arouses in us the fear of living.

And yet the women left the tomb "with fear *and great joy*." Their fear differed from that of the soldiers because, though truly frightened, the two Marys had an inkling that the powers that had crucified Jesus were defeated. The ground under their feet had shaken. His promises made in his lifetime were coming true. No matter how much money the religious authorities paid the soldiers to concoct a story about his body being stolen, these women knew that the resurrection was no deception but the truth. They say to us that it is all right to be afraid, if fear can be experienced in the context of God's having raised Jesus from the dead.

Second, the two Marys were given a job to do. They were *to go and tell the others* what the messenger of God had told them. "Go quickly and tell his disciples that he is going ahead of you to Galilee. There you'll see him." And as Matthew reports it, they ran quickly to spread the news. Easter is a message about the God who raised Jesus from the dead and who is our only hope in life and in death—our only security. The women are given the risky job of telling the story that in the perilous face of death there is God.

It's not an easy assignment. In Luke's account we read that some thought their message an idle tale and dismissed the women as irrelevant. It's not just a story of a resuscitated corpse or the miracle of the empty tomb they were to announce, but the defeat of the power of death. And that's a hard word to sell when a war is going on and when people are frantically clinging to a national invulnerability and to the notion that God is "on our side." It's a hard word to sell when people would prefer to sing "God bless America" than to say, "Let's go to Galilee."

And "to Galilee"—not so much a place on a map, as the place where Jesus had initially entered the routine of the daily lives of these disciples; where they fished and argued with one another. Galilee was not a place of power, but a less significant, marginal area; yet it was the territory where most of Jesus' ministry had been carried out. It was in Galilee, not in the holy city of Jerusalem or the power and glitter of Washington, where he promised to meet them. It was amid the routine of reading books and discussing theology, of visiting hospitals and leading youth groups, of spending a night at the shelter or demonstrating hospitality at East Lake, of writing papers and, dare I suggest, parsing Greek verbs, that Jesus promised to bring God's reign of justice and love.

Finally, as the women go about their task of witnessing to the resurrection, Jesus encounters them. He doesn't say much really, except "Greetings!" and then repeats the messenger's word that they should go into Galilee. But they are confident now that his resurrection is no longer a promise but a reality, for we read, the women *worshipped him*. Actually the narrative says that they "took hold of his feet and kissed them"—a gesture to acknowledge their total dependence on him, their complete submission to the risen Lord.

Don't dismiss this act of worship too lightly. We are not talking about a narcotic trip into another world, when worship becomes an escape. This is no "sweet hour of prayer that calls us from a world of care." In the face of an insecure world, these women were on their knees before Jesus. But the women had to let go of the feet of Jesus in order to carry the message they had to deliver. There comes the moment when we have to leave behind the sanctuary and go to meet Christ in the world. But worship, where we dare to acknowledge the insecurities of this world for the security of the risen Christ, is where it all begins. It is in this posture of self-giving that fires are ignited. To put it in Barth's famous phrase, "To clasp the hands in prayer is the beginning of an uprising against the disorder of this world."

So as we start this new academic year, our text poses the question: Where is our ultimate security to be found? What is our only "hope in life or in death"? Is it to be found in a national program of self-defense, in pistol packing pilots who are to foil the efforts of every highjacker, or is it found in the God who sends us into an insecure world to tell the story and who goes before us into the many Galilees of this world? May God give us the grace to follow the two Marys, who acknowledged their fear, who obeyed the messenger's directive to tell the story, and who worshipped the risen Christ.

[After completing the initial draft of this sermon, I came across a fine Easter sermon on the same text by Patrick Willson, pastor of the Williamsburg Presbyterian Church, Williamsburg, Virginia. I am sure I picked up some of Willson's phrases in my revision. I am grateful also to George Stroup, who read the draft and made several helpful suggestions.]

2

# Genesis 2–3 and *1 Enoch* 6–16: Two Myths of Origin and Their Ethical Implications

*Carol A. Newsom*

As is well known, origin myths are not only etiologies for how the world came to be the way it is but also statements of fundamental values and convictions. Though cast as narratives about a distant past, they have a strong normative function. The moral imaginations embedded in particular myths of origin establish perceptual frameworks that have implications for evaluating novel situations and directing appropriate decisions. Although Christian theology found its primary myth of "the Fall" in Genesis 2–3, not all strands of contemporary Judaism saw that story as the crucial explanation of the brokenness of the world. For certain apocalyptically oriented Jews the fundamental story of the origin of evil in the world was the elaboration of Gen. 6:1–4 as it is found in *1 Enoch* 6–16. The book of *1 Enoch* was also quite influential in early Christianity, though it eventually declined in popularity until it came to be regarded as authoritative only in Ethiopian Christianity. I wish to make a case, however, for the continuing theological and ethical significance of the book, particularly as that significance is seen by putting it into conversation with Genesis 2–3. In these stories one finds two narratives that tell of events that truly "shook the earth and the heavens" through the audacity of the actions of their protagonists but that also elicit a divine shaking of heaven and earth. Considering these narratives invites reflection on contemporary actions and decisions that are themselves quite as "earthshaking" and that could be seen as inviting a similar divine response: "'Yet once more, I will shake not only the earth but also the heaven'" (Heb. 12:26).

No one has done more than Walter Brueggemann to direct our attention to the forms of moral imagination in the Bible. It is with gratitude for his work that I dedicate this article to him.

These two stories are strikingly different. They pertain to different periods of the Bible's primeval history, involve different characters, and have different plots. More significantly, they articulate strikingly different moral imaginations. Nevertheless, they both employ some of the same images, figures, and themes, though these function quite differently. Here are two texts that ought to get together and have a conversation. As valuable as it might be simply to compare and contrast these two texts with one another, I think more may be elicited from such a dialogue. Every moral imagination is a way of perceiving and a way of thinking. If one can characterize the contrasting moral imaginations of these texts, might it be possible to think with their resources about a modern ethical dilemma, say, for example, the issue of cross-species genetic manipulation? Such a venture may sound far-fetched, but it might suggest a model for engaging the Bible in ethical reflection.

In what follows I wish to do three things: first, to reflect on why some of the issues raised in origin myths never go away: specifically, what the nature of the human being is and what the nature of the world is; second, to conduct a comparison of the two stories in Genesis and *1 Enoch*. In particular, I want to draw attention to what I see as an implicit conversation between the two texts concerning (1) the role of desire as constructive or destructive of the human and its world, and (2) the significance of the figure of the "monster," that is, the creature who mixes two natures. Finally, I want to show how the basic understanding of the world sketched in these two texts can lead to contrasting but equally profound moral stances toward the same issue, using for the purpose of illustration the example of cross-species genetic manipulation.

## I. THE PERSISTENCE OF ORIGIN MYTHS

Though modern culture may no longer set its stories in the long ago and far away, popular culture—novels, movies, especially science fiction—is often concerned to raise certain questions characteristic of origin myths: What does it mean to be a human being? What is the nature of the world and our proper place in it? The persistence of these questions is illuminated by the insight made by Clifford Geertz, who observed that human beings are "incomplete animals." Whereas other animals have their instincts sufficiently "hardwired" into their brains to function successfully, humans do not. Consequently, we have to complete ourselves and our worlds through the symbolic constructions of culture.[1] The question about what a human being is can never be settled once and for all because there is no final answer. The stories we tell construct possible identities, but those identities may be questioned and contested by other stories.

Whenever one tries to define something (e.g., a human being) one tends to do so by comparison or contrast. How is this like or unlike that? What is the boundary marker between this and that? Naturally enough, in the stories of origin that try to say what a human being is, one of the ways of doing so is by comparing or distinguishing humans from animals, or humans from divine beings. In our modern world we have added a third set of comparisons: humans and machines. Such boundaries, however, are always constructed rather than given and involve very specific decisions about what feature or features will mark the boundary between humans and animals, humans and machines, humans and gods. The fact that these boundary lines have to be constructed also means that they are always fragile and subject to falling apart. If language distinguishes humans from animals, what about animals who can be taught to use sign language? If the ability to think and feel is the boundary between humans and machines, what about artificial intelligence computers that some argue can actually think—and perhaps may even come to have emotions? Not only science fiction, but philosophy, too, is now puzzling over the ethical status of the machines of the future. As for the difficult boundary between humans and gods, that is the concern of Genesis 2–3, namely, the ways in which we have become "like gods" but are not gods.

These perplexities are intrinsic to the task of conceptual boundary making. But the modern world faces additional dilemmas now that science is quite literally dissolving some of the taxonomies that used to organize our world. When animal organs and tissues are placed in human bodies, when genes can be transferred from animals to plants to humans and vice versa, when we are increasingly becoming "bionic" persons, with a variety of implanted machines, the boundaries that distinguish person, animal, and machine are put in question. How to deal with the fluidity of such boundaries poses not only conceptual but ethical dilemmas. Are there some boundaries that are sacrosanct? Or is this process simply part of the creation of new life forms?

## II. GENESIS AND *1 ENOCH*

At this point I wish to examine what these two stories of origin, Genesis 2–3 and *1 Enoch* 6–16, have to say about what it means to be human, what the nature of the world is, and how it came to be the way it is today. Despite the lack of overlap in these stories, each examines what it considers to be *the* crucial episode by which the world acquired its present reality. The story in Genesis is fundamentally preoccupied with the issue of what it means to be human. It tells how what was not yet recognizable as fully human (the creature *'adam*) comes to be what we know as human (having two sexes, equipped with moral agency, pursuing life outside the garden). This story deals explicitly with the question of the boundary between the animal and the human on the one hand and the divine and the human on the other. The stories that follow, especially in Genesis 4–11, deal with the consequences for the world of the unintentionally constructed human, consequences that include the emergence of evil and its containment.

The relevant story in *1 Enoch* starts with human beings already in place. Its primary focus is not on constructing the human. Rather, it is concerned with the origin of evil in the world, how humans came to be corrupted, and why the world is a broken world.[2] It explores this topic, however, largely by means of the figure of violated boundaries, especially the boundary between the divine and the human. And in telling this story about the brokenness of the world, it does have important things to say about the nature of human existence.

From this brief characterization, it should be evident why these stories invite comparison. In Genesis the critical action starts with a desire of the human for that which belongs to the divine (the knowledge that makes one like the gods). In *1 Enoch* the action starts with a desire of the divine (the angels) for that which properly belongs to humans (sex and procreation). Desire is thus an important element in both stories, as is the role of transgressed boundaries. In both, knowledge plays an important role. Humans *take* knowledge in Genesis, and in *1 Enoch* angels *give* heavenly knowledge to humans. In Genesis humans are active agents. But in *1 Enoch* humans appear to be more sinned against than sinning—at least at first. In sum, though these two stories ostensibly narrate episodes from different periods of the mythic history of the human race, at the level of theme and imagery they appear to be very much in competition and conflict about the nature of the world and of human beings.

## A. Genesis 2–3

As many commentators have observed, the Christian theological interpretation of Genesis 2–3 simply as a narrative of a "fall" is somewhat misleading. From a comparative religions perspective, Genesis 2–3 is perhaps better described as a birth story, one that describes the birth of humans and the birth of culture. In order to tell this story, it has to construct two boundaries: the animal/human and the human/divine.

Animals are first introduced in Gen 2:18–20 in response to God's perception that "it is not good for *hā-'ādām* to be alone." The intention is to form "a helper corresponding to him." Every detail of the text appears to assert the fundamental commonality between humans and animals. Not only are they made from the same substance (the *'ădāmâ*), but God also seems to anticipate that *hā-'ādām* will find his companion among them. That is, of course, the purpose of the naming. If *hā-'ādām* gives a name to an animal that establishes some sort of linguistic relationship with his own name, then that will be the sought-for companion. But *hā-'ādām* does not in fact recognize such a helper among the animals. The pun of recognition appears only when God has decided to "subdivide" *hā-'ādām*, who declares in verse 23: "This is woman [*'iššâ*], for from man [*'îš*] she was taken." Though the episode *hints* at a difference between these not-quite-yet-humans and the animals, it ends without constructing a clear boundary between them. That boundary will emerge only later, as a consequence of the *confusion* of the boundary between humans and divine beings.

That crucial episode is the one involving the tree, the talking snake, and the conversation. The snake engages the woman in conversation about which trees are and are not off limits to the man and woman. When the woman identifies the tree of the knowledge of good and bad as the one that cannot even be touched upon pain of death, the snake refutes her judgment and insists, correctly, that the humans will not die: "But God knows that on the day you eat of it, your eyes will be opened, and you will be like gods, knowing good and bad" (3:5, author's translation). The knowledge that comes from the fruit is, as many commentators have argued, not simply knowledge of moral good and evil but rather the knowledge that makes all kinds of judgments possible, the power to make reflective, discriminating choices between what seems good and what seems bad.

The significance of the next line (3:6) is debated. It describes the woman's seeing the fruit and taking it. One might object that the woman already seems to have the power to choose between good and bad because she *chooses* to eat the fruit, even though the power of choice should be the consequence of that act. Perhaps it is the storyteller's failure in the face of a difficult narrative moment. The author of Genesis 3 knows that humans, as he experiences them, have the capacity to make rational choices; but how does one describe the act by which that capacity was achieved? I would argue, however, that the story is not being clumsy here but rather is making a subtle distinction. When the focus of the narrative shifts from the snake's words to the woman's perspective, what the narrator's words describe is simply the moment of *desire*. And desire is not the same as discriminating judgment. The sentence emphasizes the involvement of the senses and uses the vocabulary of appetite and desire: "Then the woman *saw* that the tree was good *to eat*, and that it was *pleasurable to look at*, and that it was *desirable* for making wise, and she took some of its fruit and she ate" (3:6a; author's translation, emphasis added). The desire for wisdom is described in language that suggests it is not truly a rational choice but is folded into a more enveloping experience of desire that operates on a prerational level. It is no accident that the crucial symbolic object in this story is a food rather than, for example, a talisman of some sort. Food is a basic object of desire, grounded in our physical selves. Desire is thus a quality intrinsic to our prehuman state, but it is the one that serves as the mechanism by which decisive change is set in motion.

Consequently, it is important to reflect on the structure of desire. Ever since Plato's *Symposium*, desire has been described, above all, in terms of lack. But the condition of lack is not properly a negative one. Desire is always desire *for* some thing, and so it is a form by which persons go beyond themselves, transcend themselves. In fact, desire helps to create one's sense of oneself as a self, because desire teaches one about the nature of boundaries. Anne Carson examines this element in her book on desire in early Greek poetry, *Eros the Bittersweet.* In her words, "the experience of eros [or desire] as lack alerts a person to the boundaries of himself, of other people, of things in general. It is the edge separating my tongue from the taste for which it longs."[3] Thus the thing I desire is different from me, outside of me, but I want to draw it to myself, for it to become me or at least mine. Carson notes that in the play of desire a curious shift of perspective occurs. I want it to be mine because even though I never knew I lacked it before I saw it, this thing or person now appears as a *necessary* part of myself. I am incomplete without it, and so I draw it to myself.[4] This is the brilliant artistry of Genesis 2–3. The author knows that human beings are in fact characterized by the capacity for discriminating judgment, judgment represented by the tree of knowledge. That is a necessary part of what it means to be a human being. But the story takes the reader back to the moment of desire, when this capacity to make judgments, represented symbolically by the desirable fruit, was both outside of us and yet seen and longed for, felt for the first time as a necessary part of who we are.

And the result of desire fulfilled? "And their eyes were opened and they saw that they were naked" (3:6b–7a). At this remove, it is difficult to know if the story intended this line to be humorous, though I think it likely. This perception hardly seems like wisdom of the gods. And yet it is a brilliant and densely packed symbol.[5] Mostly, the image has been associated with awakened sexuality. That is not entirely incorrect, since the fig-leaf coverings the woman and the man make for themselves serve to cover the genitals. But the recognition of sexual difference is not the primary issue here. After all, sexual difference was what the man had exclaimed so happily about when he first saw the newly created woman in Gen. 2:23. Something else is primarily at stake here. Perhaps one can get at it by considering the contexts in which the word "naked" can and cannot meaningfully be used. It is a word that can appropriately be used only of human beings. One cannot properly say of a trout or a lion or a deer that it is "naked." The concept of nakedness is one of the sharpest boundaries between the animal and the human.[6] Animals make many things: shelters, tools, perhaps even weapons. But no animal makes clothes. Or, as the

Yahwist might say, an animal is naked but not ashamed. Thus as the woman and the man confuse the boundary between themselves and the divine, that action simultaneously establishes the definitive boundary between themselves and animals. If humans have become "like gods," the consequence is that they are no longer like animals.

But what exactly is this "eye-opening" knowledge? As the philosopher and ecologist Baird Callicott observes, what the woman and the man see is *themselves*. They become *self*-aware, *self*-conscious; and this self-consciousness is the prerequisite for the experience of shame. And so they make clothes to cover themselves. That quality of self-awareness is also what distinguishes humans from the other animals.[7]

It is not self-evident, however, why the story would conceive of the ability to discriminate between good and bad *not* to have been appropriate to humans in the first place. The reason appears to be this. Humans can now choose, but all choice has to be made with reference to some center of value. And what will that be? With the emergence of self-awareness comes the possibility of self-centeredness, both individual self-centeredness and the species self-centeredness we call anthropocentrism. To grasp the full significance one has to think of the combining of desire and self-consciousness of which this story speaks. For the animals the powerful engine of desire operates within boundaries set by the hardwiring of their instincts. But in humans desire has now become conjoined with a reflective and creative self-consciousness. This is not to say that all human choices are necessarily tainted by self-centeredness. The combination of desire, with its other-directedness, and of self-consciousness, with its capacity to imagine the self *as other*, can also result in acts of great generosity. *Agapē* as well as *eros* becomes a possibility for the human. But desire, coupled with self-conscious choice, is a highly unstable and unpredictable mixture. The birth of the human changed the world forever.

The stories that follow in Genesis 4–11 play out some of the consequences of what it means that we have become human. These stories tell of the birth of civilization that follows from the birth of the human. And the arts of civilization, according to this account, variously include murder (Gen. 4:8), musical instruments (4:21), urban planning (4:17), cycles of revenge (4:23–24), metallurgy (4:22), animal husbandry (4:20), and the practice of religion (4:26). The presence of the human in the world seems to introduce a degree of creative unpredictability. Yet the human who comes to be in these narratives is a good fit for the world constructed by the text. As has long been noted, the character of God and the structure of the narrative itself seem to have an open, experimental quality. The world, as it is seen from the perspective of Genesis 2–3, has an open architecture, and the odd, non-self-identical creature that is the human seems well suited to its possibilities.

All is not free play, however. There are boundaries and limits that foreshadow the dangerousness of this creature. Humans *may not* become fully gods. As the events of Genesis 2–3 have blurred what had been the boundary of knowledge between humans and divine beings, it becomes necessary to establish the difference by another criterion. Humans are expelled from the garden to prevent access to the tree of life and thus also from immortality, which now becomes the defining difference between the human and the divine (3:22–24).

Before turning to the story of *1 Enoch*, there is one final observation to make. According to this narrative in Genesis, human beings are something very close to what we might call monsters. A monster, by dictionary definition, is "a legendary animal . . . [with] a form either partly brute and partly human or compounded of elements from several brute forms . . . abnormal," though the word also connotes "something unnaturally marvelous."[8] As this definition suggests, things that blur categories, things that transgress boundaries, are often treated as objects of fear, horror, and loathing. They are monstrous. Yet this story claims just such a monstrous identity as the very shape of the human. And though the story sees this new mixed monster as problematic, it does not recoil in horror. The reason for raising this point is that in some strands of postmodern thought the category of the monstrous has been reclaimed as a positive and ethically significant image precisely for its power to expose the various ways in which humans form identities not just by establishing boundaries but also by transgressing boundaries.[9] While Genesis 2–3 is certainly not itself a postmodern text, it has more affinities with postmodern perspectives than have yet been explored.

## B. *1 Enoch* 6–16

The relevant narrative in *1 Enoch* does not tell a story about how humans came to be humans. In fact such a story would be utterly unpalatable to *1 Enoch* because, to use philosophical categories, it perceives the world not through the category of Becoming but through the category of Being. Thus, even though *1 Enoch* 6–16 and Genesis 2–3 talk about some issues that overlap, they begin from different starting places. Though it is a noncanonical, apocalyptic text, *1 Enoch* exhibits a moral imagination strikingly similar to that of the Priestly writer, and in this sense, makes a valuable supplement to the frequent comparisons of the Yahwistic and Priestly creation narratives.

In the book of *1 Enoch* the story of the angels and their human wives occurs in chapter 6. But the preceding chapters set up the worldview within which this story is to be understood. The first chapter is a hymn that describes the final intervention of God to rescue the righteous and judge the wicked. This is followed in chapters 2–5 by a teaching in the form of a rebuke to sinners.

Characteristically, and importantly, Enoch casts this rebuke in terms of an argument from nature.

> Contemplate all the events in heaven, how the lights in heaven do not change their courses, how each rises and sets in order, each at its proper time, and they do not transgress their law. Consider the earth, and understand from the work which is done upon it . . . that no work of God changes as it becomes manifest. . . . Contemplate how the trees are covered with green leaves, and bear fruit . . . all his works serve him and do not change, but as God has decreed, so everything is done. . . . But you have not persevered, nor observed the law of the Lord. But you have transgressed, and have spoken proud and hard words with your unclean mouth against his majesty. You hard of heart! You will not have peace! (*1 En.* 2:1–5:4; trans. Knibb)[10]

For *1 Enoch* God's will is expressed in fixed categories, clear boundaries, and orderly and harmonious embodiment of those orders in the activities of creatures. The order of nature stands as exemplary for humans. Following this admonition, the story of the angels and the human women serves as the parade example of the disaster that occurs when orders are not respected and boundaries are transgressed. The authors of *1 Enoch* have picked up this story from Gen. 6:1–4, but they have elaborated on it and changed its significance substantially.

The story, according to *1 Enoch*, begins as follows:

> And it came to pass, when the sons of men had increased, that in those days there were born to them fair and beautiful daughters. And the angels, the sons of heaven, saw them and desired them. And they said to one another, "Come, let us choose for ourselves wives from the children of men, and let us beget for ourselves children." (*1 En.* 6:1–2; trans. Knibb)

Here is desire again, setting the plot in motion. But this time it is divine desire for that which pertains to the human. Here, one might say, the apple reaches out for Eve.

The very fact that angels should desire humans is significant. Human existence is not depicted as something deficient. Rather humans have something that even the angels do not have. But what, exactly? Sometimes the story has been read simply in terms of angelic lust. But that does not seem adequate. Although the desire is explicitly erotic, what the angels seek is a normal family life: marriage and children. Twice later in the story there are references to the angels' concern for their children (*1 En.* 12:5–6; 14:6–7). The trope of angelic desire for human existence is also a topic examined in contemporary popular culture, for example, in Wim Wenders's *Wings of Desire* and its remake as *City of Angels.* These films take up the motif of angels who desire aspects of human existence, but in a different way than in *1 Enoch*. The films make the point that love and delight in the full sensual world of tastes and colors and touch make mortal life not merely endurable but quite wonderful. Ultimately, however, *Wings of Desire* and *City of Angels* are sentimental and individualistic. In them the angel's decision affects no one but himself and his wife. These are merely "angelic self-realization" films and have no way to explore what the book of *1 Enoch* sees as the dark cosmic consequences of a desire that transgresses boundaries. Desire for the wrong thing—for what is off limits, out of bounds—can literally wreck a world and lead to the ultimate destruction of the desired other.

The warning about transgressive desire in the book of *1 Enoch* becomes concrete as the story describes the angels' offspring. As the story was originally told in Gen. 6:1–4, the offspring of the divine beings and the human women were the giants, who are called "the giants of old, the men of renown." That is to say, Gen 6:1–4 gives a rather positive interpretation to the giants. These were the legendary "great men," the like of whom we do not see in our diminished days. But here the book of *1 Enoch* makes its most significant change in the story. According to *1 Enoch*:

> [The women] became pregnant and bore large giants. . . . These devoured all the toil of men, until men were unable to sustain them. And the giants turned against them in order to devour men. And they began to sin against [i.e., eat] birds, and against animals, and against reptiles and against fish, and they devoured one another's flesh and drank the blood from it. (*1 En*. 7:2–5; trans. Knibb)

With this passage in *1 Enoch* one is a long way from the representation of desire for the other as the eating of a lovely piece of fruit. What the images in the *1 Enoch* story suggest is that transgressive desire takes on a life of its own and produces a distorted image of itself. The angels desired human women and the families they might produce together. But this wrongful desire, once carried out, produces only a mocking exaggeration of itself. It produces in the giants appetite without limit, desire without the possibility of satisfaction, desire in which the incorporation of the other becomes an orgy of violence. The horror of it is marked in the fact that the giants do not simply consume vegetable food, which is all that is permitted to humans at this stage of the world (see Gen. 1:29–31), but consume blood—life itself—in all categories of animals, in humans, and finally in a self-destructive cannibalistic self-consumption.

Here are monsters of a familiar type. The mixing of the human and the divine produces something ambiguous, fearful, out of control: something wholly loathsome. One should notice, however, that in *1 Enoch* the giants occupy the conceptual space that humans occupy in Genesis. They are the creatures of mixed identity, the product of blurred boundaries. But the giants are regarded with revulsion.

*First Enoch* has yet more to say concerning the full horror of the distortions of transgressive desire. The earth complains to God, and through the help of the good angels, God intervenes. A flood will cleanse the earth. The giants who remain after their internecine conflict are killed by drowning (*1 En.* 10:9–12). But like the monstrous force that it is, transgressive desire survives attempts to kill it. God has to explain the biology of monsters to Enoch. The giants were half human, half divine. The flood can kill their mortal flesh, but not their eternal spirits. Those cannot be killed. Moreover, since the giants were born on earth, it is on earth that the spirits now have their home. God continues, "And now the giants who were born from spirits and flesh[11] will be called evil spirits upon the earth, and on the earth will be their dwelling. . . . And these spirits will rise against the sons of men and against the women because they came out from them" (*1 En.* 15:8–9, 12; trans. Knibb).

The divine element of the giants, that which is directly derived from their angelic fathers, now embodies sheer malice against humans. Where the angels had erotically desired human women, the residue of their desire has now become its opposite: implacable hostility. But what about the humans? This story of how evil entered the world initially seems to contrast with Genesis 2–3 in seeing humans as passive victims rather than as initiating agents. Of course, insofar as this story is told as a sequel to the admonition in *1 Enoch* 2–5, it would be warning humans, too, about the dangers of transgressing whatever boundaries are applicable to them. But the story also says some specific things about the way in which human beings come to be implicated in the guilt of the angels.

The humans in this story are not presented simply as victims. Although the description of the angels' initial encounter with the women is very brief, the relationship does not appear to be one of rape. Instead, it seems to be presented more in terms of traditional courtship. The angels can be seen as offering wedding gifts both to the women and to their male relatives. These gifts are the "heavenly secrets" that the angels teach to the humans (*1 En.* 7:2; 8:1–4; 9:6–8). So, here, as in Genesis 2–3, the issue of knowledge enters the story. Humans receive knowledge that will make them more like divine beings. And though the humans do not initiate the quest for such knowledge, they appear to be eager recipients. This account is a variant of the common mythic motif of the gift of the arts of civilization by divine beings (for example, Prometheus's gift of fire in Greek mythology). But it turns out to be a deadly gift.

The teaching is described in chapter 8, after the women have become wives of the angels:

> And Azazel taught men to make swords, and daggers, and shields and breastplates. And he showed them metals,[12] and the art of making them: bracelets, and ornaments, and the art of making up the eyes and of beautifying the eyelids, and the most precious and choice stones and all kinds of coloured dyes. And the world was changed. And there was great impiety and much fornication, and they went astray, and all their ways became corrupt. Amezarak taught all those who cast spells and cut roots, Armaros the release of spells, and Baraqiel astrologers, and Kokabel portents, and Tamiel taught astrology, and Asradel taught the path of the moon. (*1 En.* 8:1–4; trans. Knibb)

Two things deserve note: the consequence of this gift of knowledge to humans is that "the world was changed" (8:2). And in *1 Enoch* change is not good. One should note also what was taught: the art of making weapons, the art of personal ornamentation, and the arts of magic and astrology. If one translates the concrete terms into somewhat more abstract categories, these are three of the less admirable techniques by which desire accomplishes its object: by techniques of force, by techniques of seduction, and by techniques of manipulation. The angels have infected human beings with their own transgressive desires and equipped them with the means to accomplish them, so that the world was changed.

## III. IMPLICATIONS FOR ETHICAL REFLECTION

These two narratives sketch two very different perspectives on the world, on what it means to be human, on how one might interact with the world, and on what the consequences will be. They are, in my opinion, intriguing on their own account. But stories that offer images of ourselves and our relation to the world bear—at least indirectly—on the way in which we continue to reflect on concrete ethical dilemmas. One must be careful. It is not possible simply to read Genesis or *1 Enoch* and then apply it to some modern question. Such stories do not give oracular answers, and it would also be dangerous to read them as allegories of our present situation that need only be decoded. But such narratives and their various modes of thought, general perspectives, and symbolic images do model a way of thinking about the world. To the extent that one looks through the lenses of these narratives, one will tend to see the relevant aspects of contemporary problems in a particular way, to set the parameters of the question differently, to choose different starting points and different analogies by means of which to think. Such ways of looking at things do not necessarily dictate specific conclusions, but they do direct the kind of framing perception that guides one's moral reasoning and hence the type of decisions one makes.

To make this claim more vivid, I would like to illustrate with a somewhat whimsical example, crafted in the spirit of the late Steve Allen's television program entitled *Meeting of the Minds*. What if one imagined Enoch and Eve sitting outside the Starbucks in heaven, arguing over an article in the newspaper concerning genetic engineering. It is a story about the implantation of a fish gene into a tomato plant to make it resistant to freezing weather. But of course more is at stake than codfish and tomatoes. I use this example of genetic modification, especially as it involves cross-species manipulation, since it so clearly raises issues of the nature of the world as given or constructed, the moral and metaphysical implications of changing the world, the nature of human desire and creativity, and so forth.

There is no doubt where the type of moral imagination embodied in *1 Enoch* comes out. Enoch speaks a resounding "no." His starting point is an orientation to the character of the world itself.

**Enoch**: Can you believe this, Eve? Putting fish genes into tomato plants? There is a God-given wisdom already structured into the world of nature that has to be respected. You can't make proper moral decisions by just asking what people want (like a freeze-proof tomato). People's desires don't provide an adequate moral compass because we always want what we don't have. There's no discipline to desire. It just wants what it wants. The only reliable moral compass comes from something that transcends human beings. Immanuel Kant got it right, Eve: "the starry sky above and the moral law within." Human beings have to resist the desire to tamper. Tampering breaks things. And a broken world can't be fixed.

*Eve knows she disagrees with Enoch, though she isn't quite sure why. It's just not the way she looks at things.*

**Eve:** Enoch, I don't think you have a clue as to what it means to be a human being. Desire is not a dirty word. Desire is at the root of human curiosity, human creativity. Humans have a hunger for knowledge, Enoch. To be human is to see the world as full of wonderful things to be explored. Human desire reaches out for new possibilities, things not yet imagined. This is the heart and soul of scientific inquiry. But I'd disagree that desire has no discipline. People aren't just pure appetite. We don't just grunt and point: "Me want pretty apple." We've got brains, too. We make choices based on what seems good and what seems bad. Now, I'll grant you that not every decision humans make is wise. We make some big mistakes—DDT seemed like a good idea at the time—but we face the consequences and make new and better choices.

One other thing, Enoch. I've always admired your environmental sensibilities. But your understanding of the world is so rigid. You see it as some fragile machine that's going to break at the slightest change. But change is itself part of the world. I see the world as open and adaptive. The world is always "under construction," and what humans do is part of that construction—even at the level of genes and chromosomes.

**Enoch**: Oh, good grief, Eve. A tomato with the soul of a fish is just unnatural.

**Eve**: It's not a soul, Enoch; it's a gene. But anyway, I don't think we should fear things just because they are strange, new, "unnatural." When it comes to that, we are the most "unnatural" being there is. Look, I'm not saying that I think this tomato experiment is a good one. There are all kinds of ecological and social issues to be considered. But in principle, a fish gene in a tomato plant is no more monstrous than is a human being, that cross between ape and angel. Don't you see the implications of your *way of thinking*, Enoch? You're so tied up in taxonomies and identities. "A place for every thing and everything in its place." This whole focus on identities is part of a totalizing epistemology that is a tool of repression. You ought to read some feminist science fiction, Enoch. They've transcended the binary opposition of the organic versus the technological. In their imagery of cyborgs and monstrous women created through boundary transgressions, identities are always partial and contradictory. It's by thinking the "monstrous" that we deconstruct the definitions that entrap us and "crack the matrices of domination."

*Enoch sighs. Ever since Eve read Donna Haraway's "Cyborg Manifesto"*[13] *and declared herself a cyborg feminist, they've been having this discussion. Eve keeps trying to find a way to reread her own story subversively. Enoch doesn't think that it quite works, but if anyone can pull it off, Eve can.*

**Enoch**: Look, Eve, I don't want to get into all that again. What I do want to say is that I can't believe you have such a naïve understanding of desire (or "creativity" as you want to call it) and the law of unintended consequences. You talked a minute ago as though the results of human creativity remain under our control. But that is not so. Look at the already-existing technologies, from nuclear energy to industrialized, pesticide-laced farming. These technologies, born in desire, the offspring of our spirit and material reality, acquire a life of their own. They escape our control, and when they do, they develop voracious appetites, attacking and consuming the environment in unexpected ways. And even when one tries to eliminate them, their toxic ghosts hang around, the inverted image of our original desire, now turned into something that seems full of malice toward us, their human parents.

*Growing more and more agitated, Enoch continues:*

Don't you see where this leads? Too much tampering with the God-given world, and its very structures will collapse, corrupted beyond redemption. And moral order won't survive the collapse of nature either. Transgression leads to anarchy, Eve, and the result is an orgy of violence and the betrayal of every human bond. It would take the judgment of God to clean up the mess. And maybe that's what we need. Call me a pessimist, Eve, but I don't think we can reign in our out-of-control technological desires by ourselves. I think nothing short of a global catastrophe can put an end to it. But, maybe, just maybe, out of the ruins there might be a few survivors who would understand that humility and living rightly and harmoniously with the world instead of against it is the only way. Look at the stars; look at the trees. If we lived like them, nature would bring forth its own abundance, and we could live in peace instead of greedy conflict. That's what people were intended to do.

*Momentarily shaken both by the power of Enoch's vision and his passion, Eve recovers a bit and speaks.*

**Eve**: Look Enoch, I think you've been reading too much *bad* science fiction. All this dystopian/utopian, apocalyptic fantasy is simply hysterical anxiety in mythological drag. Nevertheless, I'll concede you this much. The problem, as I think we both see it, is that people don't have much of an internal-control mechanism. It is really hard for us to say no to ourselves once we've seen a gleaming possibility. I know some of my friends in the scientific and business communities wouldn't agree with me, but we really do need some limits, limits that come from something that transcends ourselves. But pointing to the "laws of nature" is no good, Enoch. We aren't stars; we aren't trees. We're something different. But I'm not willing to say that apocalypse is the only answer. What's missing in those approaches is that they don't take seriously our status as moral agents. Call me naïve, but I really think that if human beings have a clear vision of the good, a sense of what it means to be a community of mutual responsibility, that we can commit ourselves voluntarily, bind ourselves to some limits that will protect us against our worst excesses. But I don't quite know how to envision what that would look like.

*At that moment Eve looks up and sees another friend coming out of Starbucks.*

**Eve**: Oh! Moses! Come over here. There's something we want to ask you.

As much as I would love to continue "Eve-s-dropping," it is necessary to leave them to their conversation. What I have tried to demonstrate, however, is that the stories people tell about who we are as human beings and what the world is like are stories that embody powerful moral imaginations. They are prototype stories that embody distinctive ways of perceiving and thinking. They offer forms of moral imagination that can be drawn upon when encountering new and unfamiliar issues. To the extent that people are formed by such stories, they will try to map the stories onto new issues. For someone whose moral imagination is close to that articulated in what I have called the "priestly" imagination of *1 Enoch*, the structures of the world are inviolable, and transgressing natural boundaries would be terribly wrong, fraught with almost unimaginable dangers. For someone who is formed by the exploratory imagination of Eve in the story of Genesis 2–3, the world is always "under construction," and human curiosity and desire are part of that unfolding. In this exercise of the imagination I have tried to present Enoch and Eve as both representing morally significant positions. The motivating force of this exploration, however, is not to advocate one or the other but to encourage the examination of the shapes of moral imagination as they occur in formative texts of Scripture and in other normative sources that inform contemporary ethical reflection. In this enterprise lie new possibilities for the conversation between the Bible and ethics.

## NOTES

1. Clifford Geertz, *The Interpretation of Cultures* (New York: Basic Books, 1973), 46.
2. Paolo Sacchi, *Jewish Apocalyptic and Its History*, trans. W. J. Short; JSPSup 20 (Sheffield: Sheffield Academic Press, 1990), 32–71.
3. Anne Carson, *Eros the Bittersweet* (Princeton, N.J.: Princeton University Press, 1986), 30.
4. Ibid., 33.
5. I examine this text for its general ecological implications in Carol Newsom, "Common Ground: An Ecological Reading of Genesis 2–3," in *The Earth Story in Genesis*, ed. N. C. Habel and S. Wurst (Sheffield: Sheffield Academic Press, 2002), 68–69.
6. Baird Callicott, "Genesis and John Muir," in *Covenant for a New Creation: Ethics, Religion and Public Policy*, ed. C. S. Robb and C. J. Casebolt (Maryknoll, N.Y.: Orbis Books), 123.
7. Ibid., 123–24.
8. *Webster's Third New International Dictionary* (Springfield, Mass.: Merriam-Webster, 1976), 1465.
9. E.g., Donna J. Haraway, *Simians, Cyborgs, and Women: The Reinvention of Nature* (London: Free Association Books, 1991). The tantalizing ambiguity of the monstrous is analyzed in Timothy Beal, *Religion and Its Monsters* (New York and London: Routledge, 2002), 193–96.
10. Michael Knibb, "*1 Enoch*," in *The Apocryphal Old Testament*, ed. H. D. Sparks (Oxford: Clarendon Press, 1984), 204–05.
11. Reading with one of the Greek manuscripts. See Knibb, 204, n. 13.
12. Reading with one of the Greek manuscripts. See Knibb, 190, n. 4.
13. Donna J. Haraway, "A Cyborg Manifesto: Science, Technology, and Socialist-Feminism in the Late Twentieth Century," in *Simians, Cyborgs, and Women*, 149–82.

3

# Shaking the World of Family Values

*David L. Petersen*

This paper is intended to address the theme "Shaking Earth and Heaven: Bible, Church, and the Changing Global Order" and to honor the work of Charles Cousar and Walter Brueggemann.[1] In that regard, I have tried to identify a significant issue that is shaking public conversation and that should be fruitfully addressed by the church as it is informed by the biblical witness. One such involves the family. Those in many countries around the world debate vigorously the very nature of the family. What is a family? Is there a normative family structure? Who can marry? What values are of utmost importance to families? Many who address these questions think that wrong answers will shake their societies to the point of destruction.

I have recently moved from Colorado to Georgia. While living in Denver, I was close to one of the centers for discourse about family values. The organization, Focus on the Family, is located just south of Denver in Colorado Springs. Focus on the Family is interested in sustaining the family as a part of its Christian mission. I, too, am interested in thinking about the ways in which the canonical witness—particularly the book of Genesis—can help us assist families. Hence, I was curious to see how Focus on the Family thinks about the relation of family values to biblical literature.

My first task was to find Focus on the Family's statement of mission on its Web site (www.family.org). It reads as follows:

> To cooperate with the Holy Spirit in disseminating the Gospel of Jesus Christ to as many people as possible, and, specifically, to accomplish that objective by helping to preserve traditional values and the institution of the family.

Now, as someone who worries about the niceties of texts, I noted two revealing phrases: "traditional values" and "the institution of the family." And of those two phrases, the one about which I wanted immediately to know more was "traditional values." What are the traditional values that are to be preserved? None are offered in the statement of mission.

So I looked next at the principles that undergird the organization's operations. In this statement, I read that there are five guiding principles or "pillars." The text reads, "These pillars are drawn from the Bible and the Judeo-Christian ethic, rather than from the humanistic notions of today's theorists." Again, the "traditional values" were not defined, but at least there was an appeal to their source, namely, the Bible. The five principles themselves were not constructed as statements of traditional values, but they certainly appeared to presume such values. For example, one of the five principles affirms that there is a norm of an indissoluble marriage between one man and one woman. Though the principles do not explicitly state that a family is to be equated with a husband-wife unit, that is certainly the presumption. Further, there is strong insistence on the indissolubility of this contract between the male and female, but no reference in these so-called pillars to norms regarding sexual behavior or issues such as spousal abuse. Much about the nature and values of the family remains unsaid.

Though the values espoused by Focus on the Family and similar organizations are difficult to define, I do not think it would do that organization an injustice to suggest that the primary values focus on the so-called nuclear family, one made up of a heterosexual and monogamous marriage, which has as its primary purpose the expression of certain religious sentiments and the production of children. These features are understood to conform to biblical values.

As an Old Testament scholar, I began to think about some of the marriages attested in ancient Israel. Surely the marriages of religiously prominent individuals in the Old Testament would constitute formative moments in the Judeo-Christian ethic to which Focus on the Family appeals. I thought about Abraham, who was functionally married to two women—Sarah and Hagar. I thought about Jacob, who was literally married to two sisters, Rachel and Leah. And I thought about King David—who was married to Michal (Saul's daughter), Abigail, Bathsheba (mother of Solomon), and Haggith (mother of Adonijah). I even thought about Moses who, the book of Exodus reports, sent his wife away, which is the ancient language of divorce (Exod. 18:2, see Deut. 24:1). These are not minor figures: we are dealing here with Abraham, whom the New Testament knows as "the father of faith"; with Jacob, who bears the very name of Israel; with Moses, the giver of Torah; and with David, Israel's greatest king. And yet Abraham, Jacob, Moses, and David present us with patterns of marital behavior that do not conform to the pillars of

Focus on the Family. Are we to say that the families in which these individuals lived were illicit? Are we to be embarrassed by the nature of these families? My answer is "No." These individuals lived in families that may help us define what a family is and needs to be. We might well benefit from learning something about the family values attested in our canonical literature.

There is one body of literature in the Old Testament that truly focuses on the family. Genesis 12–37 deserves to be called the ancestral or family literature. Here, more than any other place in either the Old or New Testament, the people of God is construed as a family. And it is here, more than any other place, that we should first look to discern deep insights about families and family values.

## I

I begin by pointing to a text that occurs at the outset of this ancestral literature: Genesis 12:1–3. In these verses, God directs Abraham to leave the land where he had been living and to travel. Following that command, the deity promises to Abraham that his family will become a great nation and that "by you all the families of the earth shall be blessed" (Gen. 12:3).

This is a rich and provocative statement. It offers us an insight and presents us with a question. It helps us understand the notion of family and it raises a question: What is the blessing that will come to all the families of the earth?

First, we must examine the insight about families. The Hebrew word translated family here is *mišpāḥâ*. It bears a number of meanings in the Old Testament: it can refer to one of the Israelite tribes; it can refer to a clan; and it can even refer to ethnic or linguistically defined groups. However, the word *mišpāḥâ* never, so far as I can tell, refers to what we could call the nuclear family or even one household. So, at the outset, this biblical text challenges us to think about "family" as something larger than a man and wife. The ancestral narratives ask us to enlarge our notion of family.

The family of Abraham offers a case in point. Initially, the family—understood here initially as a residential unit of people belonging to the same lineage—included Sarah, his wife, and, soon thereafter, Lot, Abraham's nephew. Then, at least according to the story line, it included Hagar, who had presumably been there since the time that Abraham and Sarah were in Egypt. She really becomes part of the family when Abraham impregnates her and she gives birth to his son. But then, of course, Hagar and Ishmael leave. Still, despite their departure, we should not think that they cease being part of the family. The biblical writer makes it very clear that Ishmael returns when his father dies, such that both Isaac and Ishmael are able to bury their father. (The text depicts them as coequals: "His sons Isaac and Ishmael buried him in the cave of Machpelah"; Gen. 25:9). Before that moment, however, Sarah dies. Abraham then marries again—to Keturah. And they have six sons, the most prominent of which is Midian. We often forget that Abraham had two wives, one concubine, and eight sons.

The ancestral literature offers us families far more complicated than our typical picture of a nuclear family in North America, a notion underscored by the use of the Hebrew noun *mišpāḥâ* to signify family in Gen. 12:3. Hence, any conversation about family values that reflects the nature of family life in the biblical witness must take account of this broader understanding of family. Families are big, complicated entities in the ancestral narratives. That is the insight embedded in Genesis 12.

## II

Now for the question. If Abraham and his family become a great nation and if they become a blessing for other families, what is the nature of that blessing? Here the biblical text is not as clear. So, let me suggest that one of the blessings that Abraham and his family might offer to those families of the earth are the family values that Abraham and his family embody. The ancestral literature presents us with a world in which husbands and wives, mothers and fathers, brothers and sisters live out their deepest concerns. What are those values?

I think the biblical text presents at least two such family values. We discover what they are when we focus on two issues in the ancestral literature: (1) the patterns of marriage and sexual access, and (2) the means by which conflict is resolved. Let me address them seriatim.

First, we must analyze the patterns of sexual access within the marriages portrayed in Genesis. The world depicted in the ancestral literature offers some patterns for sexual access and marriage that differ significantly from those practiced in North America. Abraham marries Sarah. He chose someone who was a member of his family. Sarah was the daughter of Haran, Abraham's brother. Clearly, this marital choice is one in which staying inside the family is important (anthropologists call such a pattern endogamy). Sarah, however, was unable to bear children. Since her status as wife—and hence her place in the family—depended on her ability to give birth to an heir, she devised a plan by means of which she might bring a child into the family. She commanded Abraham to have sexual intercourse with her Egyptian slave girl. Interestingly, nothing in the biblical narratives condemns Sarah's strategy. In fact, anthropologists have discovered this pattern of marriage and sexual access in other cultures. They call it polycoity—a marriage in which one male has sexual access to more than one female. The driving family value in such marriages is the provision of an heir to whom the family's property may be passed on.[2]

Abraham's family with Sarah and Hagar is not the only unusual one in Genesis. Jacob's marriage was also different from those familiar to us today. Jacob, like Abraham and Isaac before him, married within the family of Terah, Abraham's father. (Rachel and Leah were the daughters of Abraham's nephew). But Jacob's marriage was, by our standards, even more unusual than Abraham's. Jacob married two sisters: Rachel and Leah. Though the story reports that he wanted to marry only Rachel, Rachel's father, Laban, tricked Jacob to ensure that the elder daughter, Leah, would not be left without a spouse. What is reported in the biblical narrative as a trick is, in the anthropological literature, presented as a genuine pattern of marriage, namely, sororal polygyny, in which one man is married to two sisters. The goal of this familial pattern is apparently very similar to the one of polycoity, namely, to ensure that an heir will be present.

Why would this insistence on having an heir have been so important for the society pictured in Genesis 12–37? The answer is, I fear, dismayingly simple: God had made a promise that Abraham's posterity would become numerous, would possess land, and would become a blessing. In order for that promise to work out, it was incumbent on that family not to die off. Hence, a primary family value was to keep alive the line of Abraham so that God's promise would be realized. It was more important than monogamy. The existence of that family over time was a premier value. That is value number one.

We may find the second family value by examining those instances where there is conflict within the family that traces its origins to Abraham's father, Terah. I would like to focus on three such moments of conflict.

## Abraham and Lot (Gen. 13)

Early on in the ancestral narratives, Abraham and Lot settle in the land of Canaan. The biblical writer characterizes both men as wealthy, owning prodigious herds that were cared for by numerous shepherds. Though Abraham and Lot did not live in exactly the same place, their herders apparently came into regular conflict when their sheep and goats wandered over the landscape of the central highlands.

The text does not describe the nature of the acrimony, but it certainly could have led to violence between the herdsmen. As a result, Abraham proposes to Lot that he choose where he would like to live.

Abraham is often remembered for being the gracious figure, giving Lot first choice. And that is true. But he is even better remembered if we recognize that Abraham is dealing with a member of his family, his nephew. And within that family conflict, he creates a plan to resolve the strife. This plan involves distancing, separating the parties from one another. Abraham's strategy is not unknown today. Whether in family disputes or conflicts between other types of contesting parties, simple separation to avoid further conflict and violence is often necessary. Abraham and Lot went their separate ways and, in so doing, avoided an escalation of the conflict into violence.

## Jacob and Laban (Gen. 31)

Jacob and Laban present us with another time of difficulty. Jacob has been living in Laban's household. He has married two of Laban's daughters—Rachel and Leah—and prospered. Not only does he have eleven sons; he has amassed sizeable herds as well. Further, he perceives that Laban no longer is as accommodating to him as he once was. Hence he decides to return to the land of his birth. He does so while Laban is off shearing sheep. When Laban discovers that Jacob has fled, he gathers some of his family and pursues Jacob. When he finally catches up with Jacob, there is a tense scene. They exchange accusations. Laban accuses Jacob of stealing some of his religious objects. And even though Jacob hadn't stolen them, his wife, Rachel, had. Jacob accuses Laban of cheating him over the years, which was also the case. It would not be far off the mark to suggest that Jacob and Laban engage in verbal combat.

To Laban's credit, he recognizes that he and Jacob have reached an impasse. He could do Jacob harm, but in so doing he would jeopardize the fate of his daughters and grandchildren. Hence Laban proposes that he and Jacob draw up a legal decree of separation, a covenant. They will establish a boundary that neither will be permitted to cross.

Here again, the parties in conflict resolve their dispute. This time they have had words, acrimonious words. The text refers explicitly to the possibility that Laban might have done Jacob harm. Hence, one has the sense that they could not simply go their separate ways as Abraham and Lot had done. No, those strong words created the necessity of a more formal arrangement. It involved the taking of an oath, the making of a covenant, and the creation of a tangible boundary.

Sometimes in a familial dispute the differences are so great that there is a potential for violence. Simple distancing, as Abraham and Lot had done, will not suffice. After all, Abraham and Lot met again. Jacob and Laban must not meet again. Hence this dispute must be resolved differently.

Even the casual reader of Genesis 31 can see that Jacob and Laban use the legal language of covenant and oath. Less clear is the fact that they make those oaths by swearing allegiance to different gods. Laban swears by the God of Nahor, and Jacob swears by the "Fear" of his father Isaac (the NRSV capitalizes "Fear" in Gen. 31:54). We should ask, What is the significance of this reference to two different deities? The God of Nahor and the Fear of Isaac are important to the flow of the story. Two relatives, two members of the family who could trace their heritage back to Terah, not only swear never to see each other again, they now adopt different religious language. Both names—the God of Nahor and the Fear of Isaac—had existed within the family of Terah. Now, they split off from one another, with those associated with Laban developing one way of talking about God and those associated with Jacob adopting another. The familial schism becomes religiously sectarian.

The picture is clear. In effect, Jacob and Laban create something akin to a divorce. Their differences are irreconcilable. For them to remain in contact would be terrible, almost certainly leading to violence. Their relationships up to this point have been characterized by deceit and theft. There is really only one realistic option—a clear legal separation, which is now expressed in religious language. What had once been one family has now become two families.

Divorce is rarely a happy time, and the biblical writers do not depict Laban and Jacob's separation as particularly heartwarming. Laban kissed his daughters and grandchildren and returned home, never to see them again. Still, all the members of the family are alive. Laban can go back to his sons and his herds. Jacob can return to his native territory with his large family and his herds. No one was killed. The family of Terah had, again, successfully devised a strategy to deal with severe conflict. And, in this instance, the family had changed because of this act of formal separation. On narrative and theological grounds, Laban's household will no longer be viewed as part of the immediate family that bears God's promise.

## Jacob and Esau (Gen. 32)

After Jacob disengages from Laban, he knows that he must inevitably confront his brother Esau. Just as Laban and his kinsman had charged after Jacob, so now Esau and four hundred men are rushing to engage Jacob. The strategies of distancing à la Abraham and Lot and legal remedy à la Jacob and Laban are not likely to work here. Jacob is rightly worried. He prays to Yahweh, "Deliver me, please, from the hand of Esau my brother . . . he may come and kill us all, the mothers with the children" (Gen. 32:11). Based on what Esau had said earlier, namely, "I will kill my brother Jacob" (27:41), Jacob's fears are well grounded.

However, rather than waiting for the deity to save him, Jacob develops a two-fold strategy, both aspects of which are known to anthropologists. The first involves the giving of a gift. To give a gift and to have that gift accepted is a powerful act. As the French anthropologist Marcel Mauss observed many years ago, to give a gift is to put someone in your debt.[3] Apparently knowing this principle, Jacob sent Esau a gift: "two hundred female goats and twenty male goats, two hundred ewes and twelve rams, thirty milch camels and their colts, forty cows and ten bulls, twenty female donkeys and ten male donkeys" (Gen. 32:14–15)—over five hundred forty-two animals. Some commentators have viewed these animals as decoys, thinking they would head in one direction while Jacob moved in another. But such a view misses the point of Jacob's strategy; he wants to overpower Esau economically by means of this gift.

Jacob deploys his second strategy when he and Esau actually encounter each other. It is an emotional scene, but one fraught with tension. Jacob engages Esau in a verbal jousting match, a battle of wits. Based on their early history, Jacob would have good reason to think that he might win; and he does.

At first, Esau will not accept the gift. Jacob then offers a psychologically compelling speech in which he says to Esau, "Truly to see your face is like seeing the face of God—since you have received me with such favor" (Gen. 33:10). This is a highly ambiguous statement. If an individual sees God, that individual might die. So, Jacob's statement about seeing Esau's face may quietly allude to Esau's earlier threat to kill him. Then Jacob defines Esau and his band of four hundred men as constituting a favorable response to him. That is an ingenious way of redefining what Esau is actually up to. Jacob's verbal parry begins to disarm Esau. The narrator continues, "So [Jacob] urged him, and [Esau] took [the gift]" (Gen. 33:11).

One might have thought Jacob was, at that point, safe. However, we soon learn that Esau, who probably realized he had just been outwitted, intended to stay with Jacob. This time Esau takes the initiative. He initiates a dialogue with Jacob. Esau said, "'Let us journey on our way, and I will go alongside you'" (Gen. 33:12). Jacob offers a canny and quick-witted reply: "I have to move slowly with my flocks and children, while you, Esau will want to move at a more rapid pace" (Gen. 33:13–14, author's translation). Jacob even says that he will pay a visit to Esau in his own country, which, of course, he never does. Esau loses that encounter, so he makes another proposal, that some of his men remain with Jacob. Jacob responds even more brilliantly: he asks a question, a question that has the same laudatory tone evident earlier in this dialogue with Esau. Jacob says to Esau, "Why should my lord be so kind to me?" (Gen. 33:15). Esau can think of no reply, probably because he didn't intend to be kind to Jacob. As a result, Esau, like Laban before him, headed home, and Jacob continued on his way.

Genesis 33 presents a dire situation: a fraternal dialogue that might have eventuated in fratricide. That potential calamity was, however, averted by Jacob's use of the strategy of gift giving and his ability to conduct verbal warfare. Moreover, Esau played by those same rules. By accepting the gift, he agreed not to attack Jacob. And by engaging Jacob in dialogue, he opened the door to a resolution through a war of wits rather than a war of swords. Esau lost that war, but he honored the game by leaving the playing field after he had lost a second time.

Here again the family values are clear. Both Esau and Jacob engage in strategies to deal with hatred and potential violence. They avoid violence by engaging in two well-known strategies—gift giving and verbal engagement. And they achieve a solution, one of separation. They will meet again, but only once—when they bury their father Isaac. Thus ends the third scene of conflict.

## III

Let me conclude. In this brief review of the ancestral narratives and through an exploration of three moments of conflict, I have suggested several ways that we might begin to rethink the notion of family values. First, we may need to rethink our ideas of what constitutes a family. A family may be larger than a household. It may involve multiple generations and encompass individuals who live in different places. Second, family values in the ancestral narratives permitted marital patterns very different from monogamous marriage between one man and one woman. Surely the values at work in these biblical families may help us to reflect on what might be appropriate marital patterns in our own time. Third, nonviolent resolution of conflict within the family stands out as a dominant value in the ancestral narratives. Even if they didn't always love each other, these family members managed not to take each others' lives.

There is a phrase currently being used within the Jewish community as it wrestles with the issue of domestic violence. The phrase is *šālôm bayit*, which one might translate literally, "peace at home." Ancient Jewish writers took this family value, *šālôm bayit*, "peace at home," very seriously. As one scholar recently wrote, when summarizing the views of earlier sages, "the ultimate achievement of peace on earth depends upon its achievement in the smallest social unit—the family."[4] I would go further and maintain that the ancestral narratives in Genesis show us how to achieve such peace, even when family members are in conflict.

The Old Testament offers testimony about the family of Abraham, which is to serve as a source of blessing for others. This Abrahamic family on occasion harbored murderous intent. However, by using one or another strategy—distancing, oaths, contracts, legal separations, verbal combat, gifting, battles of wit—they were able to resolve that conflict without violence. In so doing they were able to create a sort of *šālôm bayit*. This Abrahamic family has offered us both a family value of nonviolent conflict resolution and strategies that can help us live out that value. It is a traditional family value, and it is true to the best of the biblical witness. Were we able to deploy this value and these strategies both inside our own families and more broadly—particularly in a world that continues to be shaken by the violence of war—it would truly be a blessing to all the families of the earth.

## NOTES

1. Portions of this presentation were included in my presidential address at the 2004 Annual Meeting of the Society of Biblical Literature, under the title "Genesis and Family Values" (San Antonio, Texas: November 20, 2004).
2. I depend here on the work of Naomi Steinberg, who has analyzed the structure of families in Genesis 12–36 in *Kinship and Marriage: A Household Economics Approach* (Minneapolis: Fortress Press, 1993).
3. Marcel Mauss, *The Gift: Forms and Functions of Exchange in Archaic Societies* (Glencoe, Ill.: Free Press, 1954).
4. Marcia Cohn Spiegel, "Spirituality for Survival: Jewish Women Healing Themselves," *JFSR* 12 (1996): 123.

4

# What Do You Do with the God You Have? The First Commandment as Political Axiom

*Patrick D. Miller*

In 1933, when Karl Barth wrote his powerful essay "The First Commandment as Theological Axiom," it was a primary weapon in his "fight against natural theology," a fight he saw as "unavoidable in view of the first commandment as an axiom of theology . . . a fight for right obedience in theology."[1] I would like to suggest that it is also a weapon in the fight against bad forms of political theology. That may need some explanation inasmuch as the term "political theology" has valid uses in reference both to a powerful theological movement in the second half of the twentieth century as well as to the fact that theology, if it is talk about God, is thoroughly political in that it deals with the governing of cosmos, church, and polities. When I talk about the fight against political theology, I have in mind resistance to indiscriminate confusion of the political and the theological, manifest in both politicizing theology and detheologizing politics. That occurs in several ways, specifically in the coalescence of God and country, the takeover of the language of faith in the speech of politics, and the confusion of loyalty with obedience.

While Barth's essay is thoroughly theological, entirely a discussion of theology, and has little or no reference of any sort to politics, to the state, or to contemporary events, it was delivered in the very first days of the Third Reich only a few days after the burning of the Reichstag and just a year before the

For over forty years Walter Brueggemann and Charles Cousar have been my friends and teachers. Their contribution to the interpretation of Scripture is immeasurable, but so is the depth of their friendship for those whose lives have come in touch with theirs. This essay, an expanded form of which has been published as *The God You Have: Politics and the First Commandment* (Minneapolis: Fortress Press, 2004), is a mere token of my gratitude to them both.

Declaration of Barmen. Halfway between the publication of this essay and the formulation of the Barmen Declaration, Barth, hoping that Reformed and Lutheran Christians could come together despite their differences, wrote these words: "Today, the conflict in the Church is not over the Lord's Supper but over the First Commandment, and we have to 'confess.'"[2]

To elaborate, then, I take as my starting point a suggestive comment by Walter Brueggemann in his editorial in a recent issue of *Journal for Preachers*.[3] There he says, "The issue for God's people is characteristically *wrong* God and not *no God*." In reflection on that assertion, let me suggest that the fundamental question is not do you believe in God, or even in one God, but *what do you do with the God you have*? That is really what the first table of the Decalogue is all about. More specifically, the first four commandments are an elaboration of the first commandment because they all have to do with what you do with the God you have.

Now, in one sense, the question formed this way is nonsensical or wrongheaded, particularly if received or heard as implying that one "has" God in some sense of power and control. If you assume that, you will find that you do not *have* God but that you have been *had*, and in the most basic sense one can imagine. In turning to the first four commandments, one must keep in mind that their whole point is that before you have God, God has you. The Commandments begin with the prologue, the first of the Ten Words: "I am the LORD your God, who brought you out . . . therefore you shall have no other gods before *me* or make images of anything and you shall not worship them because *I the LORD your God* am a jealous God" (author's translation; cf. Deut 5:6–9). All of this is held together by the first-person speech, the self-referentiality of the divine word at the beginning. Before the Commandments open up to the self and the selves who are addressed, to the person and the community, they are first-person self-presentation and self-assertion. They are from God, about God. In the humility of God, to use Barth's language, "He elected Himself . . . to be the God of Israel." You have me because I have you. Eventually you can—and must—turn to the family, the neighbor. But not before it is clear that God is given and a given, that is, given to you as the liberating Lord and a given that you cannot stroll by, acting as though the reality of God is not before you, behind you, beside you, over against you, the starting point and ending point, just as you cannot have any other gods before me, behind me, beside me, over against me, no other starting point or ending point, no other bottom line.[4] So, since you are so found, caught, constrained, led, and possessed, what now will you do with the God you have, because that God has you?

The theological claim of the prologue to the Commandments is a political announcement that means, first of all, that those who worship this God do so as those who know themselves to be set free by God's grace and mercy. There is no foundation for the claim, and no analogy to it. There is only the story of God's freeing grace and covenanting demand.

The theological claim of the prologue is a political announcement secondly because those who worship "the LORD your God" know that obedience to this God carries, as Barth put it, no *and* with it, no God *and* something else. Such obedience stands alone. Once the claim is made *upon* you, that is, in the prologue, and *by* you, that is, in the First Commandment that you have this God, then there is nothing that you can have alongside that. For Barth, the fight was over natural revelation because it was there that he saw the *and* that could produce blood and soil, that could associate God with things that belong to our natural life or to orders of creation. He already knew, however, that this was not simply an inner theological debate, but that the ground was being laid for something "beside" and "besides me," an *and*, something beside God and beside what is revealed in the first commandment, revealed in the one word that is Jesus Christ, revealed and attested in the confession that Jesus is Lord. Something "beside" that might and in Barth's situation *did* become "besides" and "over against" me (*'al pānāy* means many things).

We should not, however, reduce the issue to a single *and*, to a dualistic possibility or the question of single alternatives. The text says "other *gods*." The issue is not simply replacing the God you have with another one, but being attracted by and succumbing to *multiple* claims on our obedience. To stress the plurality, however, is not to lose the point in a vague generality of impulses and attractions. Whether with reference to the biblical story or more broadly to the picture that unfolds out of it in human history, these other gods have been dominated by two gods: *oikonomia* and *polis* (though we give them other names in the Bible and elsewhere): the *economy*, the production and distribution and consumption of things, of wealth; and the *polis*, that is, the polity or government and the governing powers and authorities. The first of these is regularly identified in the Old Testament and in the New. The other one is also clearly there, if in more subtle but no less consequential ways. It is Baal in the Old Testament and Mammon in the New. Jesus' use of the Aramaic term Mammon instead of a Greek noun for "wealth" is a confirmation of the fact that the first commandment is what is at stake, the having of other gods. But those strange and distant names cannot shield us from the lure of this god, Wealth (things, property). It is not just wealth, of course; it is the system of productivity and distribution that produces the wealth and sees that "I get mine." When Jeremiah chastises the exiles for making offerings to "other gods," in this instance the queen of heaven, they adamantly refuse to stop because when they made those offerings in the past, they "used to have plenty of food, and prospered, and saw no misfortune" (Jer. 44:17). Critical to the story of Jeremiah and the exiles is the realization that we are not talking here simply about individualized acquisitive instincts or habits, but about communal devotion to the gods of productivity and systemic efforts to elicit provision and wealth from them. That is why Mammon is not simply an abstraction—wealth—or a personal god. Mammon is what it takes to make the system more productive and provide more possibility for consumption. Most of the worship of other gods that goes on in the Scriptures is a communal enterprise. It is systemic because it has to do with the systems of making and spending, of getting and having. One of the things you can do with the God you have is to believe that you can have more with another god.

There are various texts of Scripture that illustrate and illuminate the undoing of the first commandment in the actions of the *political order* and responses to it. One of the most revealing and subtle instances is the account of the encounter between the chief priest at Bethel and the prophet Amos, who has been sent by the Lord from the south to prophesy in the northern kingdom. In their meeting, the priest tells Amos to leave town. His framing of the demand is what is revealing. Here are his words, first to the king, then to Amos:

> Then Amaziah, the priest of Bethel, sent to King Jeroboam of Israel, saying, "Amos has conspired against you in the very center of the house of Israel; the land is not able to bear all his words. For thus Amos has said,
>
> 'Jeroboam shall die by the sword,
> and Israel must go into exile away from his land.'"
>
> And Amaziah said to Amos, "O seer, go, flee away to the land of Judah, earn your bread there, and prophesy there; but never again prophesy at Bethel, for it is the king's sanctuary, and it is a temple of the kingdom."
>
> Then Amos answered Amaziah, "I am no prophet, nor a prophet's son; but I am a herdsman, and a dresser of sycamore trees, and the LORD took me from following the flock, and the LORD said to me, 'Go, prophesy to my people Israel.'" (Amos 7:10–15)

The choice of terminology is significant. "Amos has conspired against you [the king] in the very center of the house of Israel." The priest's concern is legitimate because Amos did indeed say that Jeroboam would die by the sword, but not quite that way (see below). What matters, however, is first of all that the location of the threat is described as "the *house* of Israel," surely an accurate and innocuous phrase, one of no consequence in this context. And that is the point. The consequentiality of Israel's identity as uncovered in the first commandment and the prologue has disappeared from the political scene to be replaced with an ethnic identification that has forgotten where Israel came from. When Amos responds to the priest of Bethel, the national shrine of the northern kingdom, Israel, he says that the Lord took him from following the flock and said, "Go prophesy to *my people* Israel." Not "the *house* of Israel," but "*my people* Israel," an apparently innocuous difference that conceals crucial and totally different perspectives. The political entity is understood by the political power as just that, the state, and thus under his control and subject to his will. Equally important, the religious leadership of the community, the priest anointed by the Lord, is fully complicit in this understanding. Thus Amos's response about his assignment, which recharacterizes the *polis* as "my people Israel," is an invocation of the claim of the first commandment (including the prologue) against its disappearance in the rhetoric of the religious and theological leadership.

The further words of Amaziah the priest make what has happened even more obvious, even if possibly not to him. He tells this southern prophet, Amos, to go back home to Judah and do his prophesying there, but don't ever prophesy again in Bethel, because it is—not "the house of the LORD" and/or "the temple of the LORD" but—"*the king's sanctuary*" and the "*temple of the kingdom.*" While you may be sure the moves were subtle and glossed with religiosity, the political authority has taken over the religious center and claimed it for its own. The political lord is the center of meaning and value in this sanctuary, the one who gives it identity, not "the LORD your God who brought you out of the land of Egypt, out of the house of slavery."

While resisting finding in the *polis* and its powers other gods that may draw us away from the God who has freed us in grace and mercy, we nevertheless must also ask what proper place the *polis* does have. Like the *oikonomia*, the *polis* is one of the frameworks for human flourishing without which we descend into a kind of communal and moral chaos. Jesus affirms the separation of that earthly power from the worship of God in his response to those who would test him about paying taxes. If the *economy* can be a part of human flourishing without becoming a god because you trust that what you have comes from the God you have and are willing to focus on the *God* you have more than on *what* you have, then the *polity*—the state, the civil order—can be an essential part of human community and the common good by being the context of our life with neighbors as much as it is a threat to our proper life with God. Indeed without a polity of some sort, a large common good with the neighbor is well nigh impossible either to achieve or to discover.

The apostle Paul specifically takes up the Commandments in Romans 13, which also, of course, is where we find his discourse on being subject to the governing authorities. He moves from that discourse into talking about the *second* table of the Decalogue, the commandments about the neighbor. I assume that movement results from his already being in the second table when he talks about the governing authorities. That is, Paul's discussion about honoring the political authority is a reflection of the commandment to honor parents, which, from at least the time of Deuteronomy to the present, has been understood as also directing the community about how to live in relation to the authorities and powers of the community as well as those of the household. The powers-that-be properly receive honor and respect via the injunction of the fifth commandment. But *that* is where they come into the moral framework provided by the Commandments, not in relation to the first commandment. The distinction is critical for maintaining the proper honor and respect that allows the community to function in good health and to insure that the human powers-that-be do not become other gods in whom we place all our trust and to whom our loyalty is more important than our obedience to God.

For this reason, I find myself thinking more and more of the Commandments, particularly the first one, as having to do with *obedience* rather than *loyalty*. There is a place for *civil* disobedience in the context of obedience to the only God you have. There is no place for the other gods, especially when they look like the leaders of the *polis*, the politicians, the powers-that-be. It is important to distinguish loyalty from discipleship, a notion that has its origins for both Jew and Christian precisely in the claim of the first commandment.

It is surprising and perplexing that those of us for whom the first commandment is indeed not simply a political axiom but *the* political axiom often justify our criticism of the government, its leaders, and their actions primarily on the grounds of a proper understanding of patriotism and the rights of free speech, which include dissent. That, however, is not where Christians come from. The First Commandment frees us for any and all criticism of the *polis* and politicians. The God you have is the only God you have; thus you are free from all restraints against the critique of lesser powers in this world.

My comments to this point have focused primarily on the *prohibitive* dimensions of the First Commandment. But Calvin rightly taught us that every negative command has its positive corollary and vice versa. Scripture itself makes this clear. The positive form of the First Commandment is probably most fully articulated in Deut. 13:4: "The LORD your God you shall follow, him alone you shall fear, his commandments you shall keep, his voice you shall obey, him you shall serve, and to him you shall hold fast." I suggest that this verse provides three responses to the question "What do you do with the God you have?" They are *trust*, *reverence*, and *conscience*.

First, and in brief, the final and climactic command of the verse is "to him [to the LORD] you shall hold fast." Though a form of loyalty is intended here, loyalty is inadequate to say what is really meant. The loyalty of the First Commandment is *trust*. Trust involves the possibility of living by risk and not worrying about it, living toward promise and knowing that the promise, however far off, is good. If we read the First Commandment in purely negative terms, we may forget that trust in the Lord—treating the promises of God, whatever they may be, as reliable—is a full devotion that is also fully *reciprocated*. Before we trust, we have been loved and freed. That is the structure of the Commandments. The trust that is commanded is our way through the wilderness, for that way is found precisely as one sets the Lord as the only reliable standing point for all of our life. The psalms regularly speak of trust in the Lord as manifest in finding in the God you have your only secure refuge.

> Trust in him at all time, O people;
> pour out your heart before him;
> God is a refuge for us.
> (Ps. 62:8)

The political meaning of this is self-evident but not confined to political activities alone. It means that risk is possible in the face of the power—actual and potential—of the *polis* and the lure of the economy. Both spheres are places for living and for moral reflection and action. They are not the objects of our trust. But because our refuge is elsewhere, "You do not have to be afraid." Precisely at that point the commandment comes to us as gospel, and we hear its evangelical force. And when we are undone and unable to overcome the powers that afflict our lives, the cry to God is the act of deepest trust and so an act of obedience to the first commandment.

Second, Deut. 13:4 adds to its interpretation of the First Commandment: "He [the LORD] is the one you shall fear." Under the first commandment, life is lived in the deepest *reverence* and awe before the Holy One, whose name is for us "the LORD your God." If there is reciprocity in the experience of trust, the experience of reverence and awe before the Lord your God has a different outflow. It is the possibility that in such a way before God we learn reverence not only as commandment but also as virtue. Again the political dimension of this way of feeling and being is evident and potent. Reverence means that one can no more treat the world and its populace casually and without respect than one can so treat the Lord your God. For once reverence becomes a mode of feeling and being and acting, its range is comprehensive. If, as Paul Woodruff rightly suggests, the basic components of reverence are awe, respect, and shame, then reverence makes it impossible, in the midst of war, to say, in contempt of others and without shame before God, "We wanted to kill them all but some got away."[5] It makes it impossible to count and mourn only the dead and wounded of your society and not those of your enemies or to care more about their oil fields than their artistic and cultural heritage.

Third, "His commandments you shall keep; his voice you shall obey." It is here in Deuteronomy 13's elaboration of the First Commandment that one encounters *conscience*. The familiar idiom "the voice of conscience" is apt in this instance. For it is precisely the question, To whom does one listen? that is at stake in the First Commandment, and that makes it politically axiomatic. The voice of conscience is the issue of who it is one obeys. For many, the conscience is some sort of internal moral impulse. I would rather stay with Deuteronomy and the voice. But the voice of the conscience is the Lord of the conscience, and the Lord of the conscience is the only God you have.

When the Westminster Confession of Faith takes up the matter of conscience, there are three aspects of its treatment that belong to our reflection on the first commandment. One is the fact that the subject of *conscience* is taken up immediately upon the Confession's discussion of the law as embodied in the Commandments, securing for good the connection between the Commandments and the voice of conscience. A second aspect of the confessional teaching is that conscience is taken up in the context of an understanding of Christian liberty. That means that talk about conscience in the context of Christian faith and the Commandments is about both freedom and restraint and how they are held in tension in the meaning of conscience. Thus we encounter a confessional echo of the joining of the prologue and the first commandment, the tension between being free and being under command. And the third aspect of the Confession's treatment of conscience is the fact that the Westminster divines found it necessary to provide a long concluding paragraph to the effect that there is not a contradiction between "the power which God has ordained," that is, the political power, and "the liberty which Christ has purchased." Thus Christian freedom is not to be regarded as a license for civil disobedience and rebellion against the political authorities. How one deals with this confessional safeguard and the tension it raises is not my immediate concern. What is important is that the tension is there, that the political implication of the issue of conscience, of "[the LORD's] voice you shall obey," is immediately present and unavoidable.

A final word. I do not want to let our thinking about the first commandment go without acknowledging the inherent connections with the other commandments in the first table. I will simply be suggestive and let you do the elaboration. To the extent that the first table of the Commandments is a way of learning what to do with the God you have, one may set out its movement and inner connections in the following way:

The First Commandment is a requirement that you take the God you have with ultimate seriousness; the Second Commandment, that you not take anything else too seriously; the Third Commandment is instruction not to take the Lord your God, the only God you have, too lightly; and the Sabbath commandment is there to help us take God very seriously and ourselves very lightly.

## NOTES

1. Karl Barth, "The First Commandment as an Axiom of Theology," in *The Way of Theology in Karl Barth: Essays and Comments*, ed. H. Martin Rumscheidt (Allison Park, Penn.: Pickwick, 1986), 77.
2. Arthur C. Cochrane, *The Church's Confession under Hitler* (Philadelphia: Westminster Press, 1962), 135.
3. W. Brueggemann, "Foreword," *Journal for Preachers* 26, no. 3 (2003): 1.
4. The formulation here is not simply rhetorical. Scholars debate the particular force of the prepositional phrase at the end of the First Commandment: *'al pānāy*. It can mean "before me" (i.e., in front of me or preceding me); "beside me" (i.e., alongside me); "besides me" (i.e., in my place, except me); and "over against me" (i.e., in hostile confrontation with me). The interpretive issue is not a decision to choose one over the others but to recognize that all of these meanings are present in the commandment: (a) You have no other gods *in front of* this God, taking a prior place to the Lord of Israel; (b) You have no other gods placed in a pantheon *alongside* the Lord; (c) further, no other god may *take the place* of the Lord for you; and, finally (d) you may not set any god *over against* the Lord.
5. Paul Woodruff, *Reverence: Renewing a Forgotten Virtue* (New York: Oxford University Press, 2001).

5

# Conflicting Paths to Hope in Jeremiah

*Louis Stulman*

Jeremiah is a book for our time.[1] Its haunting language of death and destruction resonates with us in strange and unexpected ways, and Jeremiah's penetrating portrayals of the horrors of war and a crumbling world are no longer unfamiliar terrain. It seems as though only yesterday they were an oddity, another's script but not our own. Siege, danger, and social chaos spoke only of faraway places, or perhaps, if we dared, of city streets in our own land, but still far, far from our settled places. Only yesterday Jeremiah's dangerous world, or the mere idea of a colloquium on the shaking of earth and heaven,[2] would have seemed alien. Our place in the world was safe and symmetrical, our lives well insulated and predictable, with only a few glitches along the way.

But all that has changed. We are currently engaged in a war that tens of millions consider deeply troubling and potentially catastrophic. Our country's foreign policy has cast a dark cloud over international law and American credibility. Like no other time in recent history, hard-wrought social programs, especially for the most vulnerable among us, are in grave danger. After careful scrutiny, trusted institutions—political, religious, judicial, and economic—are now more than suspect. Dwindling funds for basic human services and a burgeoning national debt, in part due to massive military spending, put generations to come at great risk. I am not an alarmist by any stretch of the imagination, but I am worried about the future of our country and the world and our children's part in it. It seems as though the entire global arena is coming unglued and our nation is in part a protagonist in the undoing. The terrible events of 9/11 still loom large and always will, but our grief has been

An abbreviated version of this essay appeared in the *Journal for Preachers* 27, no. 2 (2004): 18–25.

exploited in obscene ways. That terrible day has been used to polarize, to demonize, and to attack.

On September 13, 2001, I received e-mail from my friend John Hill of Melbourne College of Divinity, who expressed sympathy and wrote that eighty Australians were either dead or missing, "a large figure for us, given that the largest civil disaster in this country, a train crash about twenty-five years ago, killed about that number." Then John wrote, "We continue to pray here for strength, healing and restraint, because the political pressure to go out and attack someone will be almost irresistible." How terribly perceptive he was! And so, we are left to ponder the grotesque and unspeakable: waves of darkness and smoke; searing images of indestructible buildings dissolving; ferociously "precise" weapons ravaging innocent civilians; military occupation breeding violence and hatred; anarchy leading to riots, abduction, and rape; as well as mounting numbers of hungry, war-torn refugees. The litany of suffering does not seem to end. In stark contrast to Isaiah's vision of peace, we live in a world where plowshares are beaten into swords and pruning hooks into spears, where nations lift up sword against nation and war is the "mother tongue" (Isa. 2:4). What a collage of horror! Who would have ever thought that crippling fear, cynicism, and loss of confidence would be part of our individual and national narrative?

Over the years Walter Brueggemann has given poignant testimony to the end of past certainties. He has spoken of our situation as a "time of dislocation"[3] and has repeatedly employed the metaphor of exile, drawn in some measure from the book of Jeremiah, to speak of the church in North America.[4] But to be perfectly honest, I am not sure I actually grasped the implications of his reading until recently. Now it seems quite clear—if there were ever a doubt—that the shaking of earth and heaven speaks directly to our own moment in history.

## I. JEREMIAH AS A MAP OF HOPE FOR SHIPWRECKED EXILES

In this essay, I argue that the book of Jeremiah is a map of hope for people living on the brink of despair—for exiles in Babylon and exiles today. First of all, the text dares to speak of an experience too painful for most to utter. With candor it testifies to the end of longstanding institutions associated with God's blessings, cherished belief systems, and social structures that for centuries appeared invincible. Initially this brutal honesty may seem to have nothing whatsoever to do with newness, but truth telling, as we all well know, is the first step to healing and restoration.[5] Beyond this, the interpretive community of

Jeremiah organizes the moral and symbolic chaos into shapes that are orderly and rationally manageable. The structure of the book, for instance, bears witness to a God who "plucks up and pulls down" in chapters 1–25 *and* who "builds and plants" in chapters 26–52. Accordingly, Jeremiah moves beyond brute geopolitical forces—forces that spell death—to a God whose purposes are ultimately redemptive and salvific. At the end of the day, Jeremiah offers a path to hope that is diametrically at odds with the establishment position. Unlike the prophet Hananiah and others who would insist that the devastating events are merely bumps in the road, Jeremiah asserts that they represent a true turning point. That is, the hope that Jeremiah holds is not for a return to the old world but for a new beginning and a new community defined by justice, obedience, and inclusion. This fresh formulation, by the way, in part gave birth to Judaism. And this hope, I believe, is instructive to us in our troubled post-9/11 world.

By and large the book of Jeremiah has not been associated with hope.[6] When one is cataloging the central themes of Jeremiah, hope is usually last to be mentioned, if at all. Most read Jeremiah as a prophet of doom and gloom. Only rarely, it is maintained, does the "weeping prophet" speak words of hope (e.g., the Book of Comfort), and when he does, his utterances are obscured by a larger literary context of sin and judgment. While there is little doubt that the book of Jeremiah pulsates with such language, it nonetheless also articulates a script for new life and hope beyond disaster. In fact, Brevard Childs finds the key to the canonical shaping of Jeremiah in its "salvation oracles."[7] According to him, "regardless of the severity of the divine judgment on Israel, the ultimate goal in the divine economy was redemption."[8] Ronald Clements and Walter Brueggemann have organized their commentaries around the dual role of divine judgment and salvation. Clements goes so far as to suggest that the central message of Jeremiah is that of hope.[9] The subtitle of Brueggemann's commentary, "Exile and Homecoming," highlights his conviction that the book moves beyond dislocation and disaster to return and restoration.[10] Developing this thought, Brueggemann has recently made the case that the final form of Jeremiah is designed "to walk Jews into, through, and beyond the reality of destruction and exile."[11] Kathleen M. O'Connor has likewise proposed that disaster and survival are the "chief subjects" of the book of Jeremiah.[12] The point of the prophetic text, O'Connor suggests, is to create a world in which survivors can name the disaster, interpret it, and find hope through the persona of Jeremiah, a "survivor of disaster."[13] Following suit, I have argued that the literary organization or architecture of Jeremiah itself, governed by the prose tradition, leads the reader on a path to hope.[14] After the first scroll (Jer. 1–25) dismantles the foundations of Judah's social and theological "first principles," the second scroll (Jer. 26–52) begins to develop strategies designed to enable refugees to cope with and even thrive in their new setting in Babylon. Thus, the symbolic logic of the book paves the way for profound configurations of hope and new life. Before examining these arrangements, we must first consider the brutal honesty that makes them possible.

## II. ORGANIZING THE CHAOS INTO MANAGEABLE SHAPES

The book of Jeremiah speaks of a world under massive assault and of a people whose lives are wracked with pain. With disturbing images and raw emotion, it bears witness to a tragedy so terrible that it defies ordinary categories. Brueggemann calls it the end of Judah's known world.[15] Diamond speaks of the crisis as the "end of a culture."[16] O'Connor refers to the moment as the "colossal collapse of the world."[17] For the Judean nation, the fall of Jerusalem and exile to Babylon represented nothing less than the shaking of earth and heaven. Perhaps the most poignant words to describe this cosmic shaking appear in Jer. 4:23–26. The NRSV captures the text's cadence of terror:

> I looked on the earth, and lo, it was waste and void;
> and to the heavens, and they had no light.
> I looked on the mountains, and lo, they were quaking,
> and all the hills moved to and fro.
> I looked, and lo, there was no one at all,
> and all the birds of the air had fled.
> I looked, and lo, the fruitful land was a desert,
> and all its cities were laid in ruins
> before the LORD, before his fierce anger.

Jeremiah envisions the horrors of war. Make no mistake: enemy invasion and occupation are what the text alludes to in haunting, symbolic language. The order of creation collapses and reverts to its primeval state of chaos, "wild and waste" (cf. Gen. 1:2); the heavens become dark, mountains and hills tremble, birds take flight, fertile land turns into uninhabited desert. The earth loses its form and beauty as all is reduced to desolation and hopelessness. Ironically, this vision of chaos is meticulously structured. The parallel construction "I looked . . . I looked . . . I looked . . . I looked" is followed in each case by the Hebrew predicator of existence (*hinnēh*), "there was . . . there was . . . there was . . . there was," although no lifesigns can be found. The symmetry and repetition of the prophetic words only heighten the dread.

This text of terror is one of a myriad that speaks of unbearable suffering and loss of meaning. We also encounter in Jeremiah a surplus of disturbing metaphors: death sneaking through the windowlaces to do its insidious work (9:21), Daughter Zion being attacked and raped (13:20–27), and a dangerous (mythological) foe from the north poised to pounce on the inhabitants of Judah (e.g., 1:14; 6:22). We read of ferocious lions (2:15; 4:7), venomous snakes (8:17), as well as devouring swords, ravenous wild dogs, and vultures consuming their prey (15:3). As a result, "hands fall helpless" (6:24), sackcloth is donned (4:8; 6:26), and the bereaved of Judah outnumber the sand of the seas (15:8), which is an inversion of the ancestral promise of progeny (Gen. 22:17; 32:12). At the sight of ground zero, the tears of God, Jeremiah, and Judah inundate the world. "O that my head were a spring of water, and my eyes a fountain of tears, so that I might weep day and night for the slain of my poor people!" (Jer. 9:1). How could profound sadness not accompany the end of life as it was known?

Indeed, the first twenty-five chapters of Jeremiah broadcast the collapse of Judah's once stable world.[18] Organized around prose sermons in chapters 7, 11, 18, 21, and 25, these texts reenact the demise of the nation's sturdiest pillars, its sacred canopy: (1) *the great temple of Solomon and its systems of worship*, Jeremiah contends, will end up like Shiloh, nothing but rubble (7:1–15); (2) the *beloved covenant* between God and Israel testifies to the guilt of God's people rather than to their special place (11:1–17); (3) the *election tradition*, once a source of great confidence, is now in the service of outsiders, who enjoy the seat of honor (18:1–11); (4) strangers occupy *the land* once inhabited by Israel; and Israel in turn must live far from its home as a disenfranchised people in Babylon (21:1–10); and (5) *the dynasty*, the venerated Davidic dynasty, comes to an abrupt and screeching halt, at least as traditionally conceived (21:1–10). With Zedekiah's violent death and Jehoiachin's deportation, the kingdom and its long line of kings dies out. God has indeed "plucked up and pulled down, destroyed and overthrown." To drive home this point, by the end of the "first scroll," Jeremiah envisages the people of Judah leading the wayward nations in drinking the cup of divine wrath (25:17–29). And so, the first half of the book portrays the prophet Jeremiah frustrating every argument that God is inextricably tied to Judah's conventional religious and social systems, especially those associated with the temple and the state. Hence, nothing remains to prop up its toppling world.

The prophetic drama holds nothing back. It faces Judah's national catastrophe head on without flinching. The Jeremiah tradition courageously tells the truth about the gravity of the moment; it rejects denial; and it even claims that in some measure the people of God, especially their leaders, are coconspirators in the collapse. Judah's unfaithfulness to God and mistreatment of the poor in tandem with its royal policies of brutality and unbridled greed have brought down the walls of the city. In all this, Jeremiah, God's messenger, merely does what prophets do best: he sees through façades, shatters illusions, and grasps that such crimes are no mere misdemeanors but catastrophes that threaten the survival of the world.[19]

Not everyone buys this critique. In fact, few do. The Jerusalem establishment contends that Jeremiah is uncompromising and incendiary. It treats Jeremiah as a traitor who must be exiled or executed. His townsmen seek to silence his "eschatological" reading of the moment:

> Let us destroy the tree with its fruit,
> let us cut him off from the land of the living
> so that his name will no longer be remembered!
> (11:19)

Still others write him off as a *meshugah*—a madman—to be put "in the stocks and the collar" (29:26). Hardly anyone even entertains the possibility that Jeremiah might be speaking the word of the Lord. His detractors are sure that he is misguided when he nails the coffin shut on Judah's accepted modes of living and construals of reality (e.g., 18:18). God would never "uproot and tear down" the nation's public policies and social arrangements! Cosmic upheaval, the shaking of earth and heaven, is simply out of the question. Only time would tell how wrong they were.

## III. HOPE THROUGH THE WRECKAGE

Does Jeremiah's scathing critique of the old world close the door on the future? Does the text leave any room for hope after the wreckage? The second scroll, chapters 26–52, asserts that Israel's final chapter has not yet been inscribed. Although God "plucks up and pulls down," God also "builds and plants." Amid the destruction, seeds of hope spring forth: God sculpts new beginnings out of the rubble of fallen worlds.

The second half of the prophetic drama exploits every opportunity to show that the end has not come for the people of God. For the first time, for instance, individuals emerge who are receptive to the message of Jeremiah. These faithful few come to Jeremiah's aid when his life is on the line in the temple (26:16–19) and the royal court (36:9–19, 26), when he is thrown into a cistern (38:7–13), and during the Babylonian siege of Jerusalem (39:11–18; 40:1–6). In each case, supporters not only rescue Jeremiah from harm's way, but they protect the nation from "bringing innocent blood upon itself" (e.g., 26:15). Jeremiah's battle with prophets (Jer. 27–29), moreover, is essentially waged over the question, Which configuration of hope is "true"? Whether the nation will survive is not the issue. What is at stake is the developing character of the embattled nation. The most stunning display of hope is found in the "Book of Comfort" (Jer. 30–33). Here God reverses the judgments against Judah and outlines in their place a resilient script for the future. Even the

Baruch narrative, which recounts the suffering of Jeremiah and the fall of Jerusalem, makes the case that hope for the future lies with the exiles in Babylon and not with those remaining in the land.[20] That is to say, while the text is describing the end of one world, it is at the same time creating symbolic space for the emergence of another, albeit in a faraway land.

Finally, the three endings of Jeremiah, chapters 45, 46–51, and 52—each representing different points in the development of the book—speak of better times for the suffering people of God. The first is an oracle response to Baruch, in which God promises Jeremiah's scribe "his life as a prize of war" (45:5). The Oracles against the Nations (Jer. 46–51), another ending of the Hebrew text of the book, punctuate the book with implicit hope for exiled Judah. Specifically, the announcement of Babylon's defeat signals an epoch of hope and salvation for Judah (Jer. 50–51). And the concluding report winds up with the kind treatment of King Jehoiachin in Babylon (52:31–34), apparently whispering that the future of Judah has not come to an irrevocable end.

Despite the fact that Jeremiah's path to hope is neither unified nor systematic (cf. Ezek. 40–48), we are still able to discern its broad features. From the literary arrangement of the second scroll and from the text's recurring motifs, the following shapes emerge: First, *hope is rooted in suffering.*

> The people who survived the sword
> found grace in the wilderness. . . .
> With weeping they shall come,
> and with consolations I will lead them back. . . .
> I will turn their mourning into joy,
> I will comfort them, and give them gladness for sorrow.
> (31:2, 9a, 13cd)

Please note in these passages that sadness permeates nearly every moment of joy. Indeed, the Book of Comfort (Jer. 30–33) unites expressions of hope with suffering and marginality.[21] The first chapter of the Book of Comfort is a case in point. Its oracles of consolation are far from idyllic (e.g., 30:5–17). There is no utopian vision of the future, no garden scene, no ideal notion of peace and happiness. Instead, one encounters an assortment of disturbing images of war and invasion juxtaposed with language of embryonic hope.

> Alas! that day is so great,
> there is none like it;
> it is a time of distress for Jacob;
> yet he shall be rescued from it.
> (30:7)

Battle cries, expressions of panic, and excruciating pain pepper the literary landscape. The condition of God's people is deplorable; the prognosis is bleak

(30:12–16). Their wound is "grievous," and there is no one to mediate and nowhere to turn for help. All their lovers, or political allies, have forsaken them. Yet, unexpectedly and in a sheer act of grace, God resolves to restore and heal outcast Zion (30:17–22). God promises to redeem Israel from many troubles, but this redemption throbs with pain.

Hope is possible when the community embraces the painful realities of exile. In contrast to prophets who would deny these tragic dimensions and predict a speedy return to business as usual, Jeremiah asserts that there can be no ecstasy without mourning, no homecoming without exile, no salvation without judgment, no joyous songs without the memories of loss. Any vision of the future that avoids the real world of human suffering makes a travesty of the past and can never deal with the emotional and symbolic pain of exile. It is therefore no accident that the Book of Comfort depicts the people of God as "survivors." They have endured war, amputated hopes, splintered families, and the travail of a shattered world. Now, by the force of the prophetic word, God empowers shipwrecked people to imagine a future when none seemed possible. This is the starting point for hope and recovery.

Second, *hope involves letting go of the old world*. Jeremiah maintains that the people of God cannot return to the securities of the past. The old social world and its conventional scripts are forever gone. All that remain are ghosts. There is a powerful temptation during times of uncertainty to cling to the familiar and glamorize the ghosts of the past, no matter how destructive they may have been (see, e.g., the stories of the wilderness wanderings in Exod. 16:1–3; Num. 11:1–9). Jeremiah urges the Jewish refugees in Babylon to recognize this temptation for what it is and abandon all expectations of returning to the old world, especially one defined by a dynasty and a temple. When they do, when they relinquish the illusions of the past and its modes of power and orientation, when they surrender their old identity and accept their marginal status in Babylon, then despair loses its grip and hope is born.[22] Only then are they open to the new things that God has waiting for them. "There is hope for your future . . . for the LORD has created a new thing on the earth" (31:17a, 22c).

In his wonderful book *With Open Hands*, Henri Nouwen describes prayer as letting go and surrendering to God.[23] Nouwen tells a disturbing story of an old woman brought to a psychiatric center clenching her fist and swinging at everything in sight in fear that the doctors might take from her a penny. "It was as though she would lose her very self along with the coin." With this image Nouwen speaks of prayer as opening one's hand and heart to God. To let go of one's "small coins" is to discover the many gifts that God has in store. Indeed, with open hands one discovers God. Nouwen's story illustrates how frightening it is to let go of the "treasures" we cling to. But relinquishment is even more terrifying when the prevailing voices of the time insist that one hold on for dear life.

Jeremiah's prophetic opponent Hananiah represents one of those voices (28:1–17). According to Hananiah, there was little need to let go of the old world, for Judah's crisis was only temporary and in the long run inconsequential. After a few difficult years, life would return to normal. The nation's social structures and embroiled networks of meaning would withstand the upheaval and remain intact. "Be patient, give it some time, and the market will rebound!" With ringing authority Hananiah even gave dates and places. "'Within two years [the LORD] will bring back to this place all the vessels of the LORD's house . . . and will also bring back to this place King Jeconiah . . . and all the exiles from Judah who went to Babylon'" (28:3–4).

To Jeremiah, his opponent's appeal to traditional categories of continuity, even though grounded in Isaiah's prophecies, was not only dangerous and deceptive but also a demonstration of profound denial. Indeed, Hananiah embodies denial in the narrative account. He rejects the fissured dimension of Judah's experience in favor of unfounded hope. Anesthetized by wishful thinking, he would forget the personal and national traumas and live as if they did not really happen. Hananiah would create a pleasant, comfortable world that conforms to his own daydreams. And we, of course, do the same.[24] Yet fabricating a fictive world, no matter how appealing, cannot bring about healing and newness. Hope involves telling the truth and letting go of the old so that God's newness can break through.

Third, *hope exists on the margins and not at the center*. I think that this claim caused the most stir and incited the most opposition. And for obvious reasons. We almost instinctively link hope with power and success, with being at the hub of our little universe. It is difficult to imagine otherwise. The rush of adrenalin and the sense of euphoria that accompanies winning bear this out. For Jeremiah, however, hope is not found in triumphant nationalism, hegemony, or the customary military pomp and circumstance, that is, *in the garb of winners*. Hope emerges among the vulnerable and wounded.[25] The first readers of Jeremiah knew this all too well. Those who survived the fall of Jerusalem were no longer privileged in the old ways; they no longer enjoyed the insulation of a safe and reliable world; and they could no longer look to reassuring modes of orientation as a sign of God's blessing.

One can also look to the persona of Jeremiah, the righteous prophet and model of the new community, and his loyal scribe Baruch, to see that faithful living is not always rewarded in the traditional ways. There were no trophies for "best prophet" or "best scribe." Instead of receiving the conventional affirmations for obedience, Jeremiah suffers for God's sake. In the Confessions, moreover, God repeatedly rejects the prophet's petitions for equilibrium.

Likewise Baruch will not receive the assurances he so desperately desires: "And you [Baruch], do you seek great things for yourself? Do not seek them; for I am going to bring disaster upon all flesh, says the LORD; *but I will give you your life as a prize of war* in every place to which you may go" (45:5; emphasis added). Perhaps God blesses the faithful with "great things" in the best of times. But during the shaking of earth and heaven God promises only that they will survive. And yet survival is no sign of God's rejection or God's impotence. Living on the margins does not mean that God has forsaken suffering people, nor reneged on past promises. In the midst of all the devastation, God is present and God's purposes prevail. Only now it becomes altogether clear that God's place in the world is among the broken and dispossessed. The importance of this overture of hope cannot be overstated: by unmasking the illusion of power and by subverting conventional modes of orientation, the mystery of incarnation, and perhaps even that of the cross, is broached.

Fourth, *hope involves community building*.[26] While the new world of exile pulsates with anxiety and vexation, it also presents unique opportunities. Jeremiah encourages the exiles in Babylon to seize the moment to create genuine community. "Build houses and live in them; plant gardens and eat what they produce. . . . multiply there, and do not decrease. . . . For surely I know the plans I have for you, says the LORD, plans for your [*shalom*] and not for harm, to give you a future with hope" (29:5, 6d, 11). During their time of displacement the people of God might be tempted to sit back and do nothing or hastily follow the guidance of those who promise an imminent return to Jerusalem. So Jeremiah presses the exiles to unpack their bags, put down roots, affirm the bonds of family, and work toward peace and community building in their own neighborhoods, that is, in their own local settings in Babylon. "Seek the [*shalom*] of the city where I have sent you into exile, and pray to the LORD on its behalf, for in its [*shalom*] you will find your [*shalom*]" (29:7). Such instruction would surely not have been welcome. To pray for the welfare of their enemies, to set up homes in Babylon, and to forgo, at least for a long time, their aspirations to return to Jerusalem was anything but good news. Nonetheless, Jeremiah insists that the key to survival and hope was to join God in creating a just and compassionate counterculture, a place of new shapes and social alternatives, where violence, exploitation, and idolatry do not reign.

The second scroll in no way delineates the precise character of this "new-yet-old" community, but it does consider its rough contours. The Book of Comfort, for example, speaks of the exilic community as a place of joy, love, and embrace of the other (31:7–14); it imagines an alternative society in which one is accepted regardless of where they have been or what they have done. This war-torn community pays little attention to social position, thus leveling the playing field. Indeed, Jeremiah advocates the notion of community as inclusive and unified.

Israel's homecoming is to comprise the northern and southern kingdoms. "At that time, says the LORD, I will be the God of all the families of Israel, and they shall be my people" (31:1). All God's people are invited to the banquet, above all the most vulnerable and needy among the Jewish refugees (31:7–9). Furthermore, the knowledge of God is available to everyone, often without priestly mediation (31:34); and God showers all who return with blessing (e.g., 30:18–19; 31:1–6; 32:36–41). Hierarchical arrangements of community life, while not abandoned, are diminished. The newly imagined leader, for instance, does not wield interminable military authority, nor rule with an iron fist. The promised descendant of David is a just and righteous upholder of the social and judicial order without the traditional military trappings. As such, he is a royal savior committed to preserving justice and *shalom* (see 30:9, 21; cf. 33:14–26).

Fifth, *hope emerges in the form of a new spirituality*. The spirituality of the new world enjoys a deeply "personal" texture.[27] While the book of Jeremiah does not promote a piety that divorces the individual from the group—an idea that is clearly modern—it does envisage a community in which individuals enjoy a close relationship with God, where people's lives and personal affairs matter to God. The "new" relation, described in one place as a "new covenant" (31:31–34) and in another place as an "everlasting covenant" (32:36–44), carries with it the assurance of full acceptance before God (31:34; 33:6–8), divine favor and protection (30:10–11; 32:36–44; 33:1–9), deliverance from captivity (30:10–11, 18–21; 31:7–14, 23–25), joy (30:18–19; 31:3–6), and inner renewal (31:33; 32:39–40).

Unlike the old piety, which stressed human responsibility, this new spirituality depends far more on the extraordinary workings of God. The "if" of the divine-human relation takes a back seat to the sovereign and gracious workings of God.[28] Such a shift is absolutely necessary for people whose treasured theologies, rituals, nationalism, and ready assumptions have all failed. To address these failures, God, in a grand display of mercy, pledges to mend the broken relationship. In a bold and unprecedented move, God promises to inscribe the Torah on the hearts of the women and men who make up Israel (31:31–34). This internalization of divine instruction, this interiorization of religion, empowers victims of exile to love and obey God; and it enables them to break out of a vicious cycle of guilt and failure. The cornerstone of the new spirituality is divine forgiveness. To be sure, the new divine-human relationship hinges on God's resolve to "forgive [their] iniquity and remember [their] sin no more" (31:34). Refugees laden with guilt are granted clemency and let off the hook. Only then can the dispirited find the emotional energy to face the challenges that await them in the new world order.

Sixth, *hope is textual.* The formation of hope in Jeremiah is integrally related to a scroll, that is, to the written word of God. The prophetic scroll that authorized the undoing of the nation (25:13) now endorses the future of the surviving community of exiles (Jer. 26–52). In the second half of the book, written prophecy takes on a life of its own, often independent of the spoken words of Jeremiah. The transition from the spoken word to the written word emerges at critical junctures of the book. At the start of the second scroll, officials come to Jeremiah's defense by citing an oracle of Micah, presumably a written oracle (26:16–19). And their appeal to written prophecy, along with historical precedence, saves the day. At the end of the book, Jeremiah writes on a scroll "the disasters that would come on Babylon" (51:59–64). This symbolic action bears seeds of hope for captive peoples in Babylon, seeds that would eventuate in their liberation.

In the intervening chapters, Jeremiah sends letters to the exiles in Babylon with the intention of dispelling despair and engendering genuine hope in a faraway place (29:1–32). At the command of the Lord, Jeremiah prepares a "book" that takes dead aim at heartache and hopelessness (30:1–31:37). God instructs Jeremiah to preserve written documentation of the transaction between his cousin Hanamel and himself (32:6–44). The written materials, which Baruch places in an earthenware jar, serve as a testimony that God would one day restore the people of God. Perhaps the best-known example of the shift from spoken to written prophecy is the confrontation between King Jehoiakim and Jeremiah (36:1–32). In the narrative account, Jeremiah dictates the word of the Lord to Baruch, who reads it before Jehoiakim. The king in turn destroys the scroll of oracles only to have Jeremiah create another scroll, which contains "all the words of the scroll that King Jehoiakim of Judah had burned in the fire; and many similar words" (36:32). When all is said and done, the story affirms that this seemingly innocuous scroll trumps the king. The Word is victorious!

In all, the new epoch of hope rests firmly on Yahweh's written Word. In lieu of fallen social and theological supports—a temple and its liturgical systems, a king and a strong nation, a land and the old covenant assurances—the Word, and ultimately the God who utters it, now forms the foundation for newness. This Word matters even when "shock and awe" campaigns *appear* to render it meaningless. This Word matters even when kings conspire to tame its subversive force. Yahweh's Word matters because it disarms powers and principalities, undermines tyranny, mobilizes the faithful, and generates hope in those suffering from debilitating despair (cf. Isa. 40:1–8; 55:10–13).

Finally, *hope is found in worship*. A number of scholars have made a plausible case for the liturgical character of sections of Jeremiah.[29] It is now fairly well established, for instance, that the Confessions of Jeremiah are more than private prayers. In all likelihood, these laments are expressions of some facet of

Israel's public worship. Moreover, Mark Biddle has argued cogently that the multiple voices in Jer. 7–20 represent various constituencies participating in communal worship.[30] It is also reasonable to suppose that the Oracles against the Nations (OAN; Jer. 46–51) emanate from community worship rather than elsewhere in the social world of early diasporic Judaism. Along these lines, Brueggemann suggests that these oracles—as well as similar ones in the prophetic literature (e.g., Amos 1–2; Isa. 13–23; and Ezek. 25–32)—may have "emerged in the midst of liturgic celebrations of the sovereignty of Yahweh, and served to voice the claim that God's sovereign rule extended not simply over Israel but over all peoples."[31] Not unlike several royal psalms and hymns in the Psalter (e.g., Pss. 2, 68, 95–97, 99; see also Pss. 83, 94), the OAN both celebrate Yahweh's victory over world-destroying nations and make an array of stunning claims regarding Yahweh's reign on earth. In strange and unfamiliar garb, the OAN affirm that Yahweh, the divine ruler (46:18; 48:15; 51:57), will defeat nations resorting to the politics of arrogance and exploitation, especially Babylon. Yahweh, they declare, will not be foiled by oppressive regimes, and particularly not by rebellious vassals. And in the end, the OAN herald that Yahweh, not random geopolitical forces, controls Israel's destiny. Thus, the OAN conclude the book of Jeremiah with the triumphant note that Yahweh reigns in and through the vicissitudes of life.

Notwithstanding the force of such claims, the OAN do more than make astonishing assertions. When these texts reenact God's rule on earth, they improve the vision of exiles assembled in the synagogues of Babylon to "twenty-twenty." Through the lenses of worship, beaten down refugees in Babylon are able to see clearly that worldly power is not ultimate power, that economic-military domination is not the final word, and that God is a strong advocate for those who have been devastated by war. In this way the OAN are nothing less than "guerilla theater," a term Brueggemann has used to describe other biblical texts of resistance.[32] Such speech re-performs the fall of the powerful, without resorting to physical violence;[33] it rejects oppressive politics as normative, and it says no to despair and inertia. This public expression of faith, this subversive form of worship, sees through sinful social and political systems and in response creates its own matrix of justice and mercy. In doing so, it does not attempt to escape the fractured and troubled world or transform it through violence. Rather, this act of worship, this holy defiance, ennobles the people of God to protest and dissent, ridicule and revel, and imagine a counterview and a counter world order. For the exiles in Babylon, such worship was anything but innocuous; it was a dangerous "weapon of hope" that refused to knuckle under to political aggression and military hardware.

## IV. CONCLUSION

Hope is a rare commodity these days. In fact, despair may be one of the most debilitating diseases of our time. It is palpable, and it is everywhere. The book of Jeremiah provides an alternative script to despair, for exiles of old and exiles today. It intends to inspire hope in those whose lives have been ransacked by loss. Not the kind of hope that imagines a return to the world as it was, but one that generates faith and courage to live through the shaking of earth and heaven. Hope that is rooted in suffering. Hope that demands open hands and open hearts; hope that exists on the edge and not at the center; hope in action, building genuine community; hope that emanates from the Scriptures and that comes alive in worship. In sum the book of Jeremiah is a map of hope for the vulnerable and disenfranchised. It is a word for our troubled time.[34]

## NOTES

1. See, e.g., the many references to September 11, 2001, in the recent issue of *Word & World* 22, no. 4 (Fall 2002), which is devoted to the book of Jeremiah.
2. "Shaking Earth and Heaven: Bible, Church, and the Changing Social Order," Columbia Theological Seminary, Decatur, Georgia, on April 21–23, 2003.
3. Walter Brueggemann, "Conversations Among Exiles," *Christian Century* (July 2–9, 1997): 630.
4. See, e.g., Walter Brueggemann, *Cadences of Home: Preaching among Exiles* (Louisville, Ky.: Westminster John Knox Press, 1997).
5. On the importance of "naming the disaster," see Kathleen M. O'Connor, "Surviving Disaster in the Book of Jeremiah," *Word &World* 22, no. 4 (Fall 2002): 369–77.
6. Ezekiel and Isaiah 40–55 are the prophetic texts usually attributed to helping the Jewish exiles cope with the devastating experiences of Babylonian invasion and deportation.
7. Brevard S. Childs, *Introduction to the Old Testament as Scripture* (Philadelphia: Fortress Press, 1979), 350–52.
8. Ibid., 351.
9. Ronald E. Clements, *Jeremiah*, Interpretation (Atlanta: John Knox Press, 1988), 3; note also his earlier article, "Jeremiah. Prophet of Hope," in *Review and Expositor* 78 (1981): 345–63.
10. Walter Brueggemann, *A Commentary on Jeremiah: Exile and Homecoming* (Grand Rapids: Wm. B. Eerdmans Publishing Co., 1998); see also *Hopeful Imagination: Prophetic Voices in Exile* (Philadelphia: Fortress Press, 1986), 29–31.
11. Walter Brueggemann, "Meditation upon the Abyss: The Book of Jeremiah," *Word &World* 22, no. 4 (Fall 2002): 341.
12. O'Connor, "Surviving Disaster."
13. Ibid., 369.
14. Louis Stulman, *Order Amid Chaos: Jeremiah as Symbolic Tapestry* (Sheffield: Sheffield Academic Press, 1998), 56–98, 137–66.

15. Brueggemann, *Hopeful Imagination*, 3–7.
16. A. R. Pete Diamond, "Deceiving Hope: The Ironies of Metaphorical Beauty and Ideological Terror in Jeremiah" (paper presented at the international meeting of the Society of Biblical Literature, Rome, 2001).
17. Kathleen M. O'Connor, "Jeremiah and Formation of the Moral Character of the Community" (paper presented at the annual meeting of the Society of Biblical Literature, Toronto, 2002).
18. Stulman, *Order Amid Chaos*, 23–55.
19. Abraham Heschel, *The Prophets* (New York: Perennial Classics, 2001), 3–6.
20. In his notes in *The New Oxford Annotated Bible*, 3d ed. (Oxford and New York: Oxford University Press, 2001), Mark E. Biddle describes the failings of the Jewish communities in Judah and Egypt (Jer. 40:7–44:30) as a strategy to demonstrate that "hope for the future of God's people lies only with the Babylonian exiles" (1142).
21. Clements, *Jeremiah*, 180.
22. See Brueggemann, *Hopeful Imagination*, esp. 1–7, 10–47.
23. Henri Nouwen, *With Open Hands* (Notre Dame, Ind.: Ave Maria, 1972). This first edition of Nouwen's work includes marvelous photographs by Ron P. Van Den Bosch and Theo Robert.
24. Cf. Henri Nouwen, *The Living Reminder: Service and Prayer in Memory of Jesus Christ* (San Francisco: Harper and Row, 1984), 22.
25. An incisive treatment of the conditions of the diasporic community in Babylon can be found in Daniel L. Smith-Christopher, *A Biblical Theology of Exile*, OBT (Minneapolis: Fortress Press, 2002).
26. For a provocative anthology on hope in action, see *Hope for the World: Mission in a Global Context*, ed. Walter Brueggemann (Louisville, Ky.: Westminster John Knox Press, 2001).
27. For a critical analysis of personal religion, especially as it appears in second millennium Mesopotamian texts, see Thorkild Jacobsen, *The Treasures of Darkness: A History of Mesopotamian Religion* (New Haven, Conn.: Yale University Press, 1978), 145–64.
28. See T. A. Raitt, *A Theology of Exile: Judgment/Deliverance in Jeremiah and Ezekiel* (Philadelphia: Fortress Press, 1977).
29. See, e.g., H. G. Reventlow, *Liturgie und prophetisches Ich bei Jeremia* (Gütersloh: Gütersloher, 1966).
30. M. E. Biddle, *Polyphony and Symphony in Prophetic Literature: Rereading Jeremiah 7–20*, Studies in Old Testament Interpretation 2 (Macon, Ga.: Mercer University Press, 1996).
31. Brueggemann, *A Commentary on Jeremiah*, 418.
32. Walter Brueggemann, *Ichabod Towards Home: The Journey of God's Glory* (Grand Rapids: Wm. B. Eerdmans Publishing Co., 2001); *A Commentary on Jeremiah*, 418–24. See also Louis Stulman, *Jeremiah*, Abingdon Old Testament Commentaries (Nashville: Abingdon Press, 2005).
33. John J. Collins is surely correct that "the line between actually killing and verbal, symbolic, or imaginary violence is thin and permeable" (see "The Zeal of Phinehas: The Bible and the Legitimation of Violence," *JBL* 122, no. 1 [2003]: 4). Collins also observes that in certain instances language of violence gives "hope to the oppressed" (ibid., 18), which is likely the case in the OAN.
34. This essay is given in grateful friendship to Walter Brueggemann whose many words, both written and spoken, have been an oasis on the journey.

6

# Jeremiah's "Prophetic Imagination": Pastoral Intervention for a Shattered World

*Kathleen M. O'Connor*

Imaginative conceptions of the future in the book of Jeremiah are pastoral acts, healing interventions for people who have lost everything.[1] Since Jeremiah is a difficult and grim book, this claim seems a kind of madness, but even Jeremiah's future of impending destruction serves the moral rebuilding of the community after the fall of Jerusalem to Babylon. For Jeremiah, the future takes two radically different and contradictory shapes. One future expects impending doom and destruction, "a bad place," an inbreaking dystopia about to crush the world (Jer. 1–20). The second anticipates, briefly but no less vigorously, a future paradise, a-soon-to-come "good place," a utopia (Jer. 30–31).[2]

These future imaginings are survival strategies, theological modes of healing. They build hope when the heavens and earth have already been shattered. In our own time of terror and fear, deceit and warfare, Jeremiah's visions expand our consciousness of our fragile place in the world and invite reflection on war-ravaged places around the globe. As survival strategies, they provide pastoral insight into the impact that trauma and loss have on societies and, by analogy, on individuals whose lives have collapsed.

Jerusalem is the imagined setting of massive upheaval in both of Jeremiah's futures. The destruction of the world will occur there and so will its restoration. But in neither future does Jerusalem function as a geographical spot,

Professors Walter Brueggemann and Charles Cousar have both helped make Columbia Theological Seminary a most stimulating and amiable place to work. Both are learned, dedicated, and creative interpreters of texts. Both encourage and mentor younger scholars. Both are brilliant teachers and preachers who bring the life of the mind and the life of discipleship together for the good of the church. It is an exceedingly high honor to be their colleague and friend.

nor is the future itself the chief subject of concern. Instead, both imaginative visions use the future to address the world shattered by invasion and occupation. This means that no matter what the historical Jeremiah prophesied about looming fire and brimstone, by the time the book gains its final form, his dire prophecy is realized and Jerusalem is ravaged. The book itself testifies to this fact by its superscription, dating Jeremiah's words from "the days of King Josiah . . . until the captivity of Jerusalem" (1:1–3). The implied readers of Jeremiah reside in disaster's aftermath, *between* his two futures of impending doom and edenic new life.

Utopian visions are transparent efforts to ignite hope among the despairing, but less obvious are pastoral contributions that emerge from visions of doom. In what possible sense could Jeremiah's dismal and disturbing poetry, so utterly preoccupied with disaster, benefit survivors of disaster?[3] I begin this essay by describing disaster and its effects on survivors. Then I focus on the less obvious pastoral contributions of Jeremiah's vision of future catastrophe. Finally, I present Jeremiah's utopian vision in relation to disaster.

## I. THE SHATTERED WORLD

Babylon's three invasions of Judah (597, 587, 582 BCE) created a cascade of catastrophes. The Babylonian army destroyed cities, palace, and temple; exiled leading citizens; and became the occupier of the land. The people of Judah lost loved ones, government, daily routines of domestic life, economic livelihood, and political and military control of the land; the exiles, of course, lost the land itself.[4] Not least of the community's bleeding wounds was the collapse of the theological world that grounded its being.[5] Yet these facts only hint at the breadth and depth of loss.

### A. Human Consequences of Disaster

The most important thing about disaster is that it interrupts life on a vast scale; metaphorically, it is a cosmic destruction of creation (Jer. 4:23–28).[6] Disasters involve more than sad or tragic events.[7] A disaster is "disastrous only when events exceed the ability of the group to cope, to redefine and reconstruct" their world.[8] They crush normal human responses; devour a sense of personal safety and daily routine; and devastate economies, cultures, and theological traditions. Disasters leave people numb, physically bereft, traumatized, rudderless, and without meaning. And, as scholars who study warfare, rape, and abuse insist, physical and emotional pain destroys speech.[9] Extreme pain makes people mute, isolates them from community, and turns hearts to stone. Fear, physical deprivation, and uncertainty about survival can also create violence within the community itself. This occurs in Jeremiah when Ishmael assassinates Gedeliah, the Babylonian-appointed governor, bringing on further repression from the occupiers (Jer. 40–41). Of course, contemporary readers will not miss parallels with the American occupation of Iraq.

What do people need in the face of such colossal loss? How can they regain speech, recover meaning, and begin to heal? Can they reclaim their broken identity, rebuild the community, and create new frames of theological meaning?[10] The book of Jeremiah addresses these needs, in part, through its dual visions of the future.

Contrary to expectation, Jeremiah's dystopian future in chapters 1–20 helps the community to rebuild in the aftermath of disaster by poetically revisiting the disaster again and again. This imaginative poetry enables the community to reenter their loss symbolically and begin to come to terms with it. Following Jeremiah's call (Jer. 1), three collections of poems anticipate and relive the disaster in symbolic fashion: poems about the broken family (2:1–4:2), the mythic battle (4:3–6:30), and weeping (8:18–9:22). Chapters 11–20 enact the punishments of the broken covenant.

## 1. Family Poems (2:1–4:2)

Poems about the broken family take chaotic experience and give it meaning (2:1–4:2). No matter how thoroughly they offend contemporary Western sensibilities with their gender biases and their portrait of a violent, punishing God, they also provide a culturally appropriate explanation of the disaster that builds on the people's traditional self-understandings.[11]

Jeremiah recasts Hosea's story of God's broken family (Hos. 1–3) and presents the disaster metaphorically as the divorce of wife Judah by the brokenhearted Husband/God.[12] Judah's Husband accuses her of pursuing other lovers in heinous sexual crimes: "On every high hill . . . you . . . played the whore" (Jer. 2:20; 3:2). In accord with the culture of the ancient world, the divine husband must punish her, so God casts her off and refuses to take her back (3:1–5): "You have done all the evil you could" (3:5). Then God summons the children of the divorce to repent (3:21–25). They signify the book's readers, who are also called to repent and thereby restore the broken relationship of the community with the angry God. In this highly imaginative interpretation of the disaster, the people cause their own downfall. God has been faithful; they have not.

Self-blaming is a common survival strategy among people who have lived through disaster, trauma, or abuse. Jeremiah's blaming rhetoric gives meaning to overwhelming, life-destroying experiences. Daniel Smith-Christopher describes a similar interpretive process among Cambodian survivors of the "killing fields" under Pol Pot and the Khmer Rouge.[13] By blaming the society's fate on bad karma, Cambodians keep alive their predisaster traditions and give the present meaning in continuity with their disappeared past. Similarly, Alice Miller shows how abused children also blame themselves as a survival tactic. To blame their parents is psychologically unthinkable because the children's survival utterly depends on them, so they take the burden of guilt and responsibility upon themselves.[14]

Interpreted as a survival strategy, Jeremiah's broken family poems help the community remember its predisaster relationship with God and its former identity as a covenanted people. They show that God is not weak and did not succumb to more powerful Babylonian deities but acted according to the expectations of the culture. It is not God's failures of governance or power that brought this upon them. And these poems imply that only this God who established them in the land to begin with can save them now, if they repent. Additionally, the family poems also serve the community by offering the people a sense of agency. If they caused their suffering by their sinful life, they can also escape from it by means of their repentance.

For contemporary Western believers, Jeremiah's interpretation is not an adequate explanation of historical disaster because he employs a simplistic understanding of historical causality. Whereas human malfeasance may contribute to historical disaster, other factors are generally at play as well. It is not the sin of the Haitian people, for example, that caused the wreckage left by hurricane Jeanne but a multiplicity of factors, including a global economic system that makes Haiti the poorest nation in this hemisphere. But by assuring victims of disaster that they are agents of their own lives, the theology of human responsibility in the poetry of the broken family and elsewhere in Jeremiah offers a partial imaginative explanation of the nation's collapse. It provides a temporary measure and a way forward through suffering.[15]

## 2. War Poems (4:3–6:30)

Jeremiah's war poems function differently by reenacting the invasion itself as a coming event. The book's first twenty chapters portray doom and destruction as an onrushing, terrifying attack from the mythic foe "from the north" (1:14; 4:6).[16] By presenting the disaster as the work of this mythic "foe" (chs. 4–6; cf. chs. 7–9 and 11–20), the poems revisit the horrors of invasion and loss symbolically and, in the process, offer language for the community to name its common experience and eventually begin to face it.[17]

The battle poems amplify terror and create a frightening "symbolic geography" in which the north represents far more than a compass point.[18] In Ugaritic mythology, the north is the dwelling place of the gods. The north comes into Zion theology as Mount Saphon or Zion. Amplifying the terror is the realization that the sender of this monstrous invader is YHWH (5:15–17), the one who dwells with them in Zion and whose presence should protect them. By contrast with the foe from the north, the war poems portray the city as utterly weak and defenseless, not a warrior but a woman, Daughter Zion. In these poems, Jerusalem is an evil place, utterly defenseless before the invaders, and a dystopia from which to flee.

Imagery of sights and sounds in this inventive poetry make the advancing army live in the imagination. Trumpets call to battle (4:5b; 6:1b, 17); warriors raise standards for attack[19] as they shout, "Up, and let us attack by night and destroy her palaces!" (6:5). Zion will be under siege from invaders who "come from a distant land; . . . and [close] in around her" (4:16–17). Their approach sounds like the roaring of the sea, and they will attack Zion mercilessly (6:22–23). Horseman and archer enter forsaken towns (4:29). A frightening horde, coming from the north, a great nation equipped with superior weapons, they are cruel and merciless, grasping javelin and bow.

This is not an ordinary army; it is a mythic, superhuman force, "coming like clouds, with chariots like the whirlwind, his horses swifter than eagles" (4:13). Its attack will crush the cosmos. Light, mountains, hills, birds, and the cities will return to primeval "waste and void" (4:24–26; cf. Gen. 1:2).[20] The invader will consume all that sustains life. He

> will devour your harvest and your bread;
> he will devour[21] your sons and daughters;
> he will devour your sheep and cattle;
> he will devour your vines and your fig trees;
> he will shatter with a sword your fortified cities which you trust
> (Jer. 5:17, author's translation)

Houses, fields, and vines will be taken away and turned over to others. Institutions will fail; even the temple will be a place of injustice and heinous religious practices (7:1–8:3).

In their vivid preoccupation with the disaster, the war poems create a vocabulary of experience and build a common language within the community to name what has happened, to give it shape, and to revisit it emotionally and spiritually. Through this symbolic world, the community can see itself, what it has lost, and what it has survived. Jeremiah's dystopic future makes collective experience conscious and public. It builds a community of sufferers by offering speech to overcome the isolation and numbness that accompanies trauma. They can say, "Yes, that is the way it was," or they can argue against the text. The poems give them a way to speak about their experiences of fear and devastation.

### 3. Weeping Poems (8:18–9:22)

Jeremiah's weeping poems encourage mourning among survivors (8:18–9:23). With anticipatory grief, the mourning women further mark the totality of the disaster:

> Death has come up into our windows,
> it has entered our palaces,
> to cut off children from the streets
> and young men from the squares. . . .
> "Human corpses shall fall
> like dung upon the open field,
> like sheaves behind the reaper,
> and no one shall gather them."
> (9:21–22)

With abundant laments, and with its weeping prophet, weeping God, and weeping people, the massive sadness of the book aids survivors because it encourages tears and grief to thaw their frozen spirits.

Jeremiah's dystopia breaks open hearts of stone because it encourages grieving, lamenting, and weeping.[22] Together these poems of a coming dystopia function like the mourning women, setting out the path of sorrow and tears as the road to healing, as "the balm of Gilead." Grieving awakens traumatized, silenced survivors to enter emotionally into the pain muteness works to suppress. Hardening of hearts by denying pain and loss or by attempts to recover the good old days only work temporarily as a survival strategy. To restore its humanity, the community must grieve. Without long, deep grieving, lamentation, and weeping, new forms of life cannot be born. Only numbness and spiritual death will rule the communal spirit.

## B. The Broken Covenant

Interwoven with these three cycles of poems are further images of the breakdown of the society. The more eclectic and mixed literary materials of chapters 11–20 stress the inevitability of the future disaster. The covenant sermon (ch. 11), for example, contains no blessings, only curses, for their accomplishment is a foregone conclusion. "I am going to bring disaster upon them that they cannot escape," says YHWH (11:11). Chapters 18–20 then perform the disaster through a series of symbolic events. When Jeremiah visits the potter's house, Artist God destroys the pot symbolizing Judah (18:1–14). Then Jeremiah heralds the nation's destruction by breaking a jar before the elders who serve as legal witnesses to God's deed about to befall them all (19:1–15). Finally, the high priest Pashur imprisons Jeremiah in the stocks of the Temple, signaling the captivity of God's word and of the nation (20:1–6). Only now is the mythic "foe from the north" named Babylon. The future is here, and it is an evil place.

These texts help form Jeremiah's rhetoric of blame where the sin of the community causes the historical disaster. But they also describe the intracommunal violence that followed the invasions and convey experience of the present as bleak and brutal. Covenant relations of justice among the people and with the leadership have deteriorated. The prophet searches for one person who is righteous, first among the poor and then among the rich, and finds no one (5:1–5). The people rob and cheat and shed innocent blood (7:1–5). All are "adulterers, a band of traitors. . . . and proceed from evil to evil" (9:2–3). Prophets lie (5:30–31), saying, "'Peace, peace,' when there is no peace" (8:11). Kings, officials, priest, and prophets are idolators (2:26–27). People are duplicitous and untrustworthy, speaking friendly words, but planning ambush (9:7–9).

## C. Jeremiah's Dystopia as Pastoral Intervention

The book's depiction of disaster is symbolic and metaphoric, yet rooted deeply in the disaster in which the society finds itself. If, however, these poems are preexilic as some scholars think and come originally from Jeremiah's own mouth, they project his stark vision of the present "about to slide into nightmare."[23] His dystopian rhetoric then acts as a kind of shock therapy to frighten the community into altering its idolatrous ways and thereby avert the impending catastrophe.

But even if these poems are not Jeremiah's own, for the readers of the book who dwell in the dystopic aftermath of disaster, his words have restorative capacities. His dystopian future provides the community with an essential ingredient of ethical living, a mirror of itself, that is, knowledge of its situation in the world. It shows them they are survivors: disaster occurred, and they are still breathing. It works as a witness, a testimony to their massive losses, to the enormity of their suffering, to the destruction of their culture and the physical ruin of their cultural monuments. It grounds them in the ground-down present. This knowledge of their true condition is the only place from which rebuilding of the community can begin.

The literary world of Jeremiah's dystopia echoes, evokes, and reverberates in their real world to overcome loneliness and isolation. Jeremiah's future vision of an evil place urges the people to face all that died in their previous world. It breaks through the "blanket amnesia" and numbness that follows war and trauma.[24] It gives them poetic language, first, to see what has happened to them and, then, to speak of it. Revealing the contours of their collective experience, it restores memory lost by trauma and denial. As Chris Hedges writes about the aftermath of war, "Until there is a common vocabulary and a shared historical memory there is no peace in any society, only an absence of war."[25] Such use of language, as James Boyd White insists about other ancient texts, is a political and moral act, a performance of words that reshapes the ethical character of the society.[26]

Before they can move to hope, the community needs Jeremiah's dystopian future—not only because it offers survivors ways to begin to cope with the disaster, but because it gives credibility to Jeremiah's other future of utopian life in Zion. In the poetic world of the book, Jeremiah proves the potency of his prophetic word by prophesying the disaster before it happens. His utopian vision, therefore, must be equally reliable, a point of view that survivors may find difficult to absorb so accustomed have they become to sorrow. For the present, for the time in between the two futures, the community requires aid in assimilating their losses. Traumatized communities cannot go forward toward new life until they have begun to assimilate the truth of their past and present. Only then can Jeremiah imagine a possible future summoning Judah to live beyond the "fissure of death" and denial in which it resides.[27]

## II. JEREMIAH'S UTOPIAN IMAGINATION (JER. 30–31)

Located in the so-called "little book of consolation" (30–33), Jeremiah's radiant depiction of the future challenges the status quo with great force,[28] for "the deficiencies of the present" demand an alternative imagination.[29] Jeremiah's second future does not begin in the world of inbreaking hope but in the desolate present. These lyrically beautiful chapters interweave images of the disaster with images of an alluring, luminous world on Mount Zion. By not denying the way loss and despair govern the desperate conditions of the survivors, Jeremiah's utopia attends to life as it is.

With pastoral sensitivity Jeremiah starts with the pain of survivors. The implied readers of these chapters are survivors of the sword (31:12). They "have heard a cry of panic, of terror, of no peace" (30:3–4). The "great and incomparable day," namely, the day of military triumph over Jacob/Israel, is a time of distress from which God will rescue them (30:7). They live with incurable hurt, grievous wounds; they lack community, and someone to execute justice, and they have neither medicine nor healing (30:13). Drenched in guilt, they have turned from God, and now they have been punished (30:14–15). Zion is an "outcast" (30:17), for God's wrath has gone forth in a fierce storm (30:23–24).

It is these realities that Jeremiah's utopian future subverts, for God will break the yoke, burst the bonds, and free Jacob from servitude (30:8). Recognizing the community's suffering, Jeremiah neither ignores nor whitewashes their world. By beginning with the ways things are, the book's utopian vision not only gains a chance of being heard because it connects with the life experience of the community, but it also claims God's salvation for specific needs of survivors.[30] Finally, these chapters magnify by contrast the luminous power of the inbreaking future by acknowledging the bleak present.

## A. The Rebuilt City

Against probability, Jerusalem will be reconstituted, for God says,

> I am going to restore the fortunes of the tents of Jacob,
>   and have compassion on his dwellings;
> the city shall be rebuilt upon its mound,
> and the citadel set on its rightful site.
>
> (Jer. 30:18)

But in this vision the city is a symbolic place, not a blueprint for urban planning. Jeremiah never names it "Jerusalem," only "Zion" (30:17; 31:6, 12) or "the holy hill" (31:23), mythic terms for God's dwelling place and the setting of the destroyed temple. Exact landmarks of the city mentioned in 31:38–40 are partly mythic, indicating this utopia does not exist on a map. Of course, the tower, the gate, and the hills bounding the city may just appear to be mythic because archaeologists do not have enough information about the ancient site to locate them in the real world.[31] But the rivers around Eden in Gen. 2:10–14 provide a point of comparison. There the Tigris and Euphrates locate the idyllic garden in the real world, but the other two rivers are unknown. Although in Jeremiah's restored Zion the city assumes mythic proportions, it is still anchored in a specific historical place "hallowed by ancestral traditions."[32] The beloved rebuilt city and scope of its boundaries are, nonetheless, probably less important than the transformation of the community within.[33]

## B. Social Renewal

Drawing from the ancestral stories of Jacob's family in Genesis, as well as from earlier parts of the book of Jeremiah, these two chapters envision the society as a renewed and expanded family of Jacob. "Jacob shall return and have quiet and ease, /and no one shall make him afraid" (30:10). The weeping Rachel will regain her lost children, and the pleading child Ephraim will receive mercy (31:15–20). The restored utopian community is refigured here as the Israelite family of old. And, although Zion is the place of restoration, the people of Judah strangely do not appear explicitly. Some interpreters have explained this lack historically as an expression of Jeremiah's preexilic hope to reunite the northern and southern kingdoms under King Josiah. A better explanation might be that the book uses traditions of the now-defunct northern kingdom to imagine a world that harkens back to pristine origins in a fashion typical of utopian thinking.[34] Jeremiah uses the past to summon survivors to his alternative future, reshaping them in accord with their ancient splintered traditions. The primal past becomes their resource for connecting with their predisaster identity and starting anew in continuity with elements of that past.

Jeremiah portrays the coming utopian society impressionistically, but, typical of utopian imagination, his future world surprises because it is so unlike the present and because it emerges where it is least expected, among the feeble and the vulnerable.[35] For a people of grievous wounds and incurable pain any future at all is a surprise, let alone the possibility that they will be healed and rebuilt. In Jeremiah's utopian future they will live together in safety, merriment, and thanksgiving (30:18–20). Grace and joy, prosperity and fertility will overtake their present barren world (31:13–14). But the ones leading the procession home from exile further invert social expectations. They are the blind and the lame, the pregnant and those in labor (31:8). The former are vulnerable and physically weak; the latter as women are lowly in public stature and holders of little political power. How can the blind and the vulnerable lead? How can those giving birth march? Both groups are the new community, limping homeward. They are not kings, queens, or warriors but wounded survivors beginning life anew, broken yet fertile.

## C. The Gap between Past and Future

Even though utopian thinking uses the past to create a vision of a new society,[36] the utopian future neither continues the past nor emerges from it. Neither past nor present cause the future. Instead, a yawning gap exists between them because the utopian future does not evolve from what has gone before. It bursts into history and interrupts the present weariness without causal explanation. It makes imaginable what cannot be conceived in the dismal present.

God alone is the interrupting energy who will transform the survivors and overthrow their reigning logic. The family of Jacob cannot achieve its promised incandescent future. Only the God of the ancestors can bring it to birth in explosive new life. Only God acts to satisfy the weary and nourish the faint (31:25), to ransom Jacob and redeem him "from hands too strong for him" (31:11). Only God recreates the covenant and makes new faithful creatures by writing Torah in their hearts (31:31). Only God promises fidelity until all the mysteries of the cosmos are revealed (31:35–37).

Jeremiah's utopian vision is a vehicle of hope for survivors. These poems enflame possibility and awaken emotional yearning for a better world. They challenge the present by insisting on divine power as the enacting agent of return, by organizing a society inexplicably led by the weak and vulnerable, and by creating a communal vision of mutual sustenance where old and young, laity and priests rejoice and dance together in a watered garden, the bucolic paradise that is Zion. Yet Jeremiah's utopian future would be massively ineffective if it did not first guide the community through their story as survivors of disaster. Only then can they renew their traditions, reform as a community, and accept the generative power of the new world ahead. The book's two futures guide the community through the process of recovery and reconnection toward what is yet to be. For people who live in the in-between of the present, Jeremiah's futures generate healing and hope.

## NOTES

1. See Walter Brueggemann, *The Prophetic Imagination*, 2d ed. (Minneapolis: Fortress Press, 2001) and *Hopeful Imagination: Prophetic Voices in Exile* (Philadelphia: Fortress Press, 1986).
2. A good place is more accurately a "eutopia." "Utopia" comes from the Greek term for "no place" because the world it projects exists only in the imagination. In this essay, I use utopia in the popular sense meaning an ideal world to come.
3. For discussion of preaching as reimagination for exiles see Walter Brueggemann, *Cadences of Home: Preaching Among the Exiles* (Louisville, Ky.: Westminster John Knox Press, 1997).
4. For a thorough study of the period, see Rainer Albertz, *Israel in Exile: The History and Literature of the Sixth Century B.C.E.*, Studies in Biblical Literature 3 (Atlanta: Society of Biblical Literature, 2003).
5. See Louis Stulman, *Order Amid Chaos: Jeremiah as Symbolic Tapestry*, Biblical Seminar 57 (Sheffield: Sheffield Academic Press, 1998), 23–55.
6. See Louis Stulman's essay in this volume, chapter 5, "Conflicting Paths to Hope in Jeremiah."
7. For sociological studies of disasters and their social impacts see E. L. Quarantelli, ed., *What is a Disaster? Perspectives on the Question* (London: Routledge & Kegan Paul, 1998).
8. Daniel Smith-Christopher, *A Biblical Theology of Exile*, OBT (Minneapolis: Fortress Press, 2001), 79.
9. Elaine Scary, *The Body in Pain* (New York: Oxford University Press, 1985); Judith Lewis Herman, *Trauma and Recovery* (New York: Basic Books, 1992); and Alice Miller, *Drama of the Gifted Child* (New York: Basic Books, 1979) and *For Your Own Good: Hidden Cruelty in Children and the Roots of Violence* (New York: Farrar, Straus & Giroux, 1982).
10. Smith-Christopher, *A Biblical Theology*, 81.
11. See Renita Weems, *Battered Love: Marriage, Sex, and Violence in the Hebrew Prophets*, OBT (Minneapolis: Fortress Press, 1995).
12. A. R. Pete Diamond and Kathleen M. O'Connor, "Unfaithful Passions: Coding Women Coding Men in Jeremiah 2:1–3:25 (4:2)," in *Troubling Jeremiah*, ed. A. R. Pete Diamond et al., JSOTSup 260 (Sheffield: Sheffield Academic Press, 1999), 387–403.
13. Smith-Christopher, *A Biblical Theology*, 80.

14. Miller, *Drama* and *For Your Own Good.*
15. Biblical voices dissenting from this theology, what Walter Brueggemann names "counter testimony," appear in Job, Qoheleth, Lamentations, Psalms, and even in the book of Jeremiah itself (*Theology of the Old Testament: Testimony, Dispute, Advocacy* [Minneapolis: Fortress Press, 1997], 626). In Jeremiah's laments, also known as his "confessions," he accuses God of planting the treacherous and making them prosper (12:2) and accuses God of betrayal (15:18) and seduction (20:7).
16. John Hill, *Friend or Foe? The Figure of Babylon in the Book of Jeremiah MT*, BibInt (Leiden: E. J. Brill, 1999), 48; Ben Ollenburger, *Zion, the City of the Great King: A Theological Symbol of the Jerusalem Cult* (Sheffield: JSOT Press, 1987), 15–22. See also Leo Perdue, *The Collapse of History: Reconstructing Old Testament Theology*, OBT (Minneapolis: Fortress Press, 1994), 142–43.
17. On the terror in these poems, see especially Walter Brueggemann, *Exile & Homecoming: A Commentary on Jeremiah* (Grand Rapids: Wm. B. Eerdmans Publishing Co., 1998), 52–76.
18. John Hill, "The Threat from the North—Reflections on a Theme Both Ancient and Modern," in *Wisdom for Life*, ed. Michael A. Kelly and Mark A. O'Brien (Adelaide: Australian Theological Forum, forthcoming), 6.
19. William L. Holladay, *Jeremiah 1: A Commentary on the Book of the Prophet Jeremiah, Chapters 1–25*, Hermeneia (Philadelphia: Fortress Press, 1986), 140.
20. Although it seems to change the subject, the prose temple sermon serves as a parenthetical comment on the disaster in which insiders, not the foe from the north, threaten Jerusalem's destruction. See Louis Stulman, "The Prose Sermons as Hermeneutical Guide to Jeremiah 1–25: The Deconstruction of Judah's Symbolic World" in *Troubling Jeremiah*, 51–53.
21. Emending to the singular.
22. See Walter Brueggemann's vast repertoire on lament, most particularly essays in *The Psalms and the Life of Faith*, ed. Patrick Miller (Minneapolis: Fortress Press, 1995); *The Message of the Psalms: A Theological Commentary* (Minneapolis: Augsburg, 1984), 51–124; and *Finally Comes the Poet: Daring Speech for Proclamation* (Minneapolis: Fortress Press, 1989).
23. Chad Walsh, *From Utopia to Nightmare* (New York: Harper & Row, 1962), 138.
24. Christopher Hedges, *War is a Force that Gives Us Meaning* (New York: Anchor Books, 2003), 60, 125.
25. Ibid., 81.
26. James Boyd White, *When Words Lose Their Meaning: Constitutions and Reconstitutions of Language, Character, and Community* (Chicago: University of Chicago Press, 1984).
27. Brueggemann, *Theology of the Old Testament*, 626.
28. S. J. Schweitzer, "Exploring the Utopian Space of Chronicles: Some Spatial Anomalies" (paper presented at the Hermeneutics Task Force, Catholic Biblical Association Annual Meeting, San Francisco, Calif., August 3, 2003). Jeremiah is not writing a utopia as a full-blown literary form as in Thomas Moore's *Utopia*, but utopian thinking exists in biblical texts and utopian theory offers help in understanding the power of the imaginary world.
29. Terry Eagleton, *After Theory* (New York: Basic Books, 2003), 180.
30. Terence C. Fretheim, *Jeremiah* (Macon, Ga.: Smith & Helwys, 2002). Most likely Jeremiah 30–33 address exiles, as many interpreters recognize, for they promise a journey home.

31. For a discussion of possibilities, see Jack R. Lundbom, *Jeremiah 21–26*, AB 21B (New York: Doubleday, 2004), 490–91.
32. John J. Collins, "Models of Utopia in the Biblical Tradition," in *A Wise and Discerning Mind: Essays in Honor of Burke O. Long*, ed. Saul M. Olyan and Robert C. Culley, BJS (Providence, R.I.: Brown University Press, 2000), 67.
33. Schweitzer, "Exploring the Utopian Space," 5.
34. Roland Boer, *Novel Histories*, Playing the Text 2 (Sheffield: Sheffield Academic Press, 1997), 113.
35. Ibid. 150; Schweitzer, "Exploring the Utopian Space," 4.
36. Boer, *Novel*, 113.

# 7

# The Objects of Our Affections: Emotions and the Moral Life in Proverbs 1–9

*Christine Roy Yoder*

Interpretation of the role of emotions in the book of Proverbs has centered historically on the importance of self-restraint. Pointing to such sayings as "One who is quick-tempered acts foolishly" (14:17a) and "Those with good sense are slow to anger" (19:11a; cf. e.g., 12:16; 14:29; 17:27), scholars underline the ancient sages' concerns about rash emotional outbursts and impulsive behavior.[1] With regard to 12:16, for example, Roland Murphy notes, "The wise person exercises self-control in contrast to the fool whose emotions are immediately displayed when he is challenged."[2] Raymond van Leeuwen similarly explains that certain proverbs suggest "the damage that unrestrained emotions can do" (14:29–30),[3] the necessity of "inner strength and wisdom . . . to refrain from expressing self-defeating emotions" (12:16),[4] and, with reference to 15:28, "the inner capacity to reflect, *rather than to react emotionally*, defines the wise person."[5] Readers may thus conclude that, according to the sages, the wise characteristically control—even mute—their emotions whereas fools express theirs thoughtlessly, a contrast that the ancient Egyptian *Instruction of Amenemope* mirrors in its descriptions of the "silent man" and his rival, the "heated man."[6]

There is more to the story, however. Readers of the book of Proverbs as a whole, and chapters 1–9 in particular, encounter a text laden with language of emotion. The "motto" of the book, for example, distinguishes the wise and the foolish on the basis of their emotional attitudes: "The *fear* of the LORD[7] is the beginning of knowledge; fools *despise* wisdom and instruction" (1:7). Proverbs 1 alone refers elsewhere to greed (v. 19); love and delight (v. 22); hate (vv. 22,

I am pleased to dedicate this essay to Walter Brueggemann and Charlie Cousar, cherished colleagues and friends whose fierce love for God, the Church, the Bible, and humanity have taught me more than I can ever say about the ways of wisdom.

29, 30); terror, distress, and anguish (vv. 26–27, 33). Personified wisdom identifies herself as "delight" and rejoices before God and in the world (8:30–31). And God is said variously to love like a parent (3:12), to hate (6:16), and to revel in wisdom (8:30). Furthermore, this emotional language often occurs in contexts that refer to bodily appetites (e.g., 1:31; 5:15; 6:30; 9:5) and desires (e.g., for companionship and quick profits, 1:10–19; for sex, 6:25). These latter phenomena, while typically considered distinct from emotions, have been grouped and analyzed with them since Aristotle.[8] In short, Proverbs 1–9 does not dismiss emotions as the irrational impulses or animalistic energies long ridiculed by many moral philosophers, but rather speaks of them as constitutive elements of character.

Proverbs's concern with emotion is all the more intriguing when read today in front of the television. From terror alerts to heightened hostilities, from jubilant celebrations to palpable grief, from so-called reality shows that invite us to feel vicariously (e.g., *Fear Factor*, *What I Hate about You*) to commercials that appeal to our sentiments,[9] there is little doubt that emotions fashion the landscapes of our personal, communal, national, even global lives. Indeed, not long ago eight international scholars under the leadership of Walter Brueggemann diagnosed our present circumstances in starkly emotional terms: "The prevailing mood of humankind, *globally* considered, must be named 'despair'"—despair that is open for those who "have not" and hidden for those who "have."[10] Given this, they continued, the challenge for the Christian movement is to engage this despair and participate actively and concretely in God's work to transform it into hope. That is, for Christian proclamation and mission to be relevant—for the world to, as the old hymn suggests, "know we are Christians by our *love*" (cf. John 17:20–26)[11]—we dare not discount the emotions or downplay their ready connection to human flourishing.

Recent discussions in philosophy, ethics, psychology, and neurobiology lend credence to the notion that emotions are vital components of the moral life.[12] In fact, many argue that emotions are richly cognitive phenomena (i.e., forms of intelligence and discernment) closely connected with the way one perceives and interprets the world.[13] Philosopher Martha C. Nussbaum, a proponent of this view, suggests why:[14]

1. Emotions "are *about* something"; they have *objects*, such as people, things, symbols, ideas, situations, the natural world.
2. That "aboutness" is internal and embodies a person's way of seeing and interpreting the object. Emotions, that is, are forms of *perception*.
3. Emotions embody not only ways of seeing, but a person's *beliefs* (which are often quite complex) about the object.
4. Emotions see their object as invested with *value*, as significant for some role it plays in the person's life. Emotions thus appear to be "eudaimonistic,"[15] namely, concerned with a person's flourishing.

Accordingly, Nussbaum (and others) argue that essential to the work of moral formation is the cultivation of emotions directed "rightly" and discouragement of emotions directed "wrongly." Emotions provide people "with a sense of how the world relates to [their] own goals and projects. Without that sense, decision making and action are derailed."[16] Though this may perplex those of us raised with the modern, Western distinction between the head as the seat of cognition and the heart as the fount of emotion, the ancients resisted dichotomies between the intellect and emotions. The Hebrew term *lēb* (translated variously as "heart" and "mind"), which figures prominently in Proverbs 1–9, is used frequently as a metaphor for the inner self, the locus of *both* thoughts and feelings (e.g., 2:10; 3:1; 4:4, 23; 5:12; 6:21; note the fool "lacks 'heart,'" e.g., 6:32; 7:7; 9:4).

With Nussbaum's description of emotions as a heuristic framework, I propose that the sages of Proverbs 1–9 engage the emotions as vital forms of perception and judgment, advocating certain patterns of emotions—which they deem may be taught—as characteristic of mature, flourishing human lives. Conversely, the sages discourage patterns that constitute immaturity and lead to misery. Acknowledging the complexities of any study of emotions,[17] my aim is to consider how Proverbs 1–9 depicts these patterns, the former attributed to the wise and the latter to an assortment of fools (e.g., sinners, scoffers, fools, wicked people). I argue that the wise are urged to embrace an emotional repertoire that promotes interdependence[18] with God, wisdom, and others, while the fools' emotions alienate them from the same. Finally, I reflect briefly on some implications of this for thinking about moral formation and ministry in our changing global context.

First, it is important to say a word about the setting of Proverbs 1–9. Located in a household in an unidentified city,[19] Proverbs 1–9 contain the instructions of a parent (specifically, a father) to his son(s).[20] Although the sage's privileging of the father-son relationship as *the* authoritative context for learning offends modern, Western sensibilities, such a starting point is perhaps apt for a book about the formation of human character. While notions of family certainly vary over time and between and within different cultures, because most people have or have had a family, and the family is typically where our identities are first formed, the household appears a "natural," familiar domain for theological-ethical teaching.[21] Families often command loyalty and bear primary responsibility for initiating children into the moral beliefs, attitudes, behaviors, traditions, and institutions of the family and the community. Similarly, cities are bastions of human culture, purportedly symbols of civilizations at their most advanced. Both locations are rather conventional, though certainly value-laden,[22] places for moral education.

The parent's repeated efforts to shape the youth's emotions suggest that emotions are, to a significant extent, taught or socially constructed.[23] That is, the youth learns his emotions in much the same way he learns his beliefs, namely, through interactions with others—predominantly with parents or other caregivers in the beginning, and then later with a wider community. With the parent(s) as his first model (cf. 1:8; 6:20), the youth "tries on" various emotions that *in due course* will, it is hoped, become his own. His emotional attitudes develop over time (emotions have histories) and, arguably, even as an adult may be modified—by changes in environment (e.g., customs, institutions, laws), relationships, or thought, for instance.[24] The result is a certain emotional geography that, though never completely settled, is, as Nussbaum notes, a means by which one *maps the world* (i.e., perceives what is of value, what is not, and where both are in relation to oneself) and *maps oneself in the world* (e.g., by setting boundaries, defining relationships, and so on).[25]

## I. THE FOOL

In Proverbs 1–9, a primary charge against those who reject wisdom (e.g., sinners, scoffers, fools, wicked people) is that their emotions are skewed. The parent sketches persons of serious moral defect by, in part, pointing to their emotional confusion: they loathe the right objects (e.g., "fools despise wisdom and instruction," 1:7b) and esteem the wrong ones (e.g., a wicked man "rejoices in doing evil, and delights in the crookedness of evil," 2:14). Their moral universe is upside down, characterized by *antipathy* toward God, wisdom, other people, and even themselves. Indeed, more than any other emotion, fools are said to *hate* (cf. 1:7b, 22c, 29a, 30b; 5:12; 8:36b; 9:8a), a temperament that draws sharp boundaries around themselves and pushes others away. As Robert Roberts comments about an unsavory character in Anthony Trollope's novel *The Prime Minister*, such a "structure of [a person's] emotions explains why he does so much evil, why he has so little moral understanding, and why his life and the lives of those he touches closely are so miserable."[26] In sum, the fools' distorted emotions are emblematic of misperceiving the world—of moral depravity—and, as such, affect individual and communal misery.

Wisdom's first words signal the significance and urgency of tending to the fools' misplaced affections (1:22):

> "How long, naïve ones, will you *love* being naïve,
> [you] scoffers *delight* in ridicule,
> and [you] fools *hate* knowledge?"

Her concern is not that they have emotions, but that their emotions have such utterly wrongheaded *objects* (that is, she does not characterize any emotion—love, delight, or hate—as inherently positive or negative).[27] The callow savor their ignorance. Scoffers, known for their arrogance, cynicism, and contentious manner, enjoy making fun of others, stirring up strife (22:10), and in their effort to avoid instruction at all costs, even lash out at their teachers (9:7–8a; cf. 13:1; 15:12). And fools detest knowledge, preferring to live by their own wits, complacently and carelessly (e.g., 14:16; 28:26; 29:11). The fools' emotions variously reveal postures of hubris, wantonness, and animosity. Wisdom holds them responsible. Her rhetorical question stings, her exasperation aims to invoke their guilt, and her words caution anyone within earshot to think twice before adopting such smug ways of being in the world.

What is implicit in wisdom's question she next makes explicit, namely, that she holds out hope, however improbable, that the fools might yet accept a relationship with her: "Turn back to my reproof! See, I pour out my *rûaḥ* (NRSV "spirit") for you and make my words known to you" (1:23). Summoning them to be her students, she offers her words *and* her disposition, or *rûaḥ*, a term that in Proverbs commonly refers to one's temperament—emotions, faculties, desires, and will (e.g., 14:29; 16:32; 17:27; 18:14). Her invitation suggests, first, that she believes the fools' misdirected emotions (and the beliefs they embody) can be dismantled, unlearned. And, second, that such "radical undoing"[28] requires she cultivate in them beliefs and affections like her own. No mere "talking to," recital of facts, or logical argument is sufficient. Rather, wisdom offers a relationship—a long-term series of interactions[29]—in which she, like the parent, teaches paradigms of emotion (cf. e.g., 8:13, 17, 30–36) and the values and structures on which they depend.

Should fools refuse her invitation, wisdom foretells their grim fate: an inevitable deluge of agony. Ironically, those who deem themselves fearless are, by their own doing, *besieged by fear and despair* (1:26–27):

> As for me, I will laugh at your disaster;
>   I will mock when your *terror* comes;
> when your *terror* arrives like a storm,
>   and your disaster comes like a whirlwind,
>   when *distress* and *anguish* come upon you!

Wisdom here whips up a rhetorical tempest. She uses and repeats intense emotional language (e.g., terror, distress, anguish) and makes it personal ("*your* terror," "*your* disaster"), suggesting that what comes is what the fools fear most. Her Hebrew pelts her listeners with sharp, staccato sounds (k, b, p, ṣ). And, as is common in descriptions of emotional upheaval,[30] wisdom evokes powerful metaphors from nature—a sudden violent storm and a whirlwind—to name the gut-wrenching force of their anguish (cf. 10:25). In the face of it all, wisdom says, she will mock them (as they did her) and *laugh*, an outburst of *Schadenfreude* (joy at another's downfall). As unnerving as her response is, it may perhaps be understood as a reaction to "the absurdity of those who flaunt reality, who 'spit into the wind' and are puzzled when they get wet. It is also, perhaps, a fierce joy that the goodness of the world order and justice have been vindicated when the wicked reap what they have sown."[31] Whatever the case, such a response by people and by God is well attested in the Bible[32] and, I expect, well known to present-day readers of Proverbs. There, across the chasm of wisdom's joy and the fools' anguish, the fools will *finally* recognize their need for wisdom and cry out to her but, just as they refused her time and again, she will not answer (1:28).

Talking now *about* the fools, wisdom concludes (1:29–32):

> Because they *hated* knowledge
> and did not choose the fear of the LORD,
> did not accept my counsel,
> but *despised* all my reproof,
> therefore, they shall eat the fruit of their way
> and be sated with their own devices.
> For the waywardness of the naïve will kill them,
> and the *complacency* of fools will destroy them.

She first uses verbs of emotion (hate, despise) and cognitive resolve (did not choose, did not accept) in parallel, suggesting their interrelatedness and the significance of both in the fools' demise. She then invokes bodily appetites. Like the old adage "You are what you eat," wisdom claims that the fools satiate themselves on their misguided ways (cf. "the bread of wickedness," "the wine of violence," 4:17); the Egyptian *Instruction of Ptahhotep* claims similarly, "[The fool] lives on that by which one dies" (*AEL* 1, 75). In the end, the fools' hatred proves to be suicidal self-loathing. Like the sinners who, motivated by greed, stumble into a deadly trap of their own making (1:10–19), the fools' rejection of wisdom, God, and others ultimately claims their lives. Their *šalvâ* (NRSV "complacency"), a term used pejoratively elsewhere for the feeling of false security (e.g., Jer. 22:21; Dan. 8:25; 11:21), annihilates them. Wisdom makes this point even more pointedly later—"Those who miss me injure themselves; *all who hate me love death*" (8:36, emphasis added).

Much as wisdom describes the fools' fate in intense emotional terms, the parent later invites the youth to imagine the loss and *shame* brought on by folly (Prov. 5:8–14). The instruction weaves together a warning about sex with strangers (who also make an emotional appeal to the youth, e.g., 7:18) with caution not to reject wisdom:

> Keep your way far from [the Strange Woman],
> and do not go near the door to her house;
> lest you give your honor to others,
> and your years to the merciless,

(lest) strangers take their fill of your wealth,
and your labors go to the house of a foreigner;
And at the end of your life you groan,
as your body and flesh waste away,
and you say, "O, how I *hated* discipline,
and my heart *spurned* reproof!
I did not listen to the voice of my teachers
or incline my ear to my instructors.
Now I am at the point of utter ruin
in the assembled congregation."

Alongside the loss of vigor and wealth (particularly grievous because it is to "others," "strangers," people not of the youth's family) will be the crippling loss of personal and public respect. Shame strikes at personal value and the social appearance of worthiness. The youth will perceive that he has "fallen steeply short in worthiness or respectability of an important kind," and that the community regards him accordingly.[33] People he once rejected (e.g., his teachers) will reject him. And, like the fools overtaken by a storm of their own making, the youth alone will be responsible for his humiliation: "*I* hated . . . *my heart* spurned. . . . *I* did not listen . . . or incline *my* ear. . . . Now *I*." Notably, the youth juxtaposes verbs of emotion (hate, spurn) and perception (hear, incline the ear), indicating their correlation and the import of both for the attainment of wisdom. Withering in his old age and wracked by shame, the youth, like the fools, will lament his hatred of wisdom.

These texts highlight how critique of various fools in Proverbs 1–9 is laden with language of emotion, from indictment of their emotions to descriptions of their probable fates. The parent diagnoses moral depravity, in no small way, by pointing to the fools' emotional dispositions. Theirs is an emotional geography characterized by delusional self-sufficiency and antipathy—a sort of uniform, flat plain that is "very much like the world seen from the point of view of a far-distant sun, a world not yet humanized by the earthquakes of human love and limitation."[34] Such a world, wisdom claims, does indeed prove *inhuman*: lonely, hopeless, misshapen by upheavals of fear and shame, and ultimately deadly.

## II. THE WISE

The emotional landscape of the wise is, in contrast, marked by "fear of the LORD," love of instruction, and devotion to one's companions. Language of love predominates (e.g., 4:6b; 8:21b; 9:8b), an emotion that, unlike hate, expands personal boundaries, "picturing the self as constituted in part by strong attachments to independent things and persons."[35] Inasmuch as the wise invest a good measure of their well-being in "objects" beyond their control, they acknowledge a lack of self-sufficiency, a sense of vulnerability, a need for others in the world. In turn, they commit themselves to being accountable to those "objects" in certain ways. Proverbs 1–9 thus emphasizes certain interdependencies as vital to human flourishing.

## A. Fear of the LORD

First and foremost, the wise "*fear* YHWH." Indeed, "fear of the LORD" is Proverbs' resounding refrain, occurring thirteen times (e.g., 1:7; 2:5; 8:13; 9:10) and forming an *inclusio* around chapters 1–9 (1:7; 9:10) and the book as a whole (1:7; 31:30);[36] "fear of the LORD" is the quintessential expression of what it means to be wise (1:7).[37] Interpreters typically construe the phrase to mean a sort of convicted piety or reverence for God (akin to "having faith"),[38] and downplay or altogether dismiss its emotional connotations. For example, Richard Clifford writes, "'Fear of a god' does not refer primarily to an emotion or a general reverent attitude. Rather it means revering a particular deity by performing the god's rituals and obeying the god's commands."[39] Such parsing of "fear" in "fear of the LORD" is misleading, however.

In Proverbs, "fear of YHWH" is a broad expression encompassing dread of God's disapproval or punishment, trepidation in the presence of the holy, and a conscience defined by obedience to God. At times, as Clifford's comment suggests, "fear of YHWH" is nearly synonymous with "knowledge of God" (1:7, 29; 2:5; cf. 9:10; 30:3) and "instruction in wisdom" (15:33). Proverbs thus explicitly identifies fear of God with *cognition*, with a perception of the world that recognizes God's sovereignty and the posture of humanity (our capacities and limitations) before God and creation. Michael V. Fox rightly notes, "[T]his is fear of God as *conscience*,"[40] a state of mind that engenders humility (e.g., 3:5–8, 34; 22:4; cf. 15:33; 18:12) and is equated with *hatred* of evil (8:13; cf. 14:16; 16:6). That is, "fear of the LORD" is both cognitive *and* emotional.

At other times what motivates "fear of the LORD" is, in fact, *dread* of certain consequences, such as trouble (15:16), harm (19:23), and deadly snares (14:27; cf. 10:27). The sages admonish readers to "fear YHWH and the king" for "who knows the ruin both can bring?" (24:21–22). This suggests that distinctions between "fear of the LORD" and fear may not be drawn too sharply (cf. e.g., Exod. 20:19–21; 2 Sam. 6:6–11; Job 1–2). Certainly, given Proverbs's depiction of God as ultimately powerful, mysterious, and free (e.g., 16:1–9; 19:21; 21:30–31), one might argue that *not* to feel "some stirring of fear would indicate a profound state of spiritual numbness, if not acute mental illness,"[41] an overly domesticated conception of the divine, and/or an exaggerated sense of self. This dread, then, is not "unreflective"[42] or irrational, but emotional *and* cognitive; it reflects certain beliefs, namely, that should one act wrongly, God has the capacity to act (even adversely), God will probably do so, and the wrongdoer is both vulnerable and accountable.

Thus "fear" in "fear of the LORD" is used equivocally, to name both an emotion *and* a more complex orientation in the world (i.e., conscience) of which that emotion is a part. It manifests itself on a continuum, so that to talk of "fear of YHWH" we need to include everything from obedience to moments of terror. The whole gamut—which reflects certain beliefs about God, humanity, and the necessity of a relationship between the two—is "the beginning of wisdom" (1:7). And, like many fears that promote survival by prompting avoidance of and escape from danger (i.e., from other fears), "fear of YHWH" is associated with health ("healing for your flesh and refreshment for your body," 3:8) and enables one to avoid certain perils, most notably the storm of panic that consumes fools (3:24–26; cf. 1:33):

> If you sit down, *you will not be afraid*;
> When you lie down, your sleep will be sweet.
> *Do not be afraid* of sudden panic,
>    or of the storm that strikes the wicked;
> for the LORD will be your confidence
>    and will keep your foot from being caught.

Such an orientation in the world comes with certain accountabilities. The youth is, for example, to trust and in every way acknowledge God (3:5–6), to honor God with first fruits (3:9), and to accept God's reproof (3:11–12). In relation to others, the wise pursue "righteousness, justice, and equity" (1:3), terms that together refer comprehensively to ethical and neighborly conduct in personal and communal relationships (e.g., 3:17–32; 6:1–5; cf. 6:6–19). Fear of the LORD, in fact, demands just and gracious acts even when human laws and regulations are ineffective or silent,[43] such as fair business practices (e.g., 11:1; 16:11; cf. Lev. 25:17), respect for and deference to the elderly (Lev. 19:32), care for the physically disabled (Lev. 19:14), and support and protection of families (Lev. 25:36). Without fear of the LORD, the threads that weave together moral, equitable relations easily fray or unravel altogether.

### B. Love

Alongside "fear of the LORD," the wise are summoned to *love*—specifically, to *erotic love*—for wisdom (4:6; 8:17, 21) and for the "wife of your youth" (5:18). Love for personified wisdom is described metaphorically as the passion of a young man for a desirable bride. He is charged to seek and find her (3:13; 8:17, 35), hold fast to her (3:18), embrace her (4:8), and love and never abandon her (4:6). The youth is to call wisdom his "sister" (7:4), a term of romantic endearment (Song 4:9, 10, 12; cf. 5:2),[44] and to wait expectantly, as lovers do, "day by day" outside wisdom's house (8:34; cf. Job 31:9; Song 2:9; Sir. 14:20–25). In turn, the parent promises that wisdom will love the youth (7:17), give him a garland and a crown (items worn by a bridegroom, 4:9; cf. Song 3:11; Isa. 61:10), and lavish upon him life and prosperity.

Erotic imagery is even more sexually charged with regard to the youth's wife (5:18b–19):

> May you *rejoice* in the wife of your youth,
> a lovely deer, a graceful gazelle.
> May her breasts quench your thirst at all times;
> may you ever stagger by her *love*.

Focusing on the woman's sexual desirability, the parent first compares her—as was common in erotic speech (e.g., Song 2:7; 3:5; 4:5)—to certain animals.[45] He then makes a pun, referring to the woman's *daddayim* ("breasts" or "nipples"), a word remarkably similar to *dōdîm* ("lovemaking," cf. 7:18; cf. Song 1:2, 4; Ezek. 23:17). The parent's hope is that the woman's breasts/lovemaking will so "quench" (NRSV "satisfy") her husband's thirst (note the language of a bodily appetite) that he "staggers" around like a drunkard. Whereas elsewhere in the Old Testament, the verb "to stagger" is always used negatively, as in "to stray, to make a mistake, to do wrong" (e.g., 5:20; 19:27; 1 Sam. 26:21; Ps. 119:21, 118), the parent here uses it positively. Rather than admonishing the youth never to "stagger" (that is, to stray), despite the excitement and passion that connotes, the parent encourages him to do so and regularly ("at all times") *with his wife*. The "object" of the youth's affections, it seems, proves the difference between a life-giving sexual tryst and a deadly one. The parent underscores this point elsewhere when he warns about personified wisdom's sexually desirable counterpart, namely, the "Strange Woman" or Woman of Folly (cf. 2:16–19; 5:1–14; 7:6–27), whose fluttering eyelashes, smooth words, lips dripping sweet honey, and promises of illicit delight threaten to waylay the erotic affections of unsuspecting young men. Involvement with her—the wrong "object" of erotic love—has deadly consequences (e.g., 2:16–19; 7:21–23).

Though space does not permit detailed consideration of *eros* in Proverbs 1–9,[46] use of erotic love establishes certain expectations for the youth's relationships with wisdom and his lifelong companion. First, erotic love is *partial* and *intense*, characterized by deep longing for the other, who is seen as radiant, wonderful, and necessary for one's well-being. With regard to wisdom in particular, the parent and personified wisdom aim to cultivate such fervent desire with imperatives like love (4:6), seek and find (e.g., 2:4; 3:13), acquire (4:5, 7), cry out for (2:3), prize highly (4:8), and do not forsake (4:6), coupled with repeated celebration of wisdom's many benefits. Second, erotic love *opens* a person. Inherent is the perception that one is limited, even incomplete, and in need of the other for wholeness. So the wise assume a posture of rapt attention and receptivity to wisdom—listening, watching, inclining their hearts to instruction, accepting reproof, and practicing humility. Finally, erotic love *esteems the other as independent*, not simply a part of or submissive to the lover.[47] The parent asserts wisdom's independence variously, calling it a divine gift (2:5–6), personifying it as a woman who takes her stand in the heart of everyday life (1:20–21; 8:2–3), extolling wisdom's preeminent and mysterious relationship with God (8:22–31), and, with only one exception (5:1), never referring to wisdom as possessed by a person (e.g., "her wisdom," "their wisdom"). So though the wise hold fast to wisdom, it remains ever "other," deep and mysterious. To receive wisdom, as Alcibiades discovered in his quest to learn from Socrates,

> [the youth] must not be self-sufficient, closed against the world. He must put aside the vanity of his beauty and become, himself, in his own eyes, an object in the world: the world of the other's activity, and in the larger world of happenings that affect his dealings with the other.[48]

In sum, this consideration of the wise and their emotions reveals that interdependence is a significant part of the conception of *eudaimonia* (commonly translated "happiness"), or human flourishing, that Proverbs 1–9 advocates. Indeed, the parent claims that "fear of the LORD," love of wisdom, fidelity to and delight in one's partner prompt just that emotion, namely, *happiness*. Words translated "happy" (*'ašrê* and *mĕ'uššar*), for instance, frame the tribute to personified wisdom in 3:13–18, and she later promises that "happy [*'ašrê*] are those who keep my ways . . . happy [*'ašrê*] is the one who listens to me" (8:32–34). Moreover, wisdom identifies herself as *delight* (8:30), rejoicing always before God, in the world, and with humanity (8:30–31), so that to embrace her is to grab hold of pure joy. Like the parent before her, she exemplifies for her students the emotional disposition she aims to teach. Worthy of note is that this concept of *eudaimonia* is *not* solely or simply about individual satisfaction, about what God, wisdom, or my companion can "do for me." Rather, insofar as it summons all those who would be wise to awe of and obedience to God, humility, receptivity to and respect for others, and the lifelong pursuit of "righteousness, justice, and equity" (1:3), it values the "objects" of our affections as worthy of love and benefit for their own sake.

## III. CONCLUSION

The attention Proverbs 1–9 gives to emotions invites us to reflect carefully about several matters as we engage in moral formation and ministry at the dawn of a new millennium. First, the texts advocate a *holistic understanding of the human*. They teach to and for the whole person, resisting distinctions between the rational and the emotional as they foster certain beliefs in the inner self (the *lēb*, or "heart/mind"). "To do this," Fox writes, "more is required than sententious warnings and somber maxims or even a logical demonstration of cause and effect, for by themselves these are abstract and lack rooting" in people's experience.[49] It is not enough, that is, to proclaim but not evoke, to teach but not enable affective participation, to appeal to the intellect and not care for the body—a claim, I expect, that is not entirely new to pastors, educators, and caregivers everywhere.[50] Proverbs reminds us that the formation of moral, faithful individuals and communities urgently depends on our capacities to engage human pathos and to cultivate hope and joy.

Second, the sages' valuing of emotions as forms of judgment that can be taught, rather than as irrational impulses that must be suppressed, means that the teaching of virtue need not be construed solely as a "matter of strength, the will simply holding down the brutish impulsive elements of the personality."[51] Instead, reason infuses the whole person, so that changes in perception and beliefs provoke changes in behavior *and* emotions. Certainly, such changes are arduous; personified wisdom offers a long-term relationship—not a "quick fix"—to reform the fools' affections (1:22–33). But Proverbs 1–9 encourages us to shift our weight in moral formation from the repression of emotions to the cultivation of just, honest, good ways of perceiving the world, trusting that such quell the emergence of undesirable, even dangerous emotional judgments (e.g., misogynistic anger, hatred of others solely on the basis of race, religion, sexual orientation, and so on). Said differently, moral formation may be more about testifying to God's wisdom woven into the very fabric of creation (cf. esp. 3:18–19; 8:22–31) than the vigilant restraint of innate unruly passions.[52]

Finally, the sages remind us that we map the world and map ourselves in the world by our emotions; thus the "objects" of our affections matter deeply. The wise in Proverbs 1–9 are not "objective" and removed, but *people of passions* (even of compulsions), captivated by beauty and goodness, disgusted by wickedness, devoted to God, wisdom, and others. This relational portrait of what it means to be wise challenges our cultural tendency toward atomism, the view that every individual is a sovereign self, a "free unfettered agent" who is by nature not bound to anything or any authority; the view that rejects the idea we are creatures "embedded in a structured creation that has its own say"[53]and to which we are accountable. Taking her stand in the heart of the city, wisdom calls us away from such folly, ushering us instead into a landscape of towering loves, intoxicating fidelities, and profound responsibilities—a landscape Proverbs deems ripe for human flourishing.

## NOTES

1. Unless otherwise noted, all translations are my own. I add emphasis to highlight the language of emotion.
2. R. E. Murphy, *Proverbs*, WBC 22 (Nashville: Thomas Nelson, 1998), 91.
3. R. van Leeuwen, "Proverbs," in *The New Interpreter's Bible* (Nashville: Abingdon Press, 1997), 5:143.
4. Ibid, 127.
5. Ibid., 152. Emphasis added.
6. M. Lichtheim, *Ancient Egyptian Literature*, vol. 2, *The New Kingdom* (Berkeley: University of California Press, 1976), 146–63. Hereafter *AEL* 2.
7. See discussion below.
8. M. C. Nussbaum, "Emotions as Judgements of Value and Importance," in *Relativism, Suffering, and Beyond: Essays in Memory of Bimal K. Matilal* (Delhi: Oxford University Press, 1997), 235. See this elaborated more fully in her *Upheavals of Thought: The Intelligence of Emotions* (Cambridge: Cambridge University Press, 2001), 129–37.
9. Note, for example, Toyota's slogan "Get the Toyota feeling," or Chrysler's recent catchphrase "drive=love."
10. Walter Brueggemann, ed., *Hope for the World: Mission in a Global Context* (Louisville, Ky.: Westminster John Knox Press, 2001), 16 (emphasis original).
11. P. Scholtes, "They'll Know We are Christians by Our Love." Copyright 1966 F. E. L. Publications; assigned to the Lorenz Corporation, Dayton, Ohio.
12. See especially A. R. Damasio, *Descartes' Error: Emotion, Reason, and the Human Brain* (New York: Avon, 1994); Damasio, *The Feeling of What Happens: Body and Emotion in the Making of Consciousness* (San Diego: Harcourt, 1999); R. C. Roberts, *Emotions: An Essay in Aid of Moral Psychology* (Cambridge: Cambridge University Press, 2003); Roberts, "Emotions Among the Virtues of the Christian Life," *The Journal of Religious Ethics* 20 (1992): 37–68; R. Bondi, "The Elements of Character," *The Journal of Religious Ethics* 12 (1984): 201–18. For a recent consideration of the role of love in Deuteronomy in light of some of these discussions, see J. E. Lapsley, "Feeling Our Way: Love for God in Deuteronomy," *CBQ* 65 (2003): 350–69.
13. Nussbaum, *Upheavals of Thought*, 94.
14. I summarize here the four main points of Nussbaum's argument, which was first published in "Emotions as Judgements of Value and Importance," 231–51, and then revised and expanded in *Upheavals of Thought*, 19–88.
15. Nussbaum favors the Greek spelling of this term instead of the English ("eudaemonistic") because the former broadly includes distinct conceptions of what is good while the latter, in her view, is too narrowly associated with the notion that the supreme good is happiness (cf. *Upheavals of Thought*, 31, n. 23).
16. Ibid., 117.
17. The extent and diversity of theories about the emotions offered by various disciplines (e.g., philosophy, ethics, psychoanalysis, evolutionary biology, cultural

anthropology, neurobiology) alone demonstrates their complexity. Debates continue as to the nature of emotions; their source(s); relationship to cognition; connections to moods, motives, desires, and actions; and so on.

18. By "interdependence" I mean (a) recognizing that those whom we love are separate from us and not mere instruments of our will; (b) depending on them in certain ways (without insisting on omnipotence); and, in turn, (c) inviting others to depend on us and committing ourselves to be responsible to and for them in particular ways (see Nussbaum, *Upheavals of Thought*, 224–29).
19. See, e.g., Prov. 1:8, 20–21; 6:20; 7:6–12; 8:1–3; 9:3, 14–15.
20. The father-to-son setting is common in ancient Near Eastern wisdom literature. For example, the epilogue of the Egyptian *Instruction of Anii* is a dialogue between a father and son (*AEL* 2, 144–45) and the Sumerian *Instructions of Shuruppak* are lessons Shuruppak teaches his son (*BWL*, 92–94). Elsewhere in the Hebrew Bible, Ecclesiastes addresses "my son" (12:12). In Proverbs, the father-to-son setting continues through chapters 1–9 and is assumed occasionally elsewhere in the book (cf. 19:27; 23:15, 19, 26; 24:13, 21; 27:11). Twice, the father associates his teaching with that of his wife (1:8; 6:20), but she never speaks directly to the son.
21. So C. A. Newsom, "Woman and the Discourse of Patriarchal Wisdom: A Study of Proverbs 1–9," in *Women in the Hebrew Bible: A Reader*, ed. A. Bach (New York: Routledge & Kegan Paul, 1999), 86; first published in *Gender and Difference in Ancient Israel*, ed. P. Day (Minneapolis: Augsburg Fortress, 1989), 142–60.
22. The family setting, for example, eclipses class interests: "[T]his is not a landed aristocrat speaking, not a senior bureaucrat, not a member of the urban middle class or a disenfranchised intellectual, but 'your father'" (Newsom, "Woman and the Discourse of Patriarchal Wisdom," 86). When one looks closely, in fact, it is evident that Proverbs 1–9 was intended for young men of relatively privileged circumstances, perhaps the sons of affluent and moderately wealthy members of an urban commercial class (see, e.g., 3:9–10; 5:10; 6:1–5, 35).
23. See Roberts, *Emotions*, 351; M. C. Nussbaum, "Narrative Emotions: Beckett's Genealogy of Love," *Ethics* 1 (1988): 234–35; *Upheavals of Thought*, esp. 139–237. This is not to dispute that there may also be evolutionary origins for emotions (cf. *Upheavals of Thought*, 204).
24. The prologue of Proverbs (1:1–7) promotes the book of Proverbs as instruction for a lifetime, as a primer for the young and an advanced textbook for the more experienced (cf. 1:4). Insofar as the book conceives the quest for wisdom as a lifelong endeavor, the possibility of learning something new in adulthood (including something that modifies one's emotions) is assumed.
25. Nussbaum, *Upheavals of Thought*, 206–7.
26. Roberts, *Emotions*, 1.
27. Note, for example, that the wise hate (8:13) and the foolish love (1:22). That said, it is difficult to claim that emotions in Proverbs are all "morally neutral" (e.g., van Leeuwen, "Proverbs," 141). Hatred, for example, is most frequently construed negatively (e.g., 10:12, as stirring up strife).
28. Nussbaum, "Narrative Emotions," 233.
29. Proverbs assumes that wisdom's companionship with those who love her endures. Note, for example, that the nature and extent of lexical and thematic parallels between the descriptions of personified wisdom in Proverbs 1–9 and of the Woman of Substance in 31:10–31 suggests that the two figures essen-

tially coalesce (cf. C. Roy Yoder, *Wisdom as a Woman of Substance: A Socioeconomic Reading of Proverbs 1–9 and 31:10–31*, BZAW 304 [Berlin: Walter de Gruyter, 2001], 91–93). As such, the silent youth of Proverbs 1–9 may be seen to mature into wisdom's esteemed spouse in 31:10–31, to develop "from receptive child to responsible adult, from dependent to patriarch" (W. P. Brown, "The Pedagogy of Proverbs 10:1–31:9," in *Character & Scripture: Moral Formation, Community, and Biblical Interpretation*, ed. W. P. Brown [Grand Rapids: Wm. B. Eerdmans Publishing Co., 2002], 153).

30. Compare the following from the Egyptian *Instruction of Amenemope*: "He who does evil, the shore rejects him. / The floodwater carries him away. / The northwind descends to end his hour, / It mingles with the thunderstorm. / The storm cloud is tall, the crocodiles vicious, / You heated man, how are you now?" (*AEL* 2, 150).
31. Van Leeuwen, "Proverbs," 41.
32. See, e.g., Prov. 11:10; Job 22:19–20; Isa. 14:3–20; Pss. 2:4; 37:10–13; 52:5–7; 58; Rev. 18:20; but cf. Prov. 24:17.
33. Roberts, *Emotions*, 227.
34. Nussbaum, *Upheavals of Thought*, 88.
35. Ibid., 300.
36. See also Prov. 10:27; 14:26–27; 15:16, 33; 16:6; 19:23; 22:4; 23:17 and the imperative "fear the LORD!" three times (3:7; 14:2; 24:21).
37. According to the sages, "fear of the LORD" is the *rē'šît* of knowledge (1:7a; cf. 9:10a). The term *rē'šît* has a range of possible meanings. It may be interpreted temporally as "beginning or starting point" (cf. Gen. 10:10; Jer. 26:1), suggesting that "the fear of the LORD" is the prerequisite, the foundation for knowledge. It may also be read qualitatively, as "first, best, or epitome" (Amos 6:6; Jer. 2:3; Ezek. 48:14). Either way (and the ambiguity may well be intentional) there is no wisdom without it.
38. L. G. Perdue, *Proverbs*, Interpretation (Louisville, Ky.: Westminster John Knox Press, 2000), 74.
39. R. J. Clifford, *Proverbs*, OTL (Louisville, Ky.: Westminster John Knox Press, 1999), 35.
40. M. V. Fox, *Proverbs 1–9*, AB 18A (New York: Doubleday, 2000), 70 (emphasis original).
41. E. Davis, *Proverbs, Ecclesiastes, and the Song of Songs*, WBC (Louisville, Ky.: Westminster John Knox Press, 2000), 28.
42. So Fox, *Proverbs 1–9*, 70.
43. Ibid., 70–71.
44. Egyptian love poetry also employs "sister" as a term of romantic endearment; see, e.g., *AEL* 2:181–93.
45. In the Song of Songs, for example, the woman's breasts are likened to "two fawns, twins of a gazelle (4:5; cf. 2:7; 3:5); her eyes, to doves; her hair, to a herd of goats; and her teeth, to a flock of freshly shorn ewes (4:1–2; 6:5–6); similarly the male lover is compared to a gazelle and young stag (2:9, 17; 8:14).
46. But see R. E. Murphy, "Wisdom and Eros in Proverbs 1–9," *CBQ* 50 (1988): 600–03; and J. Green, "The Love of Wisdom and the Wisdom of Love: Eros as Metaphor in Biblical Wisdom" (Ph.D. dissertation, Princeton Theological Seminary, forthcoming).
47. Nussbaum, *Upheavals of Thought*, 470. Admittedly, the "wife of one's youth" is portrayed as less independent than wisdom. Prov. 5:15–18 emphasize the

husband's exclusive claim to her; she is "*your* cistern," "*your* well," "*your* springs," "*your* fountain," "*for yourself alone*." At the same time, however, the parent warns that if the husband does not observe sexual exclusivity, neither shall his wife. Whether by force or *by choice*, she will abandon him, a claim that suggests her capacity to act independently.

48. M. C. Nussbaum, *The Fragility of Goodness: Luck and Ethics in Greek Tragedy and Philosophy*, 2d ed. (Cambridge: Cambridge University Press, 2001), 192.
49. Fox, *Proverbs*, 349.
50. Bondi, "The Elements of Character," 215.
51. Nussbaum, *Upheavals of Thought*, 232.
52. Ibid., 232–33.
53. W. Brueggemann, "Praise to God is the End of Wisdom—What is the Beginning?" *Journal for Preachers* 12 (1989): 37; C. Taylor, *Sources of the Self: The Making of the Modern Identity* (Cambridge, Mass.: Harvard University Press, 1989), esp. 192–97.

# 8

# Life Together in the Household of God

*E. Elizabeth Johnson*

North American church and culture are aflame with debate about what constitute appropriate family values. Crowds of protesters urge federal and state legislators either to defend the institution of heterosexual marriage or to extend its benefits and privileges to gay and lesbian couples; child welfare agencies encounter increasingly harsh criticism in the face of repeated failures to protect the most vulnerable people entrusted to their care; and religious communities of every stripe wrestle with and battle over issues of human sexuality, clergy misconduct, and the proper character of family life. The Bible serves as a significant authority—or weapon—in these struggles. This essay[1] suggests that the multiple voices of the New Testament offer several different answers to the questions we raise about kinship and family life, and that this very diversity may itself prove helpful for the debate. My thesis is that there are among New Testament writers at least three ways of construing family values, dubbed for the sake of conversation apocalyptic disorientation, theological reorientation, and ecclesiastical domestication. We will consider each in turn and then ask what each contributes to our thinking about life together in the household of God and in the individual households we create within it.

## I. APOCALYPTIC DISORIENTATION[2]

The patriarchal narratives in Genesis portray human beings as divinely placed in families, with parents who bear and care for children and who, as members of clans and the nation of Israel, live, work, and worship together as the household of God.[3] That vision of family life changes profoundly under the impact of urbanization, exile, diaspora life, Greco-Roman culture, and the advent of Christian faith.

The apostle Paul, the earliest Christian writer we know, lived with an apocalyptic worldview, a phrase that deserves unpacking. The word "apocalyptic" means "revealed" or "revelatory," and it is all too often used interchangeably with the word "eschatology," although the two are by no means synonyms. Eschatology refers to convictions about the end times, the end of human history, the day of the fulfillment of God's redemption. Many Jews and Christians of the first century wrote apocalypses, books that disclosed revelations they received from heavenly beings, and those apocalypses often contain eschatology, visions of God's plan to rescue the covenant people and bring justice and healing to a fallen and broken world. Christian writers like Paul were profoundly influenced by these apocalyptic texts, but with a significant difference. In his writings, Paul does not look forward only to the Day of the Lord, but claims the new age of God's redemption has already begun in the death and resurrection of Jesus. This new creation is hardly complete, as the church and the world continue to struggle against the power of sin and under the burden of death, but it has surely begun. The resurrection of Jesus, God's justification of sinners, and the Spirit's presence in the church provide a present foretaste of the glory that is yet to come.

Paul clearly anticipates the return of the risen Lord in his own near future; we are, he says to the Corinthians, "those upon whom the end of the ages has come" (1 Cor. 10:11), and he assures them that "the appointed time has grown short" (7:29). The revelation that has changed Paul's life, though, has comparatively little to do with turning the pages on the heavenly calendar or watching the rushing hands on the cosmic clock. The apocalypse that defines Paul's gospel is rather the cross of Jesus Christ, the revelation of God's new creation. This new creation, unlike the one portrayed in Genesis, is not a matter of God's planting a garden and sharing sovereignty over it with human beings. Paul's language is much more radical. The new creation is the invasion of God's righteousness that sweeps away the old world held captive to sin and death, a new creation marked not by power but by weakness, not by human wisdom but by divine foolishness, a new world that finds life in the midst of death and glory in the midst of suffering. It is disorienting and disoriented, this new creation, because it turns upside down the most treasured of human values and replaces them with the cross of Christ.

In Flannery O'Connor's short story "A Good Man Is Hard to Find," an escaped prison convict called The Misfit comes upon a family who has just had an automobile accident on an isolated road in rural Georgia. The Misfit's accomplices murder the father and one of his children in chillingly cold blood, and they are about to shoot the mother and her other two children when the grandmother engages The Misfit in conversation, trying valiantly to stem the tide of his violence. O'Connor writes,

> Finally she found herself saying, "Jesus, Jesus," meaning, Jesus will help you, but the way she was saying it, it sounded as if she might be cursing.
>
> "Yes'm," The Misfit said as if he agreed. "Jesus thown everything off balance. It was the same case with Him as with me except He hadn't committed any crime and they could prove I had committed one. . . . I call myself The Misfit," he said, "because I can't make what all I done wrong fit what all I gone through in punishment."[4]

"Jesus thown everything off balance," says O'Connor's Misfit, and so does Paul. God's revelation of the cross throws off balance all the tidy ordering of human responsibility, of crime and punishment, guilt and innocence, and justifies not the godly but the ungodly. God's new creation invades the old one and sets aside all the neat human accounting that shows who's who and what's what, that prizes honor and scorns shame, that thanks God for the differences between insiders and outsiders, between rich and poor, Jew and Greek, slave and free, male and female, because everybody needs to be somewhere, and it's always better to be on top of the heap than on the bottom.[5]

In Gal. 3:23–29, Paul says that Christian baptism is an apocalyptic act that ends the old creation. He says much the same in 2 Cor. 5:17: "If anyone is in Christ, there is a new creation," and in Gal. 6:15: "Neither circumcision nor uncircumcision is anything; but a new creation is everything!" The part of this new creation that bears most directly on matters of family and kinship is language taken from a liturgy for baptism that Paul quotes in Gal. 3:27–28: "As many of you as were baptized into Christ have clothed yourselves with Christ. There is no longer Jew or Greek, there is no longer slave or free, there is no longer male and female; for all of you are one in Christ Jesus." The first two phrases, "Jew or Greek" and "slave or free," are parallel, but the third is slightly different, "male *and* female." The language alludes to Gen. 1:27 and turns the phrase on its head. Genesis says, "God created humankind . . . male and female," but Paul says in Christ "there is no longer male and female." The dichotomy of gender is one of the most fundamental ways people have of identifying ourselves, and Paul says baptism sets it aside. He does not say that the old hierarchies that structure human society and keep people in their proper places are somehow replaced by a new equality between male and female, slave and free, Jew and Greek. There is instead a whole new humanity in Christ living in the midst of the old.

There are concrete social consequences of this new creation. In 1 Cor. 7 Paul works out some of the implications of that "no longer male and female."

He agrees with the Corinthians who say "it is well for a man not to touch a woman" (7:1), commends those who have the charismatic gift of celibacy, wishes they would all remain unmarried as he is (7:7), and affirms the choice of married couples to refrain from sex for a season in order to "devote [themselves] to prayer" (7:5). He even deems permanently celibate partnerships preferable to sexually active marriages (7:36–38). Although he twice refrains from forbidding believers to marry (7:9, 36), he three times reiterates the superiority of celibacy (7:7, 26, 38).

This strange notion of celibacy that is preferable to marriage—or celibate seasons within otherwise ordinary marriages—might be stranger still if Paul were the only one to advocate it. In fact, there are many people in the first century who are sexually abstinent the way Paul is. Philosophers and physicians alike counsel all but the most limited sexual activity for the wise who would preserve their πνεῦμα, a word that is frequently translated "spirit," but often means "life force."[6] Other religious people, Jews and pagans both, also refrain from sex in order to participate in the holiness of God or the gods. Particularly Jews and Christians of apocalyptic persuasion are known to embrace continence as preparation for life in the new age.[7] This is not even a particularly new idea in the first century. The Bible describes Israelite soldiers who fight holy wars—that is, wars on God's behalf—as refraining from sex to prepare themselves for battle (1 Sam. 21:5). It is very likely that apocalyptic Jews like Paul or the sectarians at Qumran consider themselves troops in God's final holy war,[8] and thus under the biblical injunction to purify themselves from all sexual activity before battle (cf. 2 Sam. 11:11; Deut. 23:10).

Although Paul has this strange attitude toward "real" family life, he uses a stunning amount of kinship language to describe the Christian community. When believers are baptized into his churches, they come up out of the water crying, "*Abba*," the Aramaic word for "father" (Rom. 8:15; Gal. 4:6). Christians are adopted by God in baptism and become siblings not only of each other but of Christ himself, joint heirs with Christ of God's legacy of the Holy Spirit.[9] This is the reason Paul so frequently addresses his letters to his "brothers and sisters." He bends the family language that describes his congregations, however, when he calls himself their father as well as their brother. "I have become Onesimus's father," he tells Philemon (10), and he says to the Corinthians, "In Christ Jesus I became your father through the gospel" (1 Cor. 4:15). It is rather common, actually, for teachers in the ancient world to call themselves their students' fathers, but Paul twists the metaphor still further when he tells these same Corinthians that he has "fed [them] with milk" (3:2), something only mothers can do in a world that does not yet know about infant formula or baby bottles. He says to the Galatians that he is in labor again with them "until Christ is formed in you" (4:19), as if he were both the pregnant mother who gives birth to the congregation (a second time, no less) and the midwife who delivers their child.[10]

Nowhere, though, is Paul's jarring use of family language so prominent as in 1 Thessalonians 2, where he says, "although we might have thrown our weight around as apostles of Christ,[11] we were instead infants among you, like a wet nurse tenderly caring for her own children" (2:7).[12] Although wet nurses are frequently held up as the epitome of lovingkindness and gentle instruction among philosophers of the day, only Paul claims both the role of the infant and the nursing mother. The apostolic mission can take on the astonishing vulnerability of a newborn as well as the nurture of a mother or the authority of a father (2:11)—and all of them in the same paragraph!—only because that mission is cruciform in character, shaped by the vulnerability of the cross of Christ, invaded by God's new creation. So while Paul seems to have scant regard for conventional families, he has a remarkably high view of the church as an alternative household, a household in which God is *Abba*, the firstborn is Christ, all the children are heirs, and the rigid boundaries that prescribe life in the Greco-Roman patriarchal household are constantly blurred and bent by the demands of the gospel mission.

But surely this must be a Pauline idiosyncrasy. Surely Jesus favors traditional family life. The Gospels tell us of his welcoming children, expanding the definition of adultery to include lust, and forbidding divorce. Surely Jesus is, as they say, pro-family. Again, however, things are not entirely as they appear. In the Gospels of Mark and Matthew, Jesus calls people to leave their families and join his family instead. Rather than collecting disciples, as other rabbis do, so that they might learn how to become rabbis themselves, Jesus calls people into permanent relationships of discipleship with himself that take precedence over all other relationships. In Mark 1, for instance, Jesus has established something of a reputation in the Galilee as a preacher. When he calls the brothers James and John from their fishing business to join him, however (1:14–18), Mark makes no mention of how the family will survive without their labor, and he never says how Simon's mother-in-law, whom Jesus later heals of a fever (1:29–31), manages to put food on the table when Simon abandons the family to wander the countryside. Paul says Simon Peter and his wife eventually travel through the cities of the Mediterranean together as Christian missionaries (1 Cor. 9:5), and one cannot help but wonder who keeps the home fires burning in their absence. When James and John leave their father and boat to join Jesus' movement (Mark 1:19–20), at least they leave Zebedee with some hired hands to help, but in a culture where work is incredibly labor intensive and fishing provides at best a marginal income and is heavily taxed by the empire, children who leave home like this impoverish their families both economically and socially.

The story is even more shocking in Matthew's version (4:18–22), since when Jesus arrives at the Sea of Galilee he has established no prior reputation in that region, and Matthew deletes the reference to Zebedee's employees. In Matthew the old man is left all alone to provide for himself and the rest of his household, on no notice whatsoever. These are not traditional ancient family values that Jesus exhibits any more than they are modern ones.[13] In the Gospels, the call of Jesus trumps all other calls, even those to hearth and home. In Mark, Jesus himself does what he calls his disciples to do when he rejects his family and replaces it with his "real" mother and brothers and sisters who do God's will (3:31–35).[14]

When Jesus forbids divorce and remarriage in Matt. 19:8–12, the disciples respond that, if this is so, it is better not to marry at all. And Jesus agrees with them. Like Paul, he says that becoming a eunuch is only for those who can accept it. Although celibacy is not for everyone, it is clearly preferable to marriage because the new age will see no more marrying or giving in marriage as the old age does (24:38–41). The last days, says Matthew, will bring family disruption that is better avoided ahead of time. Woe to women who are pregnant or nursing then, and pray that the end does not come on the Sabbath, the consummate family celebration (24:19–20).[15]

Still other Gospel texts issue this radical call to abandon family because Christian discipleship creates inevitable conflict due to divided loyalties. Here there is no summons to evangelize one's household but instead a warning to anticipate its division. Siblings will betray each other and parents their children, and in-laws will be at each other's throats because of their divided loyalties (Mark 13:12–13; Matt. 10:21–22, 34–39; Luke 12:51–53; 21:16–17). One answers either the call of Jesus or the call of family. It is perhaps most telling that Mark puts this warning in the midst of his eschatological discourse (chap. 13), when Jesus talks about the end times, while Matthew places the same saying in his mission discourse (chap. 10), which means Matthew sees the disruption of traditional households as part of the church's ongoing life between now and the end times.

Some scholars think this focus on apocalyptic family disorientation is created to help believers compensate emotionally for the loss of family they experience when they convert to Christianity. Antiquity abounds with stories of people like the Egyptian Asenath, who is disowned by her family when she converts to Judaism to marry the patriarch Joseph, and we know of scores of Christians who are rejected by their households when they become believers.[16] From the ways Paul, Mark, and Matthew talk, however, being adopted into God's family does not compensate for lost families of origin but instead causes the losses in the first place. Even if becoming God's children and Jesus' brothers and sisters does not destroy someone's biological and legal kinship bonds altogether (we hear, after all, of some whole families who convert), it certainly disorients the priorities that are absolutely central to Greco-Roman—and, we might add, North American—traditional family values.

## II. THEOLOGICAL REORIENTATION

This may be one reason we also find in the New Testament somewhat modified pictures of Christian kinship, a response that I call theological reorientation. With Luke 5:1–11 we return to the episode of the fishermen who leave home. Jesus' call of the first disciples is vastly less disorienting in Luke because of the story's numerous additions. Jesus approaches the fishermen first as a preacher they already know, and he uses their boat as a pulpit from which to address the crowds. Then he tells Simon to start fishing again. Despite a fruitless night of work before this, the result is a miraculously huge catch of fish,[17] so large that the newly cleaned nets[18] are nearly breaking. The superabundance of fish signals the inbreaking of the new age of God's blessing and salvation. By adding this episode to Mark's account, Luke says not only that God's power to restore and renew life has come in unprecedented fullness in the ministry of Jesus, but also that Zebedee and his family will be cared for when the sons leave home to follow Jesus. Although the new age of God's redemptive realm places serious demands on disciples, it also makes available the riches of the Jubilee: Jesus' first sermon says he has come to announce the year of the Lord's favor (4:19).

Luke knows that Christian discipleship reorders domestic priorities: "Whoever . . . does not hate father and mother, wife and children, brothers and sisters . . . cannot be my disciple" (14:26). Luke hails celibacy as a hallmark of the redeemed life (20:35), as Matthew and Mark do, and he honors some celibate characters, like Anna the prophetess (Luke 2:36–38) or the prophetic daughters of Philip (Acts 21:9), but the Lukan vision of early Christianity is not particularly ascetic. It is people who have specific prophetic roles, like Philip's unnamed daughters and Anna, who are celibate, not the rest of the Christian community. The communal life of the church in Jerusalem, where believers share all things in common and "there [is] not a needy person among them" (Acts 4:34) shows that for Luke the church is the real family to which Christians belong, even though pictures of conventional households within the church also abound.[19] Luke envisions a pragmatic accommodation to the radical disorientation of Mark's views of family life, a theological reorientation of conventional domestic virtue. He repeatedly portrays the Christian movement in ways that do not offend prevailing cultural sensibilities when he shows one household after another responding to the Christian message at the instigation of those households' patriarchs—and, in the case of Lydia, a matriarch

(16:11–15)—even as he maintains that the good news of Jesus' resurrection and God's restoration of the world replaces the foundational cultural myth of Greco-Roman supremacy.[20]

First Peter is addressed to some Christian gatherings in Asia Minor whose members belong to predominantly non-Christian households. Although 2:13–3:9 is in many ways a traditional pagan code of household responsibilities that urges wives and slaves to submit to their husbands and masters,[21] the initial imperatives to "honor everyone, love the family of believers, fear God, and honor the emperor" subtly and subversively undercut the hierarchical values of pagan domestic virtue.[22] Honor the emperor, says 1 Peter, precisely as you honor everyone else. Fear—or religious awe—belongs properly not to the emperor nor to household patriarchs but to God alone. And the community's primary obligation is to love "the family of believers" (2:17). There do not seem to be any Christian masters in these churches, since none are addressed, but there are apparently some few Christian married couples who are exhorted to "make a home together according to knowledge. . . . in order that [their] prayers may not be hindered" (3:7, author's translation), a phrase that reminds more than one interpreter of Paul's discussion of seasons of marital celibacy in 1 Cor. 7:5.[23] Christian women married to non-Christian men, however, like Christian slaves who are owned by unbelievers, are at the mercy of the men who dominate their lives, and 1 Peter urges a kind of subversive accommodation to the inevitable that obeys the letter of the cultural law while holding fast to the assurance that Christ himself suffered unjustly and his redemptive death redefines reality. In a context where these powerless people are scorned by their families and friends simply for being Christian,[24] 1 Peter encourages them to hold on to their alternative Christian lifestyles as best they can and bear one another up under the burdens of a hostile environment they are powerless to change or control.

## III. ECCLESIASTICAL DOMESTICATION

The third group of texts comes from the end of the first century, when the church is beginning to see itself as an institution in society that must find ways to get along with its non-Christian neighbors. The passages in Eph. 5:21–6:9; Col. 3:18–4:1;1 Tim. 2:8–15; and Titus 2:1–10 that enforce ecclesiastical domestication have had perhaps the most toxic impact on Christian family life of any in Scripture. Although they are seldom read at wedding services anymore, their influence in the church and culture is pervasive. They have been used—and abused—by husbands, fathers, and slave owners to brutalize women, children, and people in bondage. They continue to hold before at least some church people ideals of family life that derive not from the gospel but from Greco-Roman pagan morality. These stereotyped lists of family responsibilities are ubiquitous among ethicists of the first century, pagan and Jewish alike, who reflect on their usefulness for maintaining order in the household that will reflect and reinforce order in the empire.[25] The structure of the patriarchal household, that is, one in which the patriarch or father reigns supreme, is somewhat modified in these Christian household codes. Ephesians, for example, prefaces its code with a call to mutual submission "out of reverence for Christ" (5:21), but that scarcely takes the sting out of the emphatic command that wives obey their husbands "in everything" (5:24).[26] We've seen how the domestic code in 1 Peter neglects to address masters, but in this third-generation Pauline context there are apparently Christian slave owners as well as slaves, and a husband, father, and master addressed here is the same man who holds all three roles as patriarch.

It is this Christianized picture of the Greco-Roman household in Ephesians, Colossians, and the Pastoral Epistles, with all its boundaries and hierarchical structure reinforced and the power of the patriarch infused with religious authority, that has been the most influential biblical voice for much of Christian history. Paul's apocalyptic preference for celibacy and the Gospels' vision of the Christian community as alternative household have had much less impact, with the notable exception of Roman Catholic and Orthodox attitudes toward clergy. Not even the reorientation of family values we find in Luke and 1 Peter has so shaped Christian household ethics as "wives, be subject to your husbands" and "slaves obey your masters."

## IV. LISTENING TO THE SEVERAL VOICES OF THE NEW TESTAMENT

It is instructive to consider the strengths and weaknesses of these three different visions of Christian family life. The power of apocalyptic disorientation is that it dethrones the cultural idol of the patriarchal household, frees those enslaved to conventional domestic roles, welcomes the radical newness of the gospel, and invites us to cruciform life as the body of Christ. We ought, I think, to pay particular attention to Paul's conviction that married sex is not the prime virtue of Christian domesticity, even though it has value and is to be honored. So also, the apocalyptic disorientation of the early church shows that a variety of household arrangements bear self-sacrificing witness to Jesus' death and serve the Christian mission. The weaknesses of such a radical view are significant, though. There are not many people who have the apocalyptic empowerment of celibacy. Both Jesus and Paul reject the notion that the church can impose celibacy on people who do not have the Spirit-given gift for it, and we should too. Charismatic life like Paul or the Synoptic Gospels envision it is difficult for mere mortals to maintain over time. The church as alternative household is not finally enough on its own to sustain people who have real toddlers or teenagers or aging parents in a society that is light years removed from Greco-Roman antiquity. We must be clear about what really happens when, as my pastor always puts it when he baptizes a baby, "Parents bring their child to the font as their daughter, and they take her home as a sister in Christ."[27] Finally, to speak lightly or carelessly of the church as family leaves dangerous room for clergy to become parents who infantilize congregations, particularly when we find it so difficult to understand ministry the way Paul does, as marked by weakness and humiliation rather than by glory and power.[28]

Luke and 1 Peter seem to offer something of a "middle way" through this thicket, although we do well to recall other "middle ways" that have compromised the church's faithfulness in the past.[29] The advantage of theological reorientation of family life is that it adapts the earlier radical lifestyle to the exigencies of life in the real world without sacrificing (too much) faithfulness. Luke and 1 Peter reappropriate some Old Testament family values like clan loyalty and the otherness of faithful life in the world. Caring for widows and orphans and sharing all things in common envisions a church in which people's needs are met even as believers respond wholeheartedly to Jesus' call to leave everything and follow him. The weaknesses of this stance are real, however. The communal life of the church in Acts is probably as idealized as is the Bible's talk about Jubilee. Luke's own story about Ananias and Sapphira (Acts 5:1–11) demonstrates the pervasive power of personal property and individual freedom to pervert and distort the Christian community's best intentions, just as I suspect there were few in ancient Israel who really freed their slaves or remitted debts at the Jubilee. Furthermore, Luke's attempt to replace the prevailing values of the empire with gospel values means he sometimes blurs the boundaries between the two: look how often it is the rich and well-born who are his models of faith. In 1 Peter, the helplessness of that Christian community in its hostile environment results in an inevitable capitulation to the evils of slavery and patriarchal household order, even if it is a subversive capitulation.

I confess that it is difficult for me to name the strengths of the ecclesiastical domestication represented by Paul's theological descendants. This is a picture of Christian family life that has done more violence to women and the African diaspora than any other, and it continues to impoverish the parts of Christ's church where people's gifts for ministry are evaluated in terms of gender, sexuality, and ethnicity. I think these Christian texts are akin to the Hebrew ones that Phyllis Trible calls "texts of terror."[30] Nevertheless, I feel impelled to listen with some (perhaps limited) empathy for the exigencies of the Pastor and the Pauline school and the forces that shaped their retreat from central elements of Pauline Christianity. Ephesians, Colossians, and the Pastoral Epistles all come from situations their authors deem threatening to the very existence of the church. Heresies within and hostility without forge in these authors a determination to preserve the church's life against its enemies at almost any cost. Their place in the canon is somewhat in-spite-of in this regard. Despite their unfortunate views of family life, their convictions about God's faithfulness to the church are particularly worth holding fast. The anti-imperial christology of the Pastoral Epistles reminds us that Christ alone is Lord, not social structures—even if the Pastor himself would surely never draw the same conclusion with me. The weaknesses of this approach are all too obvious. What is domesticated here is not only the family but the wild unpredictability and Spirit-powered transformation of the new creation. Paul's descendants reverse his conviction that the real family is the church and that individual families are created in its image. The church becomes in these texts—and for much of church history following them—instead a mirror of the Greco-Roman household, with clergy who are patriarchs who reign over their wives, slaves, and children. These texts privilege those who are already privileged in the world, and they reinforce, however inadvertently, social structures that are inimical to the gospel of Christ. As with one another, perhaps, we do well to remember Jesus' command to forgive as we are forgiven, even the Pastor and Paul's other descendants. While we may forgive the Pastor for operating more from fear than from faith as he reinstitutes pagan domestic morality, we dare not allow his words to oppress the least of Jesus' brothers and sisters.

The theological lessons offered by a comparison of these three different attitudes toward family life are as much about the Bible as they are about families and family values. We cannot harmonize these different voices lest we replace them with a synthesis of our own making. This is a perennial pitfall of attempts to do biblical theology. Since the church has historically chosen the path of ecclesiastical domestication over the other two options, perhaps we ought instead to choose another one, in an attempt to atone for the damage wrought over the centuries. If we do, however, we unavoidably place ourselves in the untenable position of trying to relive the ancient Mediterranean past in a Western, postindustrial, post-Christendom present. Moreover, reifying one form of family life rather than another scarcely undoes the injuries of the past. Might we perhaps find another way to listen for the voice of God among these competing visions that honors what is most evangelical in each of them? I see three ways to make our conversation with the Bible about family life fair and keep it open to the movement of God's Spirit without absolutizing one or another of these family portraits from the New Testament.

First, we must recognize that multiple human voices in the exegetical and theological conversation reflect the multiplicity of biblical voices. The diversity in the canon suggests a rightful and proper diversity of family configurations within the household of God. We dare not allow one particular model—whether the patriarchal household, the communal ideal of the Jerusalem church, or a charismatic preference for celibacy—to become obligatory for all.

Second, the cross as hermeneutical yardstick[31] suggests that the voices of the powerless and the marginal belong at the center of this debate, not on the edges. If you want to know where God is, you look for the least, the weakest, the most foolish. The people who matter most in this conversation are those with the quietest voices, so those of us with power are obliged to listen more carefully than we speak. That is because the cross turns everything upside down and makes the first last and the last first, the wise foolish and the foolish wise, and even the dead alive.

And third, in our somewhat myopic focus on North American, mainline Christianity's internal feuding about family values, let us not lose sight of larger and far more grave threats to family life in the world God loves and for which Christ died. Virtually every resident of homeless shelters is separated or estranged from family because of persistent poverty, mental illness, or substance abuse. Thousands of families cower in fear every night from guns and bombs while we lovingly tuck our children into bed. Palestinian and Israeli families bury their parents and children day after day after day. Iraqi and Afghan families cling to each other in the rubble of their former homes. The majority of the world's hungry are women and their children. Little ones as young as four and five huddle together every night under bridges and in doorways of Latin American cities. The most compelling Christian family values are those that finally have less to do with sex and much more to do with the love of God that seeks the lost and saves the hopeless.

In Gen. 28:14, God reminds Jacob that "all the families of the earth shall be blessed" because of the covenant God has made with Abraham and Sarah, and the writer of Ephesians echoes that promise by calling God the one "from whom every family in heaven and earth takes its name" (3:15). It is only when such covenant faithfulness and the cruciform life of the church mark our life together as the people of God that the individual households we create within it will be blessed.

## NOTES

1. These thoughts first came to speech as my inaugural address at Columbia Theological Seminary where Charlie Cousar and Walter Brueggemann, the most generous of senior colleagues, have supported, nurtured, and encouraged me

and my work. They will see their own fingerprints throughout this revision—even where they disagree!—and it is with deep thanks to God for their gracious and joyful colleagueship that I offer it. David Peterson's contribution to the Colloquium and to this volume has similarly enriched my thinking about the Bible and family life, and I also thank him for stimulating my thought.

2. This section reflects much the same argument I make in "Apocalyptic Family Values," *Interpretation* 56 (2002): 34–44.
3. See David Peterson, "Shaking the World of Family Values," chap. 3 in the present volume.
4. Flannery O'Connor, *The Complete Stories* (New York: Farrar, Straus & Giroux, 1971), 131.
5. My understanding of the way Paul's gospel is apocalyptic is indebted primarily to J. Christiaan Beker, *Paul the Apostle: The Triumph of God in Life and Thought* (Philadelphia: Fortress Press, 1980); Charles B. Cousar, *A Theology of the Cross: The Death of Jesus in the Pauline Letters* (Minneapolis: Fortress Press, 1990); and J. Louis Martyn, *Galatians*, AB 33A (New York: Doubleday, 1997); Martyn, "Apocalyptic Antinomies" and "Epistemology at the Turn of the Ages," in *Theological Issues in the Letters of Paul* (Nashville: Abingdon Press, 1997), 89–123. See also Martyn's essay in the present volume, chap. 10, "World without End or Twice-Invaded World?"
6. Dale B. Martin, *The Corinthian Body* (New Haven, Conn.: Yale University Press, 1995); Martin, "Paul Without Passion: On Paul's Rejection of Desire in Sex and Marriage," in *Constructing Early Christian Families: Family As Social Reality and Metaphor*, ed. Halvor Moxnes (London and New York: Routledge & Kegan Paul, 1997), 201–15.
7. Calvin J. Roetzel, *Paul: The Man and the Myth* (Minneapolis: Fortress Press, 1999), 135–51.
8. Compare, for instance, Rom. 6:13 where believers' bodies are either "weapons of injustice in the service of sin" or "weapons of righteousness in the service of God."
9. Marianne Meye Thompson, *The Promise of the Father: Jesus and God in the New Testament* (Louisville, Ky.: Westminster John Knox Press, 2000).
10. Beverly Roberts Gaventa, "The Maternity of Paul: An Exegetical Study of Galatians 4:19," in *The Conversation Continues: Studies in Paul and John in Honor of J. Louis Martyn*, ed. Robert T. Fortna and Beverly R. Gaventa (Nashville: Abingdon Press, 1990), 189–201; and "Our Mother St. Paul: Toward the Recovery of a Neglected Theme," *Princeton Seminary Bulletin* 17 (1996): 29–44.
11. Although the phrase ἐν βάρει εἶναι is frequently rendered "to make demands," my translation seeks to highlight the contrast between the exercise of self-important authority and Paul's relinquishment of apostolic power for the church's sake.
12. The textual problem is a thorny one. Some manuscripts say the apostles are ἤπιοι ("gentle," $X^{c}$ *A* $C^{2}$ $D^{2}$ Ψ *M* $vg^{st}$ *(sy)* $sa^{mss}$) and others say they are νήπιοι ("babies," $P^{65}$ $X^{*}$ *B C* $D^{*}$ *P* et al.). Abraham J. Malherbe argues that the image of the nurse is one frequently used by popular philosophers to describe their own gentleness in addressing people with the claims of virtue ("Gentle as a Nurse," in *Paul and the Popular Philosophers* [Minneapolis: Fortress Press, 1989], 35–48). Beverly R. Gaventa, however, makes the more compelling case for νήπιοι as not only the more difficult but also the more exegetically plausible reading ("Apostles as Babes and Nurses in 1 Thessalonians 2:7," in *Faith and*

*History: Essays in Honor of Paul W. Meyer*, ed. John T. Carroll, Charles H. Cosgrove, and E. Elizabeth Johnson [Atlanta: Scholars Press, 1991], 193–207; and Gaventa's *First and Second Thessalonians* [Louisville, Ky.: Westminster John Knox Press, 1998], 26–28).

13. See Warren Carter, *Matthew and the Margins: A Sociopolitical and Religious Reading* (Maryknoll, N.Y.: Orbis, 2000), 120–23.
14. E. Elizabeth Johnson, "'Who Is My Mother?' Family Values in the Gospel of Mark," in *Blessed One: Protestant Perspectives on Mary*, ed. Beverly R. Gaventa and Cynthia L. Rigby (Louisville, Ky.: Westminster John Knox Press, 2002), 32–46.
15. John of Patmos similarly calls the 144,000 redeemed "those who have not defiled themselves with women, for they are virgins" (Rev. 14:4).
16. See, for example, Abraham J. Malherbe, "God's New Family in Thessalonica," in *The Social World of the First Christians: Essays in Honor of Wayne A. Meeks*, ed. L. Michael White and O. Larry Yarbrough (Minneapolis: Fortress Press, 1995), 116–25; and Joel Marcus, *Mark 1–8*, AB27 (New York: Doubleday, 2000), 280.
17. See John 21:4–8, a very similar story of fruitless human labor answered by divine abundance.
18. Luke says the men are "cleaning" their nets (5:2) rather than "mending" them as in Mark 1:19 (cf. Matt. 4:21). This may suggest that Luke considers the firm of Zebedee and Sons a bit more prosperous than does Mark.
19. Cornelius, Lydia, the Philippian jailer, Priscilla and Acquila, and so on.
20. Marianne Palmer Bonz, *The Past as Legacy: Luke-Acts and Ancient Epic* (Minneapolis: Fortress Press, 2000).
21. David L. Balch, *Let Wives Be Submissive: The Domestic Code in 1 Peter*, SBLMS 26 (Chico, Calif.: Scholars Press, 1981).
22. Steven Richard Bechtler, *Following in His Steps: Suffering, Community, and Christology in 1 Peter*, SBLDS 162 (Atlanta: Scholars Press, 1998).
23. Jouette M. Bassler "ΣΚΕΥΟΣ: A Modest Proposal for Illuminating Paul's Use of Metaphor in 1 Thessalonians 4," in White and Yarbrough, eds., *The Social World of the First Christians*, 53–66.
24. "If any of you suffers as a Christian, do not count it a disgrace, but glorify God because you bear this name" (1 Pet. 4:16).
25. David L. Balch, "Household Codes," in *Greco-Roman Literature and the New Testament*, ed. David E. Aune, SBLSBS 21 (Atlanta: Scholars Press, 1988), 25–50; Carolyn Osiek and David L. Balch, *Families in the New Testament World: Households and House Churches* (Louisville, Ky.: Westminster John Knox Press, 1997).
26. E. Elizabeth Johnson, "Ephesians," in *The Women's Bible Commentary*, exp. ed., ed. Carol A. Newsom and Sharon H. Ringe (Louisville, Ky.: Westminster John Knox Press, 1998), 428–32.
27. Theodore J. Wardlaw, former Pastor of Central Presbyterian Church in Atlanta, Georgia, now President of Austin Presbyterian Theological Seminary.
28. Some assessments of clergy sexual misconduct focus on the similarities of its dynamics to those of incest. See, for example, Peter Rutter, *Sex in the Forbidden Zone: When Men in Power—Therapists, Doctors, Clergy, Teachers, and Others—Betray Women's Trust* (New York: Fawcett Crest, 1989).
29. The church in the eighteenth- and nineteenth-century southern United States often spoke of a "middle way" between the barbaric abuse of slaves and their emancipation. The result was intended as a humane, even Christian, perpetu-

ation of "the peculiar institution." See Erskine Clarke, *Wrestlin' Jacob: A Portrait of Religion in Antebellum Georgia and the Carolina Low Country* (Tuscaloosa Ala.: University of Alabama Press, 2000).

30. Phyllis Trible, *Texts of Terror: Literary-Feminist Readings of Biblical Narratives* (Philadelphia: Fortress Press, 1984).
31. See J. Christiaan Beker, "The Authority of Scripture: Normative or Incidental?" *Theology Today* 49 (1992): 376–82.

# 9

# "Turning the World Upside Down": A Reflection on the Acts of the Apostles

*Beverly Roberts Gaventa*

One bright fall morning, a student waited to speak with me after class. The course was Introduction to New Testament Exegesis, and we had just finished a discussion of 1 Thess. 4:1–12. She glanced around before saying anything, as if she needed to make certain that no one would overhear some guilty secret. Then she said, "You know, Dr. Gaventa, I'm really enjoying this class. I had no idea that people studied passages in the Bible with this kind of care—it's just so much fun!"

These words would be music to any teacher's ears, to be sure, but I detected in them symptoms of something far more important than affirmation of a particular course or pedagogical strategy. I suspected that my student had been seized by passion for the text. And it is passion for the text that produces Bible studies that engage people's hearts and minds, sermons that faithfully represent the gospel, and exegetical commentaries that freshly engage both the text and its interpretive traditions. In other words, I recognized in my student's confession the experience of being gripped by the text that so deeply characterizes the work of the two colleagues whom we honor in this volume. For that reason, it seems to me appropriate to pay tribute to these colleagues through the close examination of a single text.

The close examination of a single text is not, to be sure, a singular act. As much work in contemporary hermeneutics reminds us, what we see in a passage depends on the angle of vision, the eye of the beholder, and the communities that shape the beholder. This particular examination of a biblical text proceeds in three stages, stages that successively enlarge the angle of vision and, in so doing, enlarge our grasp of Luke's story. First, we read Acts 17:1–9 as a story of individuals in conflict, then as a story that puts Rome in its place, and finally as a story about God's cosmic intervention on behalf of humankind.

## 1. FIRST READING: ACTS 17:1–9 AS CONFLICT STORY

The text I have selected is the frequently overlooked story of the witness of Paul and Silas in Thessalonica. Standing as it does between the dramatic account of the release of Paul and Silas from the Philippian jail (16:16–40) and Paul's sermon on the Areopagus (17:16–33), this tiny vignette often escapes the attention of even careful readers. It is not that readers pass over this story because it is peculiar or unusual, as may be the case with the odd incident of Eutychus's somnolent response to Paul's preaching in 20:7–12 or the strange sojourn of Paul and his traveling companions on the island of Malta (28:1–10). In this case, readers may pass over the story because its lines are so familiar that they scarcely make an impression. Already, much the same plot has been enacted in the cities of Pisidian Antioch (13:13–52), Iconium (14:1–7),[1] Lystra (14:8–20), and Philippi (16:11–40), and its motifs will replay in Beroea (17:10–15), Corinth (18:1–17), and especially Ephesus (19:1–41). In some fundamental ways, all these incidents begin to look alike.[2] Paul and his companions arrive in a city, Paul preaches, some believe, others do not, the resisters raise a ruckus, and Paul leaves town—often in considerable haste. He makes his way to the next city, where the cycle begins all over again. At first glance, then, the story of the witness in Thessalonica is just another of what we might call Luke's Pauline conflict episodes. As my student was learning, however, the delight is in the details; we must linger with the details if we are to understand the place of this particular story.

Having arrived in Thessalonica with Silas, Paul goes to the synagogue.[3] In case we have not yet noticed that this is Paul's practice (as in, e.g., 13:5, 14; 14:1), Luke himself draws attention to it by characterizing it as Paul's custom. For a period of three Sabbaths, Paul builds his case on the basis of Scripture.

The recounting of Paul's synagogue argument is quite brief, since Luke assumes that we have read (or heard) the story beginning from 1:1,[4] and we know how to fill out the contours by now (as supplied in the speeches of 2:14–36; 3:12–26; 10:34–43; and 13:16–41). Here Luke presents instead the *Reader's Digest Condensed Version* of Christian proclamation. Two points suffice, and those have already been established as major points on Luke's theological compass. First, Scripture teaches that the Messiah must suffer and be raised from the dead. According to Luke's Gospel, the earliest witnesses to Jesus learned this fundamental point from Jesus himself on the road to Emmaus, when Jesus taught the two believers how Scripture witnessed to the Messiah and the necessity of his death (Luke 24:25–27; see also 24:46–47; Acts 3:18). In other words, this knowledge derives from Jesus' instruction of his disciples. It is not the result of the believers' own learning or their diligent exegesis of

Scripture. Indeed, in Luke's Gospel, the disciples never do grasp this point, although it is repeatedly made by Jesus (note Luke 9:22, 43b–45; 13:32–33; 17:25; 18:31–34). Lest it be lost again, Luke repeats it in the resurrection accounts, where Jesus first instructs Cleopas and his companion about the necessity of the Messiah's suffering (Luke 24:26–27) and then repeats it for the whole gathering of disciples (24:44).

The second point in this brief account of Paul's argument is that Jesus is the Messiah. Omitted from the explanation is the middle piece of the syllogism, that Jesus of Nazareth had in fact suffered and been raised from the dead. Again Luke seems to assume that his audience can by now fill in this piece of the story. Instead of recounting Jesus' story, even briefly (as Peter did in 10:39–41), Luke moves directly to this all-important point—Jesus is the Messiah.[5]

As is nearly always the case in Acts, proclamation of the gospel generates a divided response. Such division arises early in the Jerusalem witness, when Peter's proclamation of the resurrection produces both five thousand new believers (4:4) and hostile interrogation by the religious leadership (4:5–22). It continues into the last lines of Acts, when some Jews in Rome are persuaded by Paul and others are not (28:24). In Thessalonica, Luke first explains that "some of them were persuaded and joined Paul and Silas." That bland translation of the NRSV completely omits the fact that *both* verbs are passive: they were persuaded and they *were joined to*, or better, *assigned to*, Paul and Silas. The implied agent here is God, as is the case in many other places in Luke-Acts. Luke makes this point explicitly in the previous episode in Philippi, when he reports that "the Lord opened" Lydia's heart so that she would hear the preaching of Paul (16:14).[6]

Who are the people who are "joined with" Paul and Silas? Luke provides no names and few details with which to depict them. Not for Luke is the strategy of closely deciphering the demographic group so as to be able to tailor the next round of marketing to the most receptive audience. He says "some" responded—an unspecified group that presumably includes Jewish residents of Thessalonica.[7] Then he adds that those who joined also included "a great many of the devout Greeks and not a few of the leading women" (17:4). The "devout Greeks," of course, are Gentiles, people we refer to as "godfearers."[8] These are the synagogue hangers-on, not full proselytes to Judaism, not part of the inner circle.

Specifically, this group of believers includes also "not a few of the leading women." Because biblical interpretation historically has minimized—if not ignored altogether—references to women, it is important to notice that "not a few" is a figure of speech (*litotes*) that actually draws attention to the number. The same figure of speech appears when Paul later declares to Festus that the events of the gospel were "not done in a corner" (26:26). That events were "not done in a corner" means that they took place everywhere and in public.[9] When Luke refers to "not a few of the leading women," then, he draws attention to their number. From as early as the gathering of believers prior to Pentecost, Luke's second volume includes references to women among the believers (1:14). That this interest of Luke's made some later readers uncomfortable becomes clear when we see that one manuscript of Acts inserts a small change so that these women become *the wives* of the leading citizens rather than the leading women themselves.[10]

Why does Luke specify their rank? Some scholars argue that the reference to their social standing has to do with Luke's own preference for the well-placed,[11] but later the text offers another hint about that status indicator, one to which we will return below.

What is absent from this story is any sense that the synagogue leaders themselves are listening with attention and sympathy. To put the matter colloquially, the seminary graduates, the presbytery's movers and shakers are not persuaded. Only the lay people—marginal and female at that—are persuaded by Paul's exegesis.

"But the Jews became jealous," Luke says in verse 5. In his recent commentary on Acts in the *New Interpreter's Bible*, Robert Wall argues that the conflict here is exegetical, that these Jewish resisters deem Paul's exegesis unpersuasive, but I find no basis for that claim in this text.[12] To be sure, Luke does give reports of that sort elsewhere, as when Stephen debates with other Jews in Jerusalem, and Luke openly comments that they "could not resist the wisdom and the Spirit with which he spoke" (6:10). What Luke says at this point in chapter 17, however, is not that there was an exegetical debate but that some Jews were jealous. Jealousy as a provocation to resistance to the witnesses emerges early on in Acts, when the temple authorities undertake to arrest the apostles, who are themselves held in high esteem by the populace. Luke describes the temple authorities as "being filled with jealousy" (5:17). Stephen's speech, which often presents its critique of Stephen's contemporaries in the guise of a report about past events, attributes the treachery of Joseph's brothers to their jealousy of him (7:9). Earlier, in Pisidian Antioch, the enthusiastic response of residents to the preaching of Paul brings about the jealousy of some local Jews (13:45). So here it seems that the resisters are jealous, not of the eloquence of Paul's exegetical presentations, but of the appeal of the gospel. And it is here that the status of the women becomes important. Not only has Paul attracted attention for his teaching, but he has attracted the more visible and admired people in town. Again to put it in the vernacular, Paul's preaching has attracted the very people who might pay for the new education building and endow the music program. That in itself might explain the jealousy that follows.

Jealousy, in this case, erupts into action (v. 5). Here English translations have great difficulty doing justice to the Greek text, in which the group of resisters becomes the agent of every action in the remainder of this small story. It is the jealous resisters, according to Luke, who *grabbed* some evil men and made a mob (obscured by the NRSV's pallid "with the help of some ruffians"). It is this larger group, composed of the resisters and their helpers, who disrupted the city and attacked Jason's house while looking for Paul and Silas. It is still they who drag Jason and others before the officials, and who cry out accusations. And it is they who stir up the crowd and the officials. Only with verse 10 does anyone else again become the subject of action.[13]

Within this steady crescendo in the actions of the resisters, two things require attention. One is the description of the people they include in their rabble rousing. What the NRSV politely refers to as "ruffians in the marketplaces" is more literally translated as "market hangers-on." In our own jargon, they might be referred to as "thugs" or even "mall rats." In case there is any chance that the point is not obvious, Luke adds that they are "bad" people. These are not respectable citizens (by contrast with those who have been listening receptively to Paul) but those who have nothing better to do than stir up trouble. A delicious irony emerges here, as the group that now charges believers with "turning the world upside down" comprises some individuals who might easily have been charged with disturbing the peace on a regular basis.

Second, and most important for the development of Luke's story, the charges themselves are without grounding in the story. As elsewhere, it is the resisters of the gospel who stir up the difficulty, who upset the peace. In the story just prior to this one, for example, the owners of the slave girl charge Paul and Silas with disturbing the city, but it is they who stir up an unruly crowd (16:16–40). Similarly at Ephesus, Demetrius scares his fellow workers with the charge that Paul will disrupt the city, but it is the riot Demetrius stimulates that actually brings danger from the Roman authorities (19:23–41). As elsewhere, the charges reveal more about those who resist the gospel than about its witnesses.

## II. SECOND READING: THE CONTEXT OF EMPIRE

That first examination of Acts 17:1–9 approaches Luke's second volume much as the church has often read it, as a historical narrative of the difficulties and triumphs encountered by the apostles and other church leaders. Especially in a North American context, this interpretation results in understanding Acts as the story of a particular kind of voluntary organization, the church. The book of Acts becomes, in that perspective, a long series of stories of conflict between good guys and bad guys.[14] We are reading Acts as if we were watching a rerun of *Gunsmoke* playing on a twelve-inch television screen. We need a larger screen on which to see this drama.

That first reading of the story ignores a crucial element in this story, both in its literary and its historical contexts. In a word, what is missing is Rome. The first hint of this element comes when the witnesses are accused of "turning the world upside down." The NRSV's "world" translates the Greek word *oikoumenē*, a term familiar to us from its English derivatives "ecumenics" and "ecumenism." In the context of Acts 17, however, *oikoumenē* may not be as benign as its pleasant contemporary offspring. Instead of referring to the unity of Christians around the world, it refers to the entire inhabited world, *as that world is controlled and designated by the empire*. And what the accusers say is that the witnesses constitute a threat to the entire world of Roman power and influence.

Perhaps that assertion will seem to place too much stress on a single word, but the additional charge points in the same direction: "They are all acting contrary to the decrees of the emperor, saying that there is another king named Jesus" (v. 7). Whatever the meaning of "contrary to the decrees of the emperor," and that is a disputed question,[15] this sentence amplifies the earlier charge. There is no escaping the implication: the earlier statement about turning the world upside down is not a complaint about the success of these preachers in attracting folks to the mid-week Bible study and potluck supper. Taken together, the charges place the witnesses before the power of Rome and accuse them of acting against Rome.

This point touches on the long-standing debate about Luke's stance toward Rome: Is Luke an apologist for Christianity, or he is actually an apologist for Rome?[16] While it has often been argued that Luke defends the innocence of Christianity to Rome, the opposite case has also been argued, namely, that Luke wants to reassure fellow believers that they have nothing to fear from the empire. Neither position is persuasive. Luke sounds nothing like Josephus, who is all too obvious in his attempt to curry favor with Rome.[17] Neither does Luke sound like *4 Ezra*, who calls down God's own vengeance on Rome (see especially the vision of the eagle in 11:1–12:39); nor does Luke resemble the Apocalypse with its graphic depiction of the destruction of Babylon. To be sure, at times Luke depicts Roman officials who short-circuit violent attacks against Paul, as when Gallio dismisses complaints about Paul (18:12–17). Later on, Lysias interrupts the beating of Paul (21:31–36; 22:22–29) and sends him to Caesarea to forestall a plot to kill Paul (23:16–30). In addition, the final chapters of Acts depict individual representatives of Rome acting in ways that are positive, or, at least, benign. Festus and Agrippa acknowledge Paul's innocence (26:31–32). Luke goes out of his way to present the centurion Julius treating Paul well during the long and eventful voyage to Rome. Yet these details hardly constitute a stance toward the empire, and I am inclined to think that the mixed picture Luke presents derives from the fact that Luke assesses all people—Roman or otherwise—in light of their stance toward the gospel. In other words, Luke's posture toward empire may be less a matter of defending or attacking the empire than of putting it in its place.

To return to the text in Acts 17, according to the first reading the charges against Paul and others are false, because it is not Paul who upsets the peace. Instead, those who resist his proclamation are the ones who upset the public order. In the larger context of the Roman Empire and its self-interpretation, however, what Paul does may be far more subversive than Luke openly admits.

To understand that possibility, we must think again about the "whole world" as governed by Rome. The pleasant sound that the word "ecumenical" makes in the ears of contemporary Christians may not be utterly removed from its connotations in the first century, at least in the world of Roman propaganda. The *oikoumenē* is the entire civilized world at peace and ruled by Rome. No less a figure than Augustus Caesar declared his devotion to peace. Shortly before his death in the year 14 CE, Augustus wrote an account of his activities. In it he mentions, with understandable pride, that the Roman senate established an altar to *Pax Augusta* (the peace of Augustus), and he reports that the gate of Janus Quirinus was shut three times during his rule, an action taken only when there is "victorious peace" throughout the empire. Of course, as Augustus continues his chronicle, it becomes clear that the *Pax Augusta* means the subjection of other peoples and lands to the will of Rome. A few lines from Augustus will suffice as an example:

> I extended the frontiers of all the provinces of the Roman people, which had as neighbours races not obedient to our empire. I restored peace to all the provinces of Gaul and Spain and to Germany, to all that region washed by the Ocean from Gades to the mouth of the Elbe. Peace too I caused to be established in the Alps from the region nearest to the Hadriatic as far as the Tuscan sea, while no tribe was wantonly attacked by war.[18]

This blatant presentation of wars of aggression as attempts to establish peace has an eerily contemporary ring to it. It is also clear that not everyone experienced the activity of the empire as peaceful. The first-century Roman historian Tacitus imagines the speech of the British tribal leader Calgacus prior to decisive battle against Rome. Warning of Rome's tyranny, Calgacus rails against the Roman invaders as

> robbers of the world, now that earth fails their all-devastating hands, they probe even the sea: if their enemy have wealth, they have greed; if he be poor, they are ambitious; East nor West has glutted them,

> alone of mankind they covet with the same passion want as much as wealth. To plunder, butcher, steal, these things they misname empire: they make a desolation and call it peace.[19]

Yet the favored voices praised Rome. Early in the second century, Aelius Aristides characterizes Rome as a paradise and wonders which is greater: Is it the greatness of the city Rome relative to all other cities that exist, or is it the empire Rome relative to all other empires that have ever existed? Aristides continues:

> [F]or the eternal duration of this empire the whole civilized world prays all together. . . . You who hold so vast an empire and rule it with such a firm hand and with so much unlimited power have very decidedly won a great success, which is completely your own. For of all who have ever gained empire you alone rule over men who are free. Let all the gods and the children of the gods be invoked to grant that this empire and this city flourish forever and never cease until stones float upon the sea and trees cease to put forth shoots in spring.[20]

In Aelius Aristides, as in Augustus, we hear about the *oikoumenē* entirely from the point of view of Rome. In this worldview, those who are civilized are those who live by Roman rule. The world is at peace, with abundant opportunity for commerce and safety in travel, but it is a peace imposed by Rome. Those who do not submit to Roman rule will not know peace. Here we see an empire confident of its own goodness. Nevertheless, it is a peace in constant need of protection, as becomes clear in Acts 17.

In the context of an empire that talks of peace but makes destruction, Luke's two-volume narrative makes some powerful counterclaims. In the story of the conversion of Peter and Cornelius in Acts 10, when Peter preached the gospel, however unwillingly, before the household of the *Roman centurion* Cornelius, Peter declared that God preaches peace through Jesus Christ and that "he is Lord of all." Most contemporary Christian readers today probably skip past those remarks, understanding them as so much theological chatter. Yet in the context of the Roman Empire, they are nothing less than an assault on the notion that the Caesar is the ruler of all things. Just a few lines after the story of conflict in Thessalonica, Paul declares before the cultured Athenians that the *oikoumenē* is going to face judgment—not, in this instance, judgment by other powers or judgment of public opinion, but the judgment of Jesus Christ (Acts 17:31).[21] That these particular statements are not incidental to the Lukan story may be seen when we return to its very beginning. The story in Luke 2 begins by invoking the *oikoumenē* ("all the world") that Caesar wishes to control by counting it (the census); it also begins prominently with an angelic declaration that the birth of Jesus means peace for humankind—God's peace, not the *Pax Augusta* (2:14).

From this enlarged perspective on our passage, then, perhaps Paul and Silas *are* guilty of the charges made against them. They do indeed serve another king. They *are* overturning the *oikoumenē*.

## III. THIRD READING: THE CONTEXT OF THE COSMOS

That way of putting things is powerfully important, especially in a North American context where the national propaganda sounds eerily like the words of Augustus or Aelius Aristides. Yet to read this passage only in the context of empire is not sufficient, and a third reading is required. The story of Paul and Silas in Thessalonica has a cosmic context that we have not yet addressed. If it is insufficient to read this as a story of conflict between individuals, it is also not enough to read it as a subtle attack on the empire. The world is being turned upside down, but it is not Paul and Silas who are doing so.

In Luke's large story, it is God who turns the world upside down—and that is signaled as early as Mary's Magnificat:

> He has shown strength with his arm;
> he has scattered the proud in the thoughts of their hearts.
> He has brought down the powerful from their thrones,
> and lifted up the lowly;
> he has filled the hungry with good things,
> and sent the rich away empty.
> (Luke 2:51–53)

Luke is the one evangelist who situates Jesus' advent in the context of the rule of Augustus and Quirinius (Luke 2:1–2), but it is Jesus who is declared to be the "Son of the Most High."

Stories of the overturning or reversal of the status quo dot the landscape of Luke's Gospel from the birth narratives forward. John the Baptist warns that God can turn even stones into children of Abraham (Luke 3:8). Jesus overturns the identity of the "bent over" woman, naming her as daughter of Abraham (Luke 13:16). He likewise gives a new name to the rich and despised Zacchaeus, the name "child of Abraham" (19:9). God overturns not only human opposition, but Satan's own plan and even death itself in the resurrection of Jesus. Overturning continues in Luke's second volume. God overturns human resistance by opening prison doors, by preserving life during storm and shipwreck, and—perhaps most dramatically—by persuading Peter and the Jerusalem church that Gentiles too have a place among God's people.

The world is being turned upside down in this story, but it is not Paul and Silas who do the turning. Luke gives us human characters who teach and preach and heal, but Luke is not confused about the source of their power. In this tiny vignette in Acts 17, we see Paul offering exegetical insight that derives from the risen Jesus, and we see that believers are added to Paul and Silas by God's own intervention.

Nor is Luke confused about God's enemies. He has a full roster of those who openly oppose God's plan, including Satan himself first of all. The roster includes Jewish opponents, Roman resisters, and even those within the church who are not altogether happy with God's way of doing things. If Luke does not portray a Roman persecution, he does portray an empire that is full of self-confidence and self-protection, an empire that somehow knows it must constantly monitor its own safety.

The shaking of heaven and earth takes place in this story, but it does so entirely because God is the actor—not Rome, not the apostles, not their opponents.

If God is the one who turns the world upside down, then what does the story suggest for us? We might begin by examining our own convictions about who is in charge of things. In his State of the Union address (2003), President Bush spoke of the "power, wonder-working power"—a phrase that many of us know quite well from the hymn "Power in the Blood," one associated with the death of Jesus Christ. But in President Bush's speech, that "wonder-working power" is located in the "goodness and faith of the American people." Here he inverts Luke's understanding. For Luke, as it is in the hymn, the power is in God's salvific action for humankind through Jesus Christ. That is the shaking of heaven and earth—not the goodness and faith of any human group.

Instead of imagining that the "wonder-working power" lies in our hands, we might take our cues from the beginning and ending of Luke's long story. At the beginning, we listen as Mary sings about God's overturning of things as they are. And at the ending, we watch as the captive Paul persists in Rome, teaching and preaching with boldness, unhindered. Not even the shadow of the empire prevents Paul from persisting in his witness to the gospel of Jesus Christ and of the power that does indeed shake both heaven and earth.

## NOTES

1. At 14:1, the narrator helpfully indicates that the story is about to repeat itself: "The same thing occurred in Iconium. . . ."
2. Despite these shared dynamics, the distinctive details of these stories have endlessly fascinated readers. The fickle inhabitants of Lystra who first greet Paul and Barnabas as gods and then join in with the crowds who stone them are not to be confused with the true believers in Ephesus, who rightly perceive the gospel as a threat to their devotion to Artemis.

3. The evidence for a synagogue structure in Thessalonica is slender and late (see Colin J. Hemer, *The Book of Acts in the Setting of Hellenistic History*, WUNT49 [Tübingen: Mohr Siebeck, 1989], 115), but that question matters little for understanding the passage. On the much-disputed question of the ancient synagogue, see especially the major work of Lee Levine, *The Ancient Synagogue: The First Thousand Years* (New Haven, Conn.: Yale University Press, 2000).
4. In addition, 1:1 takes Luke's audience back to the Gospel itself.
5. As he does so, he shifts unexpectedly from third-person summary of Paul's instruction to first-person proclamation, emphasizing the most important point, the identity of Jesus as God's Messiah.
6. That God is the central actor in Acts is a major theme in Gaventa, *Acts of the Apostles*, ANTC (Nashville: Abingdon Press, 2003), esp. 28–31.
7. This report stands in some tension with 1 Thessalonians, where Paul appears to assume that his addressees are Gentiles (see 1:9 in particular).
8. Whether "God-fearer" is a fixed term employed for Gentiles who were attracted to the synagogue without becoming proselytes is a hotly disputed point, but not one that carries weight in the interpretation of this text. On the debate, see A. T. Kraabel, "The Disappearance of the 'God-fearers,'" *Numen* 28 (1981): 113–26; Jerome Murphy-O'Connor, "Lots of God-Fearers? *Theosebeis* in the Aphrodisias Inscription," *RB* 99 (1992): 418–24; and especially Irina Levinskaya, *The Book of Acts in Its Diaspora Setting*, Book of Acts in its First-Century Setting 5 (Grand Rapids: Wm. B. Eerdmans Publishing Co., 1996), 51–126.
9. For other examples of *litotes* in Acts, see "no small commotion" (12:18), "no small dissension and debate" (15:2), "no little disturbance" (19:23), and "no little business" (19:24). Colloquially, we would find the equivalent figure of speech in a claim that "Jane's new Porsche is 'not too shabby.'"
10. The variant appears in D (Codex Bezae). Although Luke-Acts makes frequent reference to the presence of women among Jesus' followers and within the early Christian communities, women are seldom seen in leadership roles. This has given rise to extensive debate; see the important studies by Turid Karlsen Seim, *The Double Message: Patterns of Gender in Luke-Acts* (Nashville: Abingdon Press, 1994); and Ivoni Richter-Reimer, *Women in the Acts of the Apostles: A Feminist Liberation Perspective* (Minneapolis: Fortress Press, 1995). See also my comments in *Acts of the Apostles*, 43–44.
11. Ernst Haenchen, *The Acts of the Apostles*, 14th ed. (Philadelphia: Westminster Press, 1971), 507; Luke Timothy Johnson, *The Acts of the Apostles*, Sacra Pagina (Collegeville, Minn.: Liturgical Press, 1992), 310.
12. Robert W. Wall, "Acts," in *The New Interpreter's Bible*, vol. 10, ed. Leander E. Keck et al. (Nashville: Abingdon Press, 2002), 238.
13. There is ambiguity even here, as there is no clear indication grammatically that the officials are the subject of the verbs in v. 10. Given the actions described, however, the officials necessarily are the agents.
14. This way of reading Acts and other biblical texts may contribute to the longstanding problem of anti-Judaism in Christian interpretation of biblical texts. If our reading is fixated on an anthropocentric focus, a focus that sees only human beings in conflict one another, then almost certainly Christian readers will identify nonbelievers as opponents or enemies.
15. Johnson, *The Acts of the Apostles*, 307; Fitzmyer, *Acts of the Apostles*, 596; C. K. Barrett, *The Acts of the Apostles*, vol. 2, ICC (Edinburgh: T. & T. Clark, 1998), 816.

16. For a concise review of the debate regarding Luke-Acts, see Philip F. Esler, *Community and Gospel in Luke-Acts: The Social and Political Motivations of Lucan Theology* (Cambridge: Cambridge University Press, 1987), 201–19. On the larger question of early Christianity and its relationship to Rome, see Klaus Wengst, *Pax Romana and the Peace of Jesus Christ* (Philadelphia: Fortress Press, 1987); Richard A. Horsley, ed. *Paul and Empire: Religion and Power in Roman Imperial Society* (Philadelphia: Trinity Press International, 1997); and Richard J. Cassidy, *Christians and Roman Rule in the New Testament: New Perspectives* (New York: Crossroad, 2001).
17. Steve Mason rightly cautions against interpreting Josephus as nothing more than a propagandist for Roman power, but at the very least it is clear that Josephus wants his history of the war to minimize anti-Jewish reactions in Rome; see *Josephus and the New Testament* (Peabody, Mass.: Hendrickson, 1992), 58–64.
18. *Res Gestae Divi Augusti*; the translation is found in C. K. Barrett, *The New Testament Background: Selected Documents*, rev. and exp. ed. (San Francisco: Harper and Row, 1989), 2–3.
19. *The Life of Julius Agricola* 30, in *Tacitus*, vol. 1, trans. M. Hutton and rev. R. M. Ogilvie, LCL (Cambridge, Mass.: Harvard University Press, 1980), 81. On the speech and its context, see also D. J. Mosley, "Calgacus: Clash of Roman and Native," in *Images of Empire*, ed. Loveday Alexander, JSOTSS 122 (Sheffield: Sheffield Academic Press, 1991), 107–21.
20. "Roman Oration," pars. 29, 34, 36, and 109. For the Greek text and translation, see James H. Oliver, *The Ruling Power: A Study of the Roman Empire in the Second Century after Christ through the Roman Oration of Aelius Aristides* (Philadelphia: American Philosophical Society, 1953), 895–907, 982–91. For an overview of the notion of the *Pax Romana* and its ideology, see Wengst, *Pax Romana and the Peace of Christ*, 7–54.
21. The name of Jesus is not specified in 17:31, but there can be no doubt that the "man whom he [God] has appointed" is Jesus.

# 10

# World without End or Twice-Invaded World?

*J. Louis Martyn*

We begin with a brief drama. It is Sunday morning. The family station wagon has just come into the church parking lot when Diana, seven years old, turns to her mother, Elizabeth, and says, "Mom, before we go in, I need to run over the song we will sing in the youth choir."

**Elizabeth**: Which song is it?

**Diana**: Oh, you know it. It's the Gloria.

**Elizabeth**: Alright.

*Diana sings with the enthusiasm of a seven-year-old:*

Glory be to the Father,
and to the Son, and to the Holy Ghost.
As it was in the beginning,
is now and ever shall be,
Gone with the wind. Amen! Amen!

Sure that the whole of the youth choir will be singing the traditional words, and wishing to encourage Diana, Elizabeth says, "Basically, you've got it." We, however, must pause, for we have here what biblical scholars call a text-critical problem, a text with variant readings. Is it "world without end" or "gone with the wind"?

To be sure, those who are free of grandparental bias may feel that this problem can be easily solved by surmising that Diana was in the TV den the previous evening, as her parents made a journey to the fair city of Atlanta in the company of Scarlett O'Hara and Rhett Butler.

Still, in a collection of essays focused in part on what is called "The Changing Global Order," Diana's "gone with the wind" may have more immediate pertinence than "world without end." We may seriously ask ourselves, that is, why, as though the church's task were simply to resist global change, we say,

> As it was in the beginning,
> is now and ever shall be,
> world without end.

Or, more specifically, we may ask ourselves what we mean when we sing those words, and—even more important—whether they are theologically well grounded, whether they point to the real cosmos in which we actually live.

How would things fare if we were to carry the Gloria Patri to a close friend of Charlie Cousar, the apostle Paul, asking for his theological critique? Would a Pauline assessment of the Gloria tell us something important not only about the world but also about God's relationship to the world, and consequently about the relationship of the church to the world? What would Paul say about the Gloria, especially about that last line, "world without end"?

## I. ETERNAL WORLD?

In Paul's day—indeed centuries before Paul—the eternity of the world was in fact regularly affirmed by Greek philosophers, often by identifying the world with God. Heraclitus, for example, said that the cosmos was always there, having neither beginning nor end. It was literally world without end.

In its simple and unqualified sense that is an idea we do not find in Paul's letters. The Apostle knows the world to have had a *beginning*: God created it (Rom. 1:20). And as God's creation it has an *end* that is different from both its beginning and its present existence: it has a liberated future tied to the glorious future of those who are in Christ (Rom. 8:18–25; 1 Cor. 8:6). Paul does not think of the world's having a continuous, unchanging, cosmic eternity. Indeed, that thought is fundamentally qualified by Paul's references to what he calls "*this* world." He counsels his Corinthian church, for example, to deal with the world as though not dealing with it, "for the form of *this* world—the world in its distinctive manifestation—is even now passing away" (1 Cor. 7:31).[1] That is enough to give us pause about the last line of the Gloria. It is also enough to suggest that Paul's understanding of the world is deeply indebted to his heritage from Jewish apocalyptic theology.

## II. APOCALYPTIC THEOLOGY

What do we mean by "apocalyptic theology"? It is said that apocalyptic theology addresses the question "What time is it?" And that is correct, for the question of time reflects the indelible connection between apocalyptic thinking and the future-oriented matters of divine promise and human hope. The church has never lived in a state of good health apart from secure confidence in God's triumph at the ultimate end.[2] Just now, however, we turn our attention elsewhere; for there is another apocalyptic question fully as important as the query "What time is it?" Equally crucial and equally apocalyptic is the question "What world is it?" In what world do we human beings actually live?[3]

In an effort to understand Paul's apocalyptic view of the world, it would be profitable to cite numerous passages in the publications of Charlie Cousar, notably ones in his classic volume *A Theology of the Cross*. We are also recently instructed by Beth Johnson's trenchant article on the subject of apocalyptic in *Vantage*.[4]

Let me begin with a single point. Paul's apocalyptic language is metaphorical. When the apostle says, for example, that at Christ's future coming we will be "caught up in the clouds" (1 Thess. 4:17), he is functioning neither as a weather forecaster nor as a literal cosmologist. He means exactly what he says, and promise itself is no metaphor. Paul conveys God's promise, however, in apocalyptic, metaphorical images. To take his language in a literal and wooden fashion is to avoid the real message.[5]

We might even say that Paul's apocalyptic language is full of imagination. But in saying that, we would mean that this is an imagination having its origin in God. Apocalyptic language serves to reflect God's way of imaging the whole show.[6] Bearing in mind, then, the strength of Paul's apocalyptic images precisely as divine metaphors—as *God's* poetry—we ask, How does Paul use these poetic images to refer to the real state of affairs in the real world? If Paul does not say, "world without end," what does he say?

## III. THE PERMEABLE HUMAN WORLD

Immediately striking is the fact already noted that, while Paul often refers to "the world," he also speaks several times of "*this* world" (e.g., 1 Cor. 3:19; cf. Rom. 12:2). It is an expression pointing to something that definitely exists. *This* world is indeed here. At the same time, to speak of *this* world is to suggest that there is another world, or something like another world, a matter to which we will return. For the moment we simply note that Paul distinguishes *this* world from *the* world.

For Paul, *the* world of heaven and earth was created by God in such a way as to make the earth part of it permeable. That is to say, far from being a hermetically sealed sphere, earth was subject to entry from heaven. In itself the view that the earthy human world is permeable would have surprised neither the theologians of ancient Israel nor Homer (it is assumed, of course, by our children and grandchildren who readily speak of the advent of extraterrestrial figures). The Yahwist, for example, could easily refer to messengers sent into the earth part of the world by God (see also note 8 below). When, however, Paul bears his witness by speaking of the human world's being the scene of entry, he draws on Jewish apocalyptic traditions, and he limits his references in the main to three incursions. One of these stands opposite to the gospel, while the other two are clear indications of its center.

## IV. THREE COSMIC INCURSIONS

In Paul's figurative cosmological language the first instance of incursion is Sin's entry into the human world that was itself good, having been created by God. And it is here that Paul speaks of *this* world. That is to say, *this* world has its origin at the point at which Sin enters *the* world. We would not be totally wrong to say—with the poetic language of tragedy—that Sin is virtually the *creator* of *this* world; for in Paul's language it is the cosmic incursion of Sin that has caused *the* world to become *this* world.[7] In what later became traditional formulations, *this* world is the "fallen" world, but as we will see, there is much more to Paul's view of *this* world than a mere "fall." And it is important for us not to press Paul's theology into the framework of later thinkers. Paul never speaks of the world as fallen. Considering the God-created world to be both good and permeable, he speaks of its being *entered* by Sin (Rom. 5:12).

The second cosmic incursion is chronologically later, being God's redemptive entry into *this* world in the person of Christ, the Son of God who, being sent out by God, and being "born of a woman, born under the power of the Law" (Gal. 4:4), "emptied himself, taking the form of a slave" in *this* world (Phil. 2:7).[8]

And the third incursion is Christ's future coming, an event explicitly identified by Paul with the word *apocalypse*, and referred to as the exalted Christ's coming into the world from heaven (1 Thess. 4:16; 1 Cor. 1:7; Phil. 3:20). From beginning to end the center of Paul's fundamentally apocalyptic theology accents the verb *to come*. His apocalyptic language is, then, a matter of speech about God "that is based on and determined by '*the coming of God*' . . . [speech that] means both *adventus* and *futurum*, God's making himself present today and in the future."[9]

As I indicated earlier, in the present essay our focus lies on the first and second of these cosmic incursions.

## A. The Incursion of Sin: This World

Startling even to church folk is the fact that Paul speaks of the entry into the world of Sin *as a power*, a power *foreign* to God's good creation (Rom. 5:12). We here encounter the crucial distinction between what we will call "sins in the plural" and "Sin in the singular." Used in the plural and written with a lower case *s*, sins are discrete, partially volitional, rebellious missteps of human beings. These discrete, individually committed sins constitute, according to Emily Dickinson "a distinguished Precipice *Others* must resist."[10]

Although Paul seems to have lacked Dickinson's enviable sense of humor, he could agree. He does indeed recognize sins in the plural, and they have a certain importance, pointing both to a degree of human accountability and to the accompanying matter of God's role as absolute judge (1 Cor. 11:32; 2 Cor. 5:10; Rom. 3:19). These plural sins do not provide, however, the major clue to the real state of affairs; and because Paul is a realist, plural sins are not his chief concern. For the genesis of what he calls "*this* world" lies in the arrival of the suprahuman *power* called Sin, referred to by him in the singular, and best translated into English with a capital *S*.[11]

The power Paul calls Sin is not, then, a private and individual affair, whether discrete or indiscrete. Neither is it simply and entirely volitional. Sin is precisely a powerful, cosmic enemy of God, and an enemy of every human being. That it is an enemy of us all is clear from the fact that as a power Sin brings in its wake an event that is indeed universal, namely Death (Rom. 5:13; 6:16, 23).[12]

Given Sin's Adamic, cosmic breaking and entering, Paul is compelled to speak in dark tones when he refers to times prior to Christ. Speaking of divinely ordained points—rather than of a simple and continuous line that can be traced by human beings—he can indeed refer positively to the Abrahamic promise, to the establishing of the Law, to the witness of the prophets, and fundamentally in that same way to the indelible election of Israel as God's people. Referring to the period before the coming of Christ, Paul affirms, that is, the story of God's elective *points* (Rom. 9:4–13), while denying a *linearity* available to the claims and prognoses of human beings.[13] *This* world is the Adamic world that precedes Abraham and follows him, that precedes Moses and follows him, that precedes the prophets and follows them. Even after Abraham's faith, Moses' Law, and the prophets' witness, "all, both Jews and Greeks, are enslaved under the power of Sin" (Rom. 3:9).

## The Tragic Three-Actor Drama of This World

Attending to Paul's references to Sin, we begin to sense his view of the human story as the cosmic tragedy that involves three actors. That is to say, because *this* world is the result of a breaking and entering by the power called Sin, it is the cosmic tragedy in which there are actors—malignant actors—in addition to God and human beings, the major one of these additional actors being Sin itself.

### *Sin as Actor*

We note, then, that in portraying the real state of affairs Paul allows Sin to be the subject of verbs. God acts; human beings act; Sin acts! Sin does things. It establishes a reign, for example, making a slave of every human being, so that the problem is far greater than guilt for discrete sins (Rom. 5:21). And, as we have noted, in establishing its reign, Sin brings Death in its wake. We are perhaps astonished to find Paul saying that, as an active power, Sin deceives and slays human beings, even using the Law to that end (Rom. 7:9–11)![14] Sin as actor is the major key, then, to the presence of deceit and evil and lethal violence in *this* world, causing *this* world to be itself a tragic drama to which Paul refers as "the present evil age" (Gal. 1:4).

Having its own foolish wisdom (1 Cor. 1:20–21), even its own god (2 Cor. 4:4), and linked as it is with the power of Sin, *this* world is indeed a drama with a calamitous character that is catastrophic for human beings. To analyze this cosmic drama as though we did not live in a fundamentally flawed world is to walk about in the dark, with all of the dangers attendant to doing that. Consider, for example, our liturgical tendency to reduce the power of Sin to discrete, volitionally committed sins, and thence to a scenario that runs from specific sins to personal guilt to volitional repentance, and to the forgiveness that is conditional on the individual's repentance for those sins. This reducing of Sin to sins—and the remainder of that scenario as well—is utterly foreign to Paul, for it involves pretending that by repenting for sins one can climb out of the world that has been tragically entered by Sin.

We can see indeed that for Paul the real world—*this* world—is the scene of genuine tragedy because it is anthropologically and theologically "out of control." *The* world was created by God. *This* world, however, "the present evil age," is not under the immediate and exclusive hegemony either of God or of human beings. And for that reason, caught under the reign of Sin and Death, *this* world is the frightening, horrifying scene of genuine and profound disaster. The psalmist, you will recall, could say with confidence,

> The earth is the LORD's and the fullness thereof,
> the world and those who dwell therein.
>
> (Ps. 24:1)

That form of cosmic, theological monism—the assurance that other than God there are no real, extrahuman powers on the earth—finds no proper echo in Paul's letters.[15] To be sure, God created the world (Rom. 1:20). The incursion of Sin, however, has caused the cosmos to slip—at least partially—from God's omnipotent and gracious grasp, for, as we have noted, Sin can use even God's Law to its own lethally deceptive ends.[16]

Luther spoke in the mode of Pauline apocalyptic when he penned "A Mighty Fortress," with its reference to powers other than God, and other than human beings. He spoke, that is, with realism about the global order that actually exists when he referred to

> . . . our ancient foe,
> Who seeks to work us woe,
> Whose craft and power are great,
> And, armed with cruel hate,
> On earth is not his equal.

Notably at funerals we can say with confidence that

> neither death, nor life,
> nor angels, nor rulers, . . .
> nor anything else in all creation,
> will be able to separate us from the love of God
> in Christ Jesus our Lord.
> (Rom. 8:38–39)

But, as things presently stand in what Paul realistically called "*this* world," those powers do exist, and they threaten us with destruction, by being stronger and more deceptively clever than we are; and by being in a significant sense unavoidable. Unavoidable because—as Leander Keck puts it in a forthcoming commentary on Romans—we cannot emigrate from the orb of these powers by deciding to leave it.

Centrally Paul does not speak, then, of a new line of human movement, as though, by repenting for our discrete sins and asking for forgiveness, we human beings could escape from *this* world, at least in effect, deciding to transfer from a life of sins to a life of righteousness (1 Cor. 5:10).[17]

## B. The Invasion of God

Paul refers rather to a quite different line of movement. He speaks of the second instance of cosmic *in*cursion, for the line in which redemption dawns does not trace human movement *away from* this world but rather God's movement *into* it (Gal. 4:4).[18] We live in the twice-invaded world. For permeable as it was and is to the breaking and entering of the malevolent power of Sin, the world was climactically and determinatively invaded not by Sin, but rather by God. Here we can draw on the title of the present volume, speaking of "the shaking of heaven and earth." Given the advent of Christ, that is, Paul can say with what we might call cosmic emphasis that the world will never be what it was previously (Gal. 6:14–15; 2 Cor. 5:17). Here begins the cosmic movement that is "on the way" to the parousia and the total victory of the One God.[19] Being the inauguration of the whole gospel story of God's redemptive movement, Christ's advent is itself fundamentally decisive, for after that event the world is not what it was before.

To be sure, speaking of what the world was prior to Christ's advent, we are again reminded of the fact that God has been here before, being both the world's creator and the One God who issued the covenantal promise to Abraham, instituted the Mosaic Law, and spoke to his people Israel via the prophets. Indeed God continues to speak through the prophets even now at the juncture of the ages (1 Cor. 10:11; Gal. 4:21; Rom. 9:27, 29; 10:20).[20] The relationship between God's earlier acts and his advent in Christ presents Paul with several major issues that, while not subject to analysis in the present essay, serve to identify Paul's God with the God of Israel.[21] Here we simply stay with God's apocalyptic invasion in Christ, the decisive enactment of God's firstness, of God's taking the initiative, of God's refusal to wait for human beings to repent.

For in Christ, God has invaded this Sin-enslaved world *unconditionally* in order to bring it under his gracious and liberating control. And here the term "invasion" is altogether necessary, reflecting, as it does, the dynamism of Paul's apocalyptic. Paul can speak of the unveiling of God's secret wisdom, decreed before the ages (1 Cor. 2:6–10). The center of the apostle's apocalyptic thinking does not lie, however, in God's making visible some *thing* previously enclosed behind a curtain, now revealed by pulling the curtain aside. Rather, the *One* who has been on the other side rips the curtain apart, steps through to our side, altering irrevocably our time and space. What specifically ensues from this cosmic invasion of God?

To begin with, Paul is sure that the true discernment of Sin's power is itself a result of God's invasion of the world in Christ. We do not and cannot truly take the measure of Sin apart from that redemptive event. As we have seen, there is here much more, for example, than the scenario of sins, guilt, repentance, and forgiveness. There is enslavement and liberation, deliverance from the *power* of Sin and its allies. And noting Paul's repeated references to liberation from Sin, we see two major characteristics of the twice-invaded world: first, apocalyptic warfare; second, the new creation.

## C. Apocalyptic Warfare

Given the bloody history of the literal sword in the literal hands of literal Christians, we have very strong reasons for wanting to declare an absolute divorce between the term "war" and the Prince of Peace, Jesus Christ. Even if we were to think only of our own time, leaving behind the bloody "Christian Crusades" and other religious wars of the Middle Ages, we would be slow indeed to employ in a positive, redemptive sense the expression "apocalyptic warfare." Highly religious Protestants and equally religious Catholics in Northern Ireland remain daily in a volatile war zone, as do faithful Palestinians and observant Israelis. Beyond the horrors of the European holocaust in the 1940s, the spring of 1994 in Rwanda can serve by itself as a searing reminder of the connections between religion and violence: a Christian bishop remarked that many of his "most faithful" church members—along with others—took up the machetes with which approximately eight thousand persons were slaughtered every day for one hundred days.[22]

Here, however, we are patiently interviewing Paul on the subject of the twice-invaded world, and part of his witness is the insistence that to deal with this real world is to talk about war. Indeed, it is not surprising that, as Paul displays a perspective focused on divine invasion, he draws several images of war from ancient apocalyptic traditions and from the popular philosophers of his day.[23] Two examples will suffice: Sin found in the Mosaic commandment "a base of military operations" for killing human beings (reflecting the full translation of the Greek term *aphormē* in Rom. 7:11). Moreover, since God's invasion of the world, the Spirit of Christ and the Impulsive Desire of the Flesh are a pair of opposites "at war with one another" (Gal. 5:17).[24] That is to say, in the act of invading the territory of the malevolent powers, God has turned the world into hotly contested territory. Those enslaving powers do not peacefully yield their turf to God, as every parish minister knows well.

About this struggle three points are clear. First it is emphatically not a religious war, not an instance of sacred violence.[25] To be sure, Paul himself participated in some form of sacred violence when he attempted to exterminate the church (Gal. 1:13, 23; Phil. 3:6; 1 Cor. 15:9). All of that came to a decisive end in Christ. For the God whose invasion has commenced this war is the God whose advent in Christ spells the end of religious differentiations that make religious wars possible, as the baptismal formula of Gal. 3:28 announces.

Second, God's war is wholly unlike *all* wars that mere human beings carry out against mere human beings. Without exception—including struggles waged for "noble ideals"—wars inaugurated by us place one group of humans against another group of humans. And in the Pauline frame of reference that means that *all* instances of human bellicosity lie under the deceptive power of

Sin. Indeed, they set the power of Sin loose to bring Death in its wake: "We had to obliterate the village in order to liberate it." Focused on the cruciform invasion in Christ, however, God's war-like advent is fought not with the power of the sword but rather with the power of grace.[26] Having studied at the apostle's feet, so to speak, the author of Ephesians spoke for Paul when he said, "Our struggle is not against enemies of blood and flesh, but against . . . the cosmic powers of this present darkness, against the spiritual forces of evil in the heavenly places" (Eph. 6:12; cf. 2 Cor. 10:3–6).

Third, this struggle is far from being a draw. Paul is certain that "the rulers of this age"—including Sin—are themselves utterly doomed. Indeed they doomed themselves precisely in their act of crucifying the Lord of Glory (1 Cor. 2:6–8). Here we recall another Pauline line in Luther's "A Mighty Fortress":

> The prince of darkness grim,
> We tremble not for him;
> His rage we can endure,
> For lo! his doom is sure,
> One little word will fell him.

The malevolent rulers of this world are doomed, for, in spite of frequent appearances to the contrary, the victory in God's war of liberation belongs solely to God. With God's militant invasion, the human race is set on a course that, however torturous and tragic, is indelibly oriented back to the first commandment: "You shall have no other Gods before me" (Deut. 5:7). And the victory being enacted by the God of the first commandment means quite specifically the ultimate deliverance of the captives from the deceptive and lethal influence of all other gods and lords (1 Cor. 8:5–6).[27]

That assurance brings us, finally, to the climactic result of God's gracious and powerful invasion of the world: the new creation.

## V. THE NEW CREATION

I mentioned earlier that when Paul speaks of *this* world, he implies that there must be another world, or something like another world. Now, rereading Paul's letters while contemplating the twice-invaded world, we detect the identity of that contrasting other. To speak of it, Paul borrows from Isaiah and from apocalyptic traditions the expression "the new creation," a locution accenting the motif of radical, uncompromising newness (Isa. 65:17–25; *Jub.* 4:26; Gal. 6:15; 2 Cor. 5:17). The expression "new creation" does not refer to the result of merely repairing *this* world. In fundamental contrast to *this* world, God's new creation is *the* new. We close, then, by attending to three questions:

When is God's new creation? Where is God's new creation? What is God's new creation?

*When*? Presumably Paul will tell us that the new creation lies in the future. If it is genuinely, radically new, then it will surely be God's gift at the ultimate end. Not so! With the advent of Christ, God's new creation is dawning even now. Just as the world in its distinctive manifestation is already passing away, just as its malevolent rulers have already sealed their own doom by crucifying the Lord Christ, so God's new creation is already dawning.

*Where*, then, is it? Where is it dawning? Borrowing a note from the most Pauline of the Gospels, Mark, we can say with homiletic license that God's new creation is not dawning in the garden of Eden, but rather in the garden of Gethsemane, and in a place called Golgotha, with a tomb nearby.[28] In the ensuing resurrection there is victory, but it is not individualistic; it is not obvious; and it is certainly not idyllic. God's new creation does not dawn during a romantic walk in the garden while the dew is still on the roses. It dawns in the cross itself, and it continues to dawn in our participation in the cross, in the rough and tumble of daily life. And that takes us back to God's liberating war.

Just as God's new creation is the genuinely new, so the war in which it is dawning is utterly new, being inaugurated neither in the glorious power of Caesar and his legions nor in the unbelievable staying power of a Christ who can take everything the Roman soldiers can deal out, and, as it were, ask for more. The crucified Son of God is not a hero. On the cross that was reserved in his time for hideous criminals he dies a fully humiliating death, cursed by the Law itself (Gal. 3:13). The war of God's liberation opens, then, when Christ is "crucified in weakness" (2 Cor. 13:4), and it continues to take its character from the humiliating defeat he suffered for us.

There is, to be sure, a fundamental reversal on Easter morning. But Christ's resurrection does not leave the cross behind, making the crucifixion a mere way station on the journey to glory. "The theology of the resurrection is a chapter in the theology of the cross, not the excelling of it."[29] Seen through resurrection lenses, the cross itself remains the event of God's weak power, the event in which power is, in fact, transfigured and thus fundamentally redefined (2 Cor. 10–13; Rom. 12:1–2).[30]

Here we begin to see the decisive difference between the cross as *religious symbol* and the cross as *apocalyptic sign*. At numerous points in the last two millennia persons calling themselves Christians have held up the cross—literally or figuratively—as a symbol of their power over other peoples, often over Jews. Such manipulative use of the cross is as despicable and vile as it is un-Pauline. For the apostle the cross is no symbol. It is the continuing sign of Christ's powerful weakness and of the Christian's participation in that powerful weakness for the sake of others, indeed for the sake of *all others now*. When Paul describes his own cross-centered ministry, he speaks of the enactment of God's strangely weak power:

> I think that God has exhibited us apostles as last of all, as though sentenced to death, because we have become a spectacle to the world, to angels and to mortals. . . . We are afflicted in every way . . . always carrying in the body the death of Jesus, so that the life of Jesus may also be made visible in our bodies. (1 Cor. 4:9; 2 Cor. 4:8–10)

As God's thoughts are not our thoughts, as God's ways are not our ways (Isa. 55:8), so God has inaugurated our deliverance in the figure of one who is weak and despised, rejected by others.

Paul cannot speak of God's new creation, then, without at the same time speaking of the horrifying and unglorious event of the *new-creating crucifixion*. Nor can he speak of the new creation itself without referring both to his own participation in Christ's crucifixion and to the capacity of that horrifying event to kill old patterns of enslaving dominance by transfiguring *this* world's power into the victory of God's powerful weakness. In short, he speaks simultaneously of the *crucifixion of this world* and of the dawning of the new creation:

> As for me God forbid that I should boast in anything except the cross of our Lord Jesus Christ, by which the world has been crucified to me and I to the world. For neither is circumcision anything nor is uncircumcision anything. What is something is the new creation. (Gal. 6:14–15)

We ask finally, then, *what* this new creation is. How does Paul speak of the specific, bodily identity of the new creation? Born in the resurrection that consistently refers to and interprets the crucifixion, born precisely in the midst of God's weak power enacted daily in God's strange war of liberation, God's new creation is nothing other than the new community, the cross-bearing church in the here and now. In and under the cross the new creation is the community of those who—while free of sadistic masochism—are conformed to the crucified one for the sake of others. That is to say, in the word of the cross God is calling the nonexistent into existence, the new creation that is the new liberated and liberating society in the midst of the old.

In sum, then, we can see the true church and its vocation only when we truly see the church in relationship with the world as God sees and deals with the world, as God makes it the twice-invaded world. For the church is the community that invasively engages the world as the invasive God engages the world.[31]

What, then, are we to say of the world when we speak from the pulpit, and when in unison we lift our voices in song? Fundamentally, when we look the real world full in the face, we are led to speak not of its unchanging eternity, but rather of its having already been twice invaded. And we are led to speak of those invasions as events that are dramatically asymmetrical. Both are real, but they are not of equal power. Referring to the much more powerful invasion of God in Christ, we are led, then, to proclaim the Lord's death until he comes, thus finding ways in our everyday lives for actively confessing that in the paradoxical cross of Christ the world is now being reclaimed by God from its bondage to Sin and Death.

And who is this God? As the authors of the Gloria intended to say, this is the God who as Father, Son, and Holy Spirit is eternal. God is the one who is emphatically "without end." But this eternal God is not concerned to preserve to eternity what was in the beginning, *world* without end! Given the incursion of Sin and the mortal threat posed to the whole of the human race by the power of Sin, this is the invading God, the God of action, the God of action now, the God whose invasion of the world has unleashed the strange war of liberation that brings in the new creation by taking its bearings from the cross as apocalyptic sign. And this is the God who, equipping *us* with the power of the graceful Spirit, calls us to vigorous and passionate action, by placing us—under the sign of the cross—precisely in the front trenches of the war in which God is graciously and victoriously reclaiming the world.

It is in this cross-led war that we find the church's vocation as God's landing troops, thrust confidently onto the beaches of the occupied territory that is *this* world. This is the war that is fought for the whole of humanity. This is the war that is fought with the Spirit's weapons of love, joy, peace, patience, kindness, generosity, and faith itself (Gal. 5:22; Eph. 6:13–17). And this is the war that finds its daily climax, and its ultimate end, in God's life-giving victory, the formation of God's new creation in which each is the servant of the other (Gal. 5:13).

## NOTES

1. Biblical quotations and paraphrases are the author's translations, sometimes identical with NRSV, sometimes modifications of it.
2. See John T. Carroll with Alexandra R. Brown, Claudia J. Setzer, and Jeffrey S. Siker, *The Return of Jesus in Early Christianity* (Peabody, Mass.: Hendrickson, 2000); Richard Bauckham, "The Future of Jesus Christ," *The Cambridge Companion to Jesus*, ed. M. Bockmuehl (Cambridge: Cambridge University Press, 2001), 265–81.
3. See Adela Y. Collins, *Cosmology and Eschatology in Jewish and Christian Apocalypticism* (Leiden: E. J. Brill, 1996); Edward Adams, *Constructing the World: A Study in Paul's Cosmological Language* (Edinburgh: T. & T. Clark, 2000).
4. "Teaching 'Apocalyptic' Today," *Vantage* 94, no. 3 (2003): 4.
5. See Charles B. Cousar, *A Theology of the Cross: The Death of Jesus in the Pauline Letters*, OBT (Minneapolis: Fortress Press, 1990), 84–87; Paul S. Minear, *The Bible and the Historian: Breaking the Silence About God in Biblical Studies*

(Nashville: Abingdon Press, 2002), especially the first chapter, "The Musician Versus the Grammarian: An Early Storm Warning." I hardly need to add that the apocalyptic theology with which we are concerned in the present study is wholly unrelated to the so-called apocalypticism perniciously purveyed in the *Left Behind* series. See J. Byassee, "En-raptured," *The Christian Century* (April 20, 2004): 18–22.

6. See W. Lowe, "Prospects for a Postmodern Christian Thought: Apocalyptic without Reserve," *Modern Theology* 15 (1999): 17–24. See also Garrett Green, *Theology, Hermeneutics, and Imagination* (New York: Cambridge University Press, 2000).
7. To say that Sin is virtually the creator, the cause, of *this* world is to be reminded of Marcion's Demiurge, the wrathful creator god (see John J. Clabeaux, "Marcion" in *Anchor Bible Dictionary* [New York: Doubleday, 1992], 4:514–16). Radically unlike Marcion, however, Paul paints a picture that is distinctly apocalyptic. For Paul's picture involves a provisional apocalyptic dualism in which the words "cosmos" and "age" are to an extent interchangeable. He can speak of "*this* world" as "the present evil age," using both expressions to point to an entity distinguished from *the* world as God graciously created it (see J. Louis Martyn, *Galatians* [New York: Doubleday, 1997], 98). Paul's apocalyptic dualism is thus basically different from Marcion's ontological dualism. For Paul, Sin came in after God, *the Father of Jesus Christ*, created the good world.
8. Regarding God's "sending" of Christ there is important comparative material in, for example, the LXX pattern of the sending of Moses. Cf. also the Stoic references to the philosopher's being sent by Zeus, and see E. Schweizer, "What Do We Really Mean When We Say, 'God Sent His Son'?" in *Faith and History: Essays in Honor of Paul W. Meyer*, ed. John T. Carroll, Charles H. Cosgrove and E. Elizabeth Johnson (Atlanta: Scholars Press, 1990; reprinted Wipf and Stock, 2003), 298–312. Cf. J. Louis Martyn, *Galatians*, 406–8.
9. G. Sauter, "Begriff und Aufgabe der Eschatologie," *NZST* 30 (1988): 199, first italics added.
10. Emily Dickinson, "The Bible is an Antique Volume," *The Complete Poems of Emily Dickinson* (Boston: Little and Brown, 1960), no. 1545 (italics added).
11. As George Lindbeck puts it, part of the church's task is to learn and relearn its own language, relating it, to be sure, to modern parlance, but without equating the two (*The Nature of Doctrine* [Philadelphia: Westminster Press 1984]). In that process we may indeed compare Paul's theological analysis of Sin with our own references to current forms of systemic evil that, engulfing all human beings, cannot be traced to a specific individual. We can then find places in our church liturgy for explicit references to Sin (as distinct from sins), even following Paul by using Sin as the subject of verbs. See section below titled "Sin as Actor."
12. See Martinus C. de Boer, *The Defeat of Death* (Sheffield: JSOT Press, 1988); idem, "Paul, Theologian of God's Apocalypse," *Interpretation* 56 (2002): 21–33.
13. On Paul's theology and the kind of linearity one finds in a simple narrative, see Bruce W. Longenecker (ed.), *Narrative Dynamics in Paul* (Louisville, Ky.: Westminster John Knox Press, 2002), especially the chapter by John M. G. Barclay, "Paul's Story: Theology as Testimony" (133–56).
14. In Paul W. Meyer's *The Word in This World* (Louisville, Ky.: Westminster John Knox Press, 2004) see the fifth chapter, "The Worm at the Core of the Apple: Exegetical Reflections on Romans 7"; also J. Louis Martyn, "*Nomos* Plus Gen-

itive Noun in Paul: The History of God's Law," in *Early Christianity and Classical Culture: Comparative Studies in Honor of Abraham J. Malherbe*, ed. J. T. Fitzgerald, T. H. Olbricht, and L. M. White (Leiden: E. J. Brill, 2003), 575–87. On Paul's view of the Law in the context of the whole of his theology see now the sterling contribution of S. Westerholm, *Perspectives Old and New on Paul* (Grand Rapids: Wm. B. Eerdmans Publishing Co., 2004).

15. Paul's quotation of Ps. 24:1 in 1 Cor. 10:26 does not qualify the portrait he draws of *this* world under the power of Sin.
16. See note 14 above.
17. *Pace* E. P. Sanders, *Paul, the Law, and the Jewish People* (Philadelphia: Fortress Press, 1983), 7. Like the popular philosophers of his time Paul could occasionally make positive use of the language of conversion, reminding members of his Thessalonian church, for example, that, seized by the power of the gospel, they *turned* to God from idols (1 Thess. 1:9; contrast Gal. 4:9). Without exception, however, Paul understood such a conversion to be an act elicited by the prior and powerful word of the gospel (Rom. 10:17), something quite other than an autonomous human decision to convert.
18. See Meyer, *The Word in This World*, 5–18: "The This-Worldliness of the New Testament."
19. Cf. W. Schrage, *Unterwegs zur Einheit und Einzigheit Gottes* (Neukirchen: Neukirchener, 2002).
20. On Paul's view of Isaiah as proclaimer of the gospel see the extraordinarily perceptive work of Ross Wagner, *Heralds of the Good News: Isaiah and Paul in Concert* (Leiden: E. J. Brill, 2002). See also Francis Watson, *Paul and the Hermeneutics of Faith* (London: T. & T. Clark, 2004).
21. These issues emerge sharply when we compare with one another Gal. 3–4 (especially 3:16, 20–21; 4:21), 1 Cor. 10, 2 Cor. 3, and Rom. 9–11. On these four texts see (a) J. Louis Martyn, *Galatians*; (b) W. Schrage, *Der Erste Brief an die Korinther*, EKK 7:2 (Solothum: Benziger, 1995); Richard B. Hays, *First Corinthians*, Interpretation (Louisville, Ky.: Westminster John Knox Press, 1997); (c) Victor P. Furnish, *II Corinthians*, AB 32A (Garden City: Doubleday, 1984); Margaret E. Thrall, *Second Epistle to the Corinthians*, ICC (Edinburgh: T. & T. Clark, 1994–2000); A. Lindemann, "Die biblische Hermeneutic des Paulus. Beobachtungen zu 2 Kor 3," in *Paulus, Apostel und Lehrer der Kirche* (Tübingen: Mohr/Siebeck, 1999), 37–63; (d) Nikolaus Walter, "Zur Interpretation von Römer 9–11," *ZTK* 81 (1984): 172–195; Meyer, *The Word in This World*, 194–205; E. Elizabeth Johnson, *The Function of Apocalyptic and Wisdom Traditions in Romans 9–11* (Atlanta: Scholars Press, 1989); Wayne A. Meeks, "On Trusting an Unpredictable God: A Hermeneutical Meditation on Romans 9–11;" Meeks, *In Search of the Early Christians* (New Haven, Conn.: Yale University Press, 2002), 210–29; Wagner, *Heralds*; George Lindbeck, "The Church as Israel," *Jews and Christians: People of God*, ed. C. E. Braaten and R. W. Jenson (Grand Rapids: Wm. B. Eerdmans Publishing Co., 2003), 78–94.
22. In the context of the genocidal war in Rwanda a negotiator recalled sensing that in several of his conversations he was not talking to human beings but rather to evil itself. See PBS *Frontline*, April 1, 2004: "Ghosts of Rwanda."
23. See David Hellholm, ed., *Apocalypticism in the Mediterranean World and the Near East* (Tübingen: Mohr/Siebeck, 1983), especially the chapter by G. Widengren. Also M. de Boer, "Paul and Apocalyptic Eschatology," *Encyclopedia of Apocalypticism*, vol. 1, ed. J. J. Collins (New York: Continuum, 1998), 345–83.

Note the individualistic Antisthenic tradition perceptively analyzed by A. J. Malherbe, in *Paul and the Popular Philosophers* (Minneapolis: Fortress Press, 1989): "Antisthenes and Odysseus, and Paul at War" and "The Beasts at Ephesus." We also bear in mind, however, that, apart from 2 Cor. 10:3–6 and 1 Cor. 15:32, Paul typically employs military imagery to refer not to the individual but rather to the new community of the church of Jesus Christ.

24. Other passages marked by military imagery include 1 Thess. 5:8; 2 Cor. 2:14; 10:3–6; Rom. 6:12–13; 13:12; Col. 2:15; Eph. 6:10–17. See "The Galatians' Role in the Spirit's War of Liberation," in Martyn, *Galatians*, 524–36, 542–43.
25. See R. G. Hamerton-Kelly, *Sacred Violence: Paul's Hermeneutic of the Cross* (Minneapolis: Fortress Press, 1992); C. B. Cousar, "Review of Hamerton-Kelly, *Sacred Violence*," *Critical Review of Books in Religion* (1994): 196–99; M. Jurgensmeyer, *Terror in the Mind of God: The Global Rise of Religious Violence* (Berkeley: University of California Press, 2000).
26. See J. Louis Martyn, "From Paul to Flannery O'Connor with the Power of Grace," *Theological Issues in the Letters of Paul* (Edinburgh: T. & T. Clark; Nashville: Abingdon Press, 1997), 279–97; and cf. A. Bodiou, *Saint Paul: The Foundation of Universalism* (Stanford, Calif.: Stanford University Press, 2003).
27. See again Schrage, *Unterwegs* (note 19 above).
28. On Paul and Mark see Joel Marcus, *Mark 1–8*, AB 27 (New York: Doubleday, 2000), 73–75.
29. E. Käsemann, *Perspectives on Paul* (London: SCM, 1971), 59. See the explication, enrichment, and correction of Käsemann in Cousar, *Theology of the Cross.*
30. See Paul L. Lehmann, *The Transfiguration of Politics* (New York: Harper & Row, 1975).
31. Because the church's true way of engaging the world is consistently derived from God's way of engaging the world, human agency in the ecclesial new creation is itself newly and corporately fashioned by the divine agency of the Spirit of Christ. See "The Galatians' Role in the Spirit's War of Liberation" (note 24 above). See also John M. G. Barclay, *Obeying the Truth: A Study of Paul's Ethics in Galatians* (Edinburgh: T. & T. Clark, 1988); Stanley Hauerwas and William H. Willimon, *Resident Aliens: Life in the Christian Colony* (Nashville: Abingdon Press, 1989); Douglas Harink, *Paul Among the Postliberals* (Grand Rapids: Brazos, 2003).

# 11

# What If Paul Was Right?

*Leander E. Keck*

What if Paul was right?

> *What a dumb question! you may be thinking. Of course he was right. He insisted on justification by faith, didn't he? He also wrote that nice chapter on love that we read at weddings. Besides, doesn't asking whether Paul was right call into question the authority of the Bible?*

Not really. The question actually expresses the Bible's authority, for asking the question itself shows that it matters whether Paul was right. We can ask the same question about the letters of Ignatius or about any Christian writer, and we might well be instructed by what they have to say, but we are not obligated to come to terms with it because they are not part of Scripture. The canonical status of Paul's letters means that we are perpetually confronted by his thought, and must decide, again and again, whether he was right and what difference that makes.

> *Right about what? Everything?*

No, for he wrote about many things; so we have to make a judgment about what really matters and what does not.

> *What does it mean to grant that Paul was right about important things? That everyone else is wrong?*

Not at all. To say that Paul was right is to say that I find what he said to be so insightful, so penetrating, so compelling, that I am prepared to agree with him. Saying that he was right is to make a confessional statement.

> *So is that decision really a matter of preference, of feeling more comfortable with Paul than with John or Hebrews, for example?*

Not really, though of course there is such a thing as having a sense of affinity with a particular thinker. But even so, when it comes to Paul we may actually discover something else—that the more we are persuaded that he was right, the more uncomfortable we become. As Professor Cousar put it, "Paul's interpretation of Jesus' death and its impact on the Christian life may be terribly difficult to hear."[1]

*Why does Paul make us uncomfortable?*

Because Paul makes us ask whether *we ourselves* are wrong, whether we have seen deeply and clearly enough into the gospel, the character of God, and our own condition. In other words, to affirm that Paul was right is to allow ourselves to be challenged by his grasp of reality. And when that happens, we are drawn into engagement with him; that is, we find ourselves thinking theologically with him about the subject matter, and perhaps thinking against him. That's how we ourselves become serious theologians.

*Why bring all this up just now, when we are celebrating the work of Professors Brueggemann and Cousar?*

Because we honor them best by taking seriously what they took seriously enough to devote their gifts and energies to. They are not just describers of ideas in ancient texts. They are interpreters of Scripture in a community of interpreters, a community that includes the church no less than the academy, as Professor Cousar emphasized in his book on Paul's letters.[2]

So, having begun by interviewing myself, I want to pursue the question "What if Paul was right?" by reflecting on central themes in Paul's letter to the Romans, which is the earliest Christian theology of mission. And since much of today's church seems to be uncertain about its mission and confused about its message, Romans is a good place to see what difference it makes if Paul was right. My aim is neither to argue that he was right, nor to make it easier to conclude that he was. Rather, my aim is to state as sharply as I can some of Paul's basic convictions in order to identify those with which we must struggle.

## I

When Paul begins his letter to Christians in Rome, most of whom he does not yet know, he presents himself as Christ's slave, set apart for the gospel of God that God promised beforehand through the prophets in Scripture concerning his Son (Rom. 1:1–3). This self-presentation gives the three themes of my remarks: God, the Son of God, and Scripture. A few lines later, Paul says that the gospel is God's power for salvation for everyone who believes, because in it God's righteousness, God's rectitude, is revealed (1:16–17). Romans is about God. So in asking whether Paul was right about God the stakes are very high. Indeed, if Paul was right, we have the opportunity to renew the message of the church.

If we are to consider whether Paul was right, we have to think with him about the subject matter, the character of God. To think with Paul one must begin where he began. Then we must detect the logic by which he moved from his opening assertions about God and the gospel to what he goes on to say. We do not know, of course, how his mind moved from A to B, but we can infer the rationale that makes sense of the result. For theological exegesis of texts, that is what matters. Paul's theological reasoning did not begin from scratch because as an ardent Pharisee he already had a theology, and he was so convinced that he was right that he tried to stamp out new groups that insisted the Messiah is Jesus. The starting point that matters, then, is the one that convinced him that he had been wrong. We might say it was Paul's conversion, but that does not really tell us what converted him, and that is what matters for understanding his thought and thinking with him.

There is no doubt about what was the transforming starting point: the conviction that God raised the crucified Jesus from the dead. That starting point, and the conclusions Paul drew from it, accounts not only for the boldness of Paul's thought in his own time but also for the strangeness of his thought in our day. Why is that? Largely because many of us do not start where Paul started. His Christian theological thinking was set in motion by an awesome event that was compellingly real, but real only for those who believed it happened—God resurrected Jesus, the crucified.

Whoever allows *that* event to determine one's life is bound to look strange. Paul knew very well that it looked absurd. He was also convinced that without that strangeness there is no good news, because if that strangeness were eliminated, the gospel would lose its power to save us from the illusion that ordinary reality—the reality we take for granted—is the only reality. But Paul did not try to make sense of Jesus' resurrection in light of the world as we know it; instead, he tried to make sense of the world in light of God's resurrecting Jesus. We can think with Paul only if we start here.

To begin with, already as a Pharisee Paul assumed that resurrection is not resuscitation but transformation. Had he thought Jesus had been resuscitated, he would have remained a Pharisee; and he should have, because theologically even resuscitation after three days is only an amazing exception to the rules. What makes the resurrection of this particular Jew significant is another assumption: that resurrection is not an isolated event; it is always connected with something world transforming, the coming of the new age. So if resurrection happens, the new age is under way. In other words, resurrection makes sense only in the framework of Jewish apocalyptic thinking, which contrasts this age (all of history) with the age to come, a wholly new future.

The new age is not the outgrowth of the present age, but the God-given alternative to it. It is a new reality in which everything will be what it ought to be, when everything will be made right—not as the result of human achievement but by God's action. And God will make it right because God *is* right, righteous. So making everything right expresses God's righteousness, God's own rectitude. In short, *God's rectitude rectifies.* What we call justification is really rectification. And since this rectification occurs with the coming of the new age signaled by Jesus' resurrection, Paul can say in Rom. 4:25 that Jesus "was raised for our rectification." According to Paul's thinking, had Jesus not been raised or had he been merely resuscitated, everything would still be as it had been since Adam. In short, for Paul, resurrection, new age, and rectification are inseparable. Once we grasp that, we can think with Paul as he draws conclusions from Jesus' resurrection as an event.

Here is one conclusion he draws: since the reality of the new age and its rectifying effects are the result of God's action alone, in Christ God's rectitude rectifies apart from the law—that is, apart from obeying the rules, even God's rules. And since the coming of the new age rectifies whatever and whoever is not right, everybody can be rectified apart from the law, especially we Gentiles when we believe the news that God resurrected the crucified Jesus. On this side of the Easter event, it does not matter who you are, what your gender is, what group you belong to or do not belong to, what you have done or left undone, or how screwed up your life in relation to God may be; everyone can be rectified because God's rectitude rectifies apart from the law. In bringing the new age, God did not improve the old one; God brought about a whole new ball game. God did not change; God changed the situation, though that is not yet visible because only Jesus was resurrected. And that can only be believed.

So if Paul was right, what does this way of thinking tell us about God? Two things at least. First, if God's character is made evident in the event of Jesus' resurrection, one cannot think about God apart from that event. Theologically, God and Christ are distinguishable but not separable. Second, if God brings the rectifying new age apart from the law, then we must reckon with the freedom of God, the freedom of God to exercise Godhood on God's own terms. The freedom of God is the unstated theme of Romans, and of Paul's theology as a whole. And the freedom of God is the sign of the otherness of God. Only a God who is truly other can resurrect a dead Jesus and bring in the new age.

What difference does it make whether Paul was right about the freedom and otherness of God? Why is that important? Because how we understand that mysterious power we call God has consequences for everything else, for God is the ground of being and value—what is really real and what is worth living by and dying for. One place where this is evident is in Rom. 1, where Paul says, "the wrath of God is revealed . . . against all ungodliness and wickedness of those who by their wickedness suppress the truth" (Rom. 1:18). Here is the point: only the God who is other is against *all* human wickedness. When God's otherness is obscured, we soon think that God's wrath is against those we are against. Then we are convinced that when God's rectitude is activated, everyone gets exactly what is deserved—especially the "others." Then God rectifies, God justifies, the godly but not the ungodly (see Rom. 4:5). Then God is like all the gods, for they can be counted on to justify the godly. That is their business. But then the deep mystery we call God becomes our patron, and our theology turns into ideology—the rationalization of the status and power we already have or strive to acquire. Then God's ways become our ways, and God loses the freedom to make everything and everyone right on God's terms.

## II

How, then, did Paul's starting point affect his understanding of Jesus? Because of the resurrection, Paul thinks theologically about the event of Jesus as a whole. In other words, he asks, What does it mean theologically that there was a crucified Jesus at all, and that he and no one else was resurrected? After all, God did not resurrect just anyone. So what does God's resurrecting him tell us about Jesus? To come right to the point, the whole Jesus event occurred as God's way of bursting the new age into the present; it was an act of God's freedom on our behalf. We didn't deserve such an act. In other words, the Jesus event as a whole is sheer mercy and grace, an expression of God's love. That is why Paul could make the astounding claim that "God proves his love for us in that while we were still sinners Christ died for us" (Rom. 5:8). This is Paul's understanding of Jesus' significance in a nutshell. And it is decisive. In a word, Paul's understanding of God is christomorphic, and his understanding of Christ is theocentric.

Paul's assertion in Rom. 5:8 still shocks us because we are not sure that Paul was right. How could *God's* love be shown by *Christ's* death? Didn't Christ's acceptance of the cross show his love for God? Paul would not deny it. But if the accent is on Jesus' love for God, then the Jesus event tells us nothing about God that we did not know apart from Jesus. We already know that Roman power—indeed any powerful institution—often destroys those whom it regards as a threat, that the truly devout are sometimes killed because of their loyalty to God. Did Jesus have to die simply to confirm that? But if his death and resurrection (two sides of one event) disclose something definitive about God, then Christ is the self-expression of God, God's own self-giving become an event. That's why Paul calls Jesus, "the Son of God," for the Son expresses the Father.

If Paul was right in the way he thought theologically about Jesus, then we learn how to preach the Jesus reported in the Gospels—not simply as a challenging teacher who told us about God, but as a person who embodied God's love unto death itself. If Paul was right, Jesus is good news when he is preached as a gift before being preached as a requirement. Nothing is easier than preaching Jesus as a requirement, and nothing is harder than preaching Jesus as a gift. The gospel is God's power for salvation for all who believe when the hearer knows that a gift is being given. Only when the gift is received does Jesus become mandatory. Only when Jesus is a received gift are we rectified apart from the law.

## III

If Paul is right, what does that tell us about the law, indeed, about the Old Testament as a whole? Every interpreter of Romans has to come to terms with the fact that this letter refers to Scripture more often than any other. It is not difficult to show how Paul's method of citing Scripture often resembles that of other Jewish interpreters of the time. But his conclusions differ because his starting point is the resurrection of Jesus and what that implies for the new age. Scripture must now be interpreted in light of that event; it must not be set aside because of that event. So Paul does not find the meaning of the Christ event by looking at it through the lens of the law. Rather, he looks at the law through the lens of the Christ event. This event did not have to be squared with the law; now the law had to be squared with the event. No wonder the synagogue authorities gave Paul thirty-nine lashes five times (2 Cor. 11:24).

When Paul read Scripture in light of Christ, he did not read it as historical background leading up to Christ, nor as the capstone of salvation history, both of which are popular today. Had he done that, he would have implied that the new age completed the old instead of being an alternative to it. Instead, he found the meaning of the Christ event anticipated, foreshadowed, in Scripture. That's why he could describe Abraham's faith in language that fits Christian faith. Indeed, it was Abraham who believed in "the God who justifies the ungodly" (Rom. 4:5); it was Abraham who believed in the God "who gives life to the dead and calls into existence the things that do not exist" (Rom. 4:17). Abraham too was rectified by faith apart from the law. The divine grace enacted in the Christ event and in bringing in the new age by resurrection was the same grace by which God chose Jacob over Esau before the twins were born, before either one of them could deserve to be chosen (Rom. 9:10–11).

Not to be overlooked is that again and again Paul uses the language, concepts, and images of Scripture when he interprets Christ in its light. That

God's rectitude manifests itself in rectifying, in a saving activity, Paul learned from the book of Isaiah; that God requires holiness because God is holy, Paul learned from Leviticus. That God's purpose in choosing Abraham included the nations, Paul learned from Genesis. That the people of God, now including Gentiles, are called "saints," and that the Christian community is *ekklesia*, the assembled people of God, Paul also learned from Scripture. In short, because the God who resurrected Jesus is the God of Scripture, Paul could not abandon Scripture's witness to God's identity and character.

If Paul was right also about this, then we have serious theological work to do. Just now I want to mention only one segment of that work: recovering the theological significance of the fact that the Scripture of the church contains the Scripture of the synagogue—not as the Hebrew Bible (as if it were a foreign element)—but as a faithful, reliable, complex witness to the God who raised Jesus from the dead. The promised land that I glimpse from afar is not inhabited by Christian exegetes whose ingenuity enables them to find all sorts of references to Jesus hidden in Old Testament passages where no one suspects them—the way airport screeners now look for dangerous items in our luggage. That land is inhabited rather by Christian theologians, exegetes of both Testaments, who see that the entire Christian Bible is about the Holy One of Israel who is at once the God and Father of Jesus Christ and the empowering presence of the Spirit. If that is neglected or forgotten, then we Christians have created another God. For such theologians, the Old Testament is neither prologue to the New, nor the history of Israel's search for God, but the literary precipitate of the painful, redemptive encounters with the Holy One who is other, and whose otherness puts all human wickedness under wrath but also brought Jesus out of death itself. Unless we Gentile Jesus people look to that God, we will continue to adore a deity who is always and only loving. Such a deity, being neither gracious nor merciful (for grace and mercy depend on otherness), does not and cannot rectify the ungodly, for only the Holy One who is other can do such a thing. That is what Easter is all about.

So, if Paul is right about God, the Son, and Scripture, there is good news, and there is plenty to think about. But we do not go alone; we have teachers who have shown us the way—Walter Brueggemann and Charlie Cousar. They too are gifts of grace. And we are grateful.

## NOTES

1. Charles B. Cousar, *A Theology of the Cross: The Death of Jesus in the Pauline Letters*, OBT (Minneapolis: Fortress Press, 1990), xii.
2. Charles B. Cousar, *The Letters of Paul*, IBT (Nashville: Abingdon Press, 1996), 19.

12

# Between Blessing and Curse: Reading, Hearing, and Performing the Apocalypse in a World of Terror

*Stanley P. Saunders*

> Blessed is the one who reads aloud the words of the prophecy, and blessed are those who hear and who keep what is written in it; for the time is near.
>
> *(Rev. 1:3)*

On September 11, 2001, the United States suffered the deadliest terrorist attack to date on its own soil, a tragedy that has marked a turning point in American consciousness and the end of an era of relative security and stability. The rhetoric of a global war against terrorism now dominates the media and our attention. For many people, it seems that earth and heaven have indeed been shaken and that a new day, if not the last days, are upon us. Among the ominous signs of the times is the role religion is playing in both fueling and shaping current conflicts. Various forms of fundamentalism—whether Islamic, Jewish, or Christian—continue to generate and bless violence and

The material in this essay came to life as part of a workshop (co-led by Professor Carlos Cardoza-Orlandi) offered during the colloquium honoring the ministries, scholarship, and lives of Charles Cousar and Walter Brueggemann. I have learned much from Charlie and Walter about apocalyptic, the theology of the cross, theological imagination and integrity, and worship—themes that are the focus of this essay. Walter and Charlie have given faithful witness by their lives and their scholarship to the God who is shaking earth and heaven!

Some of the material in this essay has been developed more thoroughly in "Revelation and Resistance: Narrative and Worship in John's Apocalypse," in *Narrative Reading, Narrative Preaching: Reuniting New Testament Interpretation and Proclamation*, ed. Joel B. Green and Michael Pasquarello, III (Grand Rapids: Baker Academic, 2003): 117–50.

terror in the name of God.[1] Military and religious rhetoric now seem too often to blend seamlessly in our daily discourse. Without doubt, these are times that require careful discernment on the part of all people of faith, and times when Christians rightly are turning again to the Scriptures for hope and for answers.

In a world where terror is all around, we should not be surprised to see a renewal of interest particularly in John's Apocalypse, which has now emerged as a focal document in the New Testament for Christians of all varieties. While Revelation has long been the cause of embarrassment and the object of scorn among many "mainstream" Christians, it also continues to engender hope of liberation among the poor, as well as triumphalist visions of Armageddon and divine judgment among adherents of popular Christianity in America. According to *Newsweek*, the *Left Behind* series of apocalyptic Christian novels, which are based primarily on Revelation, is now outselling Stephen King, John Grisham, and every other American pop novelist.[2] Some even say that Revelation is playing a key role in shaping evangelical politics in North America, with ripples felt around the world, not least in the Middle East.

Revelation is not only the center of the canon for a variety of dispensationalist readers, for whom it provides a road map of the last, dark days before the end, but also the one New Testament document read by a generation of young people—many of them not "religious" by conventional standards—for whom "terrifying, mesmerizing violence" is the last meaningful gesture at their disposal to fight back against the emptiness of contemporary North American culture.[3] They, like many of their elders, see in the pages of Revelation not only "a guidebook on how the world will end," but "a manual on how to end the world," in other words, "an invitation to participate in the fury and terror of God."[4]

What then are we to make of this book, which has given rise to such disparate readings and reactions over the centuries? My primary claim is simple: mainstream Christians can no longer afford to ignore John's Revelation, to treat it as an embarrassment or a curiosity, or to cede its interpretation to literalists or code breakers. Revelation belongs again in our Bible studies, our church schools, and especially our worship services, where it can shape a people who see clearly the truth about the world around them and who, by their faithful worship of the Lamb, give witness to the power of the One who has overwhelmed death itself. As it calls its audience to leave behind the false gods of wealth, power, violence, and empire, Revelation offers a remarkable example of the creative use of language, image, myth, and ritual to mold a people of endurance and faithful resistance. In order to function in these ways, however, and in order not to be used in the service either of terror or of triumphalism, Revelation must be heard and experienced on its own terms, that is,

1. as the story of Jesus Christ, the Lamb who was slain, and his triumph over the powers of violence and terror;
2. as an oral performance meant for use in the eucharistic assemblies of the church; and
3. as a model of the creative use of myth and ritual to construct a people for whom worship is the primary embodiment of resistance to domination and violence.

## I. THE STORY OF JESUS CHRIST

From the very beginning of the Apocalypse, John the Seer makes clear that this is the story of Jesus Christ. In antiquity, the first words of a document often functioned as its title,[5] providing audiences with the most important information they needed in order to make sense of the work. While our Bibles typically now carry the title "The Revelation to John," the first words of this performance, in fact, are "the revelation of Jesus Christ." We should hear this phrase as a reference to Jesus Christ, both as the content of the revelation (the one revealed) and as the author of the revelation (the one doing the revealing). The author goes on to say that the revelation (or "unveiling," "uncovering," "disclosure") was given to Jesus Christ by God to show to his servants (1:1). John himself is the servant through whom this takes place. In short, the Apocalypse identifies itself not primarily as "John's Revelation" nor "a revelation of the end times" (although it does speak of "what is about to take place"), but as the unveiling of Jesus Christ. It is *Jesus'* story, told in a new way and with new images,[6] not primarily the story of the world's judgment and destruction, and neither the story of the rapture (an image not found in Revelation, in fact) nor an affirmation of the triumph of individual Christians.

As in the letters of Paul, the story of Jesus recounted by the Seer focuses in particular on his death and resurrection. Like the authors of the Gospels, the Seer uses the juxtaposition of sometimes disparate images and metaphors to challenge the audience's expectations and to open their imagination to a startling new vision of reality. The Seer, like Paul and the evangelists, would have understood well the realities of Roman power, especially the use of the cross as an instrument of human terror and a crucial tool in the pacification of peoples dominated by the empire.[7] And like the writings of Paul and the evangelists, Revelation tells the story of Jesus Christ in ways that parody and burlesque these very human notions and expressions of power that masquerade as reality. Thus, while the beast is powerful, it is no match for the Lamb who was slain. While the whore is seductive, Revelation exposes the violence and emptiness of her seductions. And while "Babylon" is a powerful force and impressive edifice, its end is certain. Revelation's images of the slain Lamb and the blood of the martyrs depict a divine power that overwhelms all the devices of domination offered by the world's powers. And the resurrection of the Lamb and the martyrs strips away even the powers of violence, terror, and death. As Lee Griffith notes,

> Bloodshed is the means by which mighty empires and terrorists of all stripes seek to claim their victories, but Revelation unveils that it is precisely their own shedding of blood that is the means by which the powers are defeated. The shed blood of the Lamb and of the martyrs becomes the instrument of God's victory. Terrorists great and small believe that every drop of blood that is shed brings them closer to victory. The exact opposite is true. Every drop of blood that is shed confirms their ultimate defeat, confirms that their fate is already sealed.[8]

The Seer's story of Jesus Christ, crucified and raised, thus depicts the ultimate counterterrorism campaign, unleashed by God against those who put their faith in the power of violence and death.

The Apocalypse begins the story of Jesus Christ with his appearance at the throne of God, where he is identified as "the Lion of the tribe of Judah, the Root of David" (5:5) yet also described as a slaughtered Lamb with seven horns and seven eyes, symbols of perfect power and wisdom. This image provides the defining paradoxes that run throughout the Apocalypse, juxtaposing weakness and vulnerability with divine power, the slain (crucified) Lamb with the conquest of death itself, and messianic hopes with cruciform sacrifice. The Lamb is the only one found worthy to open the scroll that God holds in his right hand as he sits upon the heavenly throne. No other heavenly or earthly being, and no human being, regardless of their status or power, can open the scroll and unveil the true end of history. The story of Jesus Christ thus undoes all human pretensions to power and honor. There is only one who is worthy of honor, praise, and worship: the Lamb who now sits beside God on the throne.

In the climactic visions of the Apocalypse, following the Seer's description of the destruction of "Babylon," the beast and whore that terrorized and seduced human beings, John describes the Lamb as a groom ready for marriage to a bride clothed in the righteous deeds of the saints (19:7–8). In a subsequent surprise, the bride turns out to be the heavenly Jerusalem (21:2, 9–10). The story of Jesus Christ thus culminates in a new heaven and new earth; the Lamb's own body is joined with the heavenly city to form a perfect dwelling for God with human beings, a habitation that runs beyond the limits of human language and transcends all the constraints of human space and time.

The Lamb's story thus transcends all the images of violence and terror that fill the pages of Revelation. Those who revel in this story's images of destruction and violence visited upon the unrighteous, or those who hope for divine rescue from the suffering of this world, miss the main point: the story of Jesus Christ is about the conquest of terror, violence, and death through the cross and resurrection of Jesus Christ. Those who trust in military might to bring about God's reign, those who gloat over images of divine judgment against those they deem less righteous, and those who put their trust in human wisdom and progress to resolve the world's problems all merely perpetuate the terrors of this world. It is the martyrs—those who worship God and the Lamb and give witness to the Lamb's power with their own blood—who tell with their words and their bodies the truth of God, the story of Jesus Christ.

## II. AN ORAL PERFORMANCE

The introductory lines of Revelation include a blessing upon those who "read aloud" the words of prophecy, as well as those who both hear and keep (obey) what is written (1:3). The closing sentences of the performance balance this blessing with a warning:

> I warn everyone who hears the words of the prophecy of this book: if anyone adds to them, God will add to that person the plagues described in this book; if anyone takes away from the words of the book of this prophecy, God will take away that person's share in the tree of life and in the holy city, which are described in this book. (22:18–19)

John's initial blessing and closing warning, which the Seer intends to be taken with utmost seriousness, highlight the oral, performative, and holistic character of the Apocalypse. The Seer meant for the Revelation to be read aloud in the worshiping (probably eucharistic) assemblies of the early Christians, that is, to be performed as a whole and to be heard by gathered communities of believers.[9] While this claim may not startle, it has profound implications for the way we experience and make sense of the Apocalypse. The oral performance of Revelation within and as part of the ritual life of a community produces an experience fundamentally different from reading the Apocalypse as most of us have: in bits and pieces, silently, and by ourselves. No other New Testament document has suffered more distortion and abuse under the regime of modern, text-based reading strategies than John's Apocalypse. And probably no other New Testament document, when misappropriated under such regimes, has more potential for engendering suffering. As Eugene Peterson pointed out over thirty years ago, wrenching Revelation from its roots in oral media, into the foreign atmosphere of literary texts and the kinds of interpretive operations we have come to impose on the written word, has profound cultural and interpretive consequences:

> The literary medium . . . separates the event from my experience of it. Furthermore, it fragments the event itself by phonetically separating it into individual words. Events come to be experienced in linear fashion. Life is fragmented into pieces. A person no longer lives with his whole sensorium in operation. The senses are suppressed and atrophy as the medium of the written word dominates the learning life.[10]

Cultures that are primarily oriented toward texts rather than oral communication tend to perceive the written word as more authoritative than oral communication and will turn to authoritative texts to affirm dogma and measure deviance. They are also more likely to develop sharply differentiated and polemical interpretive approaches to authoritative texts. As Catherine Bell notes, "In comparison to oral societies, therefore, change in literate societies is much more apt to be deliberate, debated, ridden with factions, explosive, and concerned with fundamentals"[11] (an apt description of much Protestant biblical interpretation!). The shift in the West from oral culture to predominantly literate, text-based culture coincided with shifts toward more linear patterns of logic and linear ways of reckoning time. All of this has contributed to the tendency among modern readers to seek to render the biblical texts, including Revelation, in abstract and propositional terms, and to impose linear notions of time on the Seer's eschatological imagination. The result has been a fixation, especially among those who affirm that the Bible must be read "literally," on timetables and decoding tactics as the appropriate interpretive frames through which to approach the Apocalypse. Such approaches unwittingly impose on Revelation interpretive agendas and strategies that are alien to the world in which and for which the Seer wrote. And when such approaches are matched with theological triumphalism, the Apocalypse is no longer read as the story of the Lamb who was slain, but as the victory of those who purport to hold the correct road map. In this frame, Revelation becomes a text of terror rather than a performance designed to liberate humankind from terror.

Scholarship is increasingly aware, however, that the biblical documents were produced in cultures that, unlike our own, did not rely on print media as the primary mode of communication. While the Christian Scriptures have been passed down in written form, the vast majority of the faithful during the history of Christianity would have experienced the Scriptures in oral/aural rather than textual form.[12] While literacy is closely associated in modern experience with the image of a solitary reader, oral cultures tend to be more holistic and communally oriented, producing "intensely participatory societies, with all the senses heightened and matured by constant use."[13] Oral people "know" what they hear. The word used in the New Testament for "reading" literally means "to know again," that is, to recognize the written characters used to transcribe what was originally heard.

The audiences that first heard performances of John's Apocalypse were well trained and richly experienced in making sense of sophisticated, subtle, and complex oral presentations, especially stories. While only a small percentage of ancient people were "literate" (able to read and write texts), nearly everyone was "auraliterate," that is, practiced in the arts of hearing something read aloud, and "oraliterate," able to recall and recite oral performances.[14] The oral performances they heard, which included the Gospels and the letters of Paul as well as sermons, were meant to shape the identities and practices of whole communities. They did so by appealing to the whole person, to physical senses, intellect, emotions, experience, and custom.

More than any other New Testament document, Revelation works on the range of human feeling and senses. The Apocalypse invokes fear, joy, patience, endurance, dread, and hope. It is the noisiest book in the New Testament.[15] Both sounds—voices, thunder, songs—and silence are important in the visions John recounts, as are visual imagination of composite beasts and people and the senses of touch, smell, and taste. It is significant that attempts to render these sensory experiences literally or pictorially typically fail miserably. Images of a slain Lamb, with seven horns and seven eyes (5:6), or of a "sea of glass mingled with fire" (15:2), or even of a city/bride that is perfectly four-square, built of jasper, pure gold, and every kind of jewel (21:2, 15–21) do not really work well as visual representations, but in orally mediated imagination they are powerful indeed.

In predominantly oral cultures, sounded words carry powers to bless, to curse, to transform, to call worlds into being—to make real what we in text-based cultures experience merely as words on a page. As a consequence, the focus of our attention ought to be not so much on *what* Revelation means as *how* it means and persuades.[16] Just as the discourse of Revelation cannot be captured in visual imagery, it also cannot be adequately represented in conceptual, propositional language,[17] for it is meant to evoke imaginative participation—a different kind of knowledge than one gains when reading ideas on a page.[18] For the early Christians, performance of Revelation was itself an event, "a movement in time, completely lacking the thing-like repose of the written or printed word."[19] In short, as an oral performance, the Apocalypse generates an array of experiences and reactions, not merely in order to fashion ideas and convictions but to transform both performer and audience and the social spaces they inhabit.

Revelation is not meant for silent reading but for public performance, not for textual or exegetical dissection but for performance as a whole. It is meant to be heard, that is, experienced and kept, thereby transforming its auditors into faithful witnesses to the slain Lamb who now reigns in heaven with God.

## III. WORSHIP, RITUAL, AND RESISTANCE TO THE MYTHS AND PRACTICES OF EMPIRE

The recognition that the Apocalypse was meant to be performed in the worshiping assemblies of the early church is closely related to its critical and creative engagement with myth and ritual. In the imperial cult, myth and ritual worked together virtually as a seamless whole to invoke and maintain the visions of reality and social practices that supported the empire. The imperial cults, which focused on the worship of the emperor and his family, drew upon prevailing stories about the mythic origins of the world, stories filled with violence and conflict embracing both human and divine realms. In Greco-Roman thought, the violence of this world mirrored that of the divine world. But the imperial dynasty also represented itself as the embodiment of a "new world order." Caesar was hailed as "savior" (*sōtēr*), a god among humans, whose birth marked the beginning of the good news (*euangelia*, gospel) for the cosmos.[20] The court poet Virgil celebrated the reign of Augustus (and his successors) as a "dominion without end," an age of peace, faith (*pistis*), and sustained righteousness (or justice).[21] This new order united cosmogony with eschatology, representing Roman rule as both the culmination of ancient origins and the realization of divine will, purpose, and order within history.

The imperial cult represented itself ritually throughout the social structures and spatial patterns of everyday life. Even in the cities of Asia to which the Apocalypse is addressed, temple structures dedicated to the emperor and members of the imperial family reminded citizens of the reality of Roman rule. Imperial cult activity also took place in civic institutions such as gymnasia and theaters, and even within local households. Steven Friesen claims that "no other symbolic system had such a range of effective meaning."[22] By means of the skillful employment of myth and ritual, the imperial cult thus established a comprehensive and pervasive mythological and religious framework that supported and affirmed Roman domination, even justifying and idealizing the exploitation, violence, and terror of the imperial order.

It was necessary for the first Christians, as they proclaimed the good news of Jesus Christ and established communities of faith across the Mediterranean basin, to contest this comprehensive system of imperial myth and ritual in every way they could. No other New Testament document so deftly uses mythic reinvention and ritual performance to challenge imperial myth and practice than Revelation. Because many rich discussions of the ways the Seer develops mythic alternatives to the empire can be found in the literature on Revelation,[23] I will briefly develop but one example, then turn to a more extended discussion of Revelation and ritual.

The Apocalypse is riddled with the language and imagery of ancient Near Eastern and Roman myth but most prominently with the combat myths that depicted the defeat of chaos by a heroic warrior. In imperial expressions of this myth, it was Caesar who embodied the role of the divine warrior. John's depiction of the victorious Christ as the slaughtered lamb not only displaces the imperial myth of Caesar as divine with a more powerful alternative, but it disrupts the conventional notions of power that legitimated Roman systems of domination. Still more important is the fact that John depicts Jesus in the role of divine warrior (cf. 19:11–16) without having him exercise violence to bring true peace. In rich irony, Satan is defeated not by military violence but by the blood of the Lamb and by the word of the martyrs' testimony (12:11).

As the combat myth is developed in Revelation, the true nature of imperial power is unmasked: the seductive power exercised by the empire does not bring peace and order but violence, terror, and death. John associates the empire alternately with a dragon, the beast from the sea, a harlot, and Babylon, the city of Israel's captivity—all images that incorporate seduction and violence. But as the story of Jesus Christ progresses during the performance of the Apocalypse, the beast meets its end at the hands of the Lamb, and the whore/Babylon is reduced to smoke. The vindication of the Lamb in the final visions of the performance brings the end of violence itself. The followers of the Lamb never take up arms themselves but offer resistance by their prayers and worship (e.g., 8:3–5). Even when Christ is depicted as a warrior on a white horse in 19:11–21, the "weapons" he wields are his own blood and "the sword of his mouth." It is not the divine exercise of violence that brings the empire to its end but the power of the resurrected Lamb, the living Word that names and evokes the reality of God's new creation.

It would not have been possible for the Christian movement to survive and flourish in this context, however, merely by the proclamation of the gospel alone, nor merely by challenging the myths of the empire on an intellectual or ideological level. John's critical engagement with empire is not merely a contest of ideas but comes to expression also in its use of many of the features of ritual. Scholars have long been aware of the many references to and images of worship in the Apocalypse, as well as the probable ritual setting in which the Apocalypse was meant to be performed. The language and images of worship frame and structure the whole story (4:2–11; 5:8–14; 7:9–17; 11:15–18; 13:1–15; 14:1–5; 15:2–4; 19:1–8). The Seer's visions take place in the Spirit on the Lord's Day (1:10), and shift repeatedly between the terror and violence of the earthly realm and the worship that is simultaneously taking place in the presence of God and the Lamb. Worship is the defining activity to which John's visions call the community.[24] The Seer uses the Psalms—especially Psalms 95–100, which celebrate the victory and enthronement of the divine warrior over all the gods of the nations—as the primary source for the form and content of the worship scenes in Revelation.[25] But the Seer also reveals that the conquering warrior is really the Lamb who was slain, thereby dramatically and provocatively recasting the mythic understandings associated with the image of the divine warrior throughout the ancient world.[26] The Seer's startling vision of a triumphant Lamb and warrior whose weapons are his own blood and the sword of his mouth would also have functioned powerfully in conjunction with the ritual of the Lord's Supper in the early Christian assemblies.[27]

Revelation's setting in the ritual life of the early Christian assemblies, its descriptions of heavenly worship, and its calls to the martyrs and saints to join their worship to that of the heavenly host do not, however, begin to exhaust the ritual repertoire at work in the Apocalypse. In addition to these references to ritual activity, the Apocalypse includes an array of intrinsic factors that mimic the characteristics and functions of ritual itself. Revelation thus not only describes and calls for worship but itself embodies the ritual elements that would draw its performers and audiences out of empire and into the reign of the Lamb. As an oral performance, the Apocalypse itself embodies many of the primary characteristics of ritual. In her survey of the main genres of ritual, ritual theorist Catherine Bell includes "rites of passage" (e.g., baptisms, weddings, funerals); "calendrical and commemorative rites" (e.g., eucharist, Christmas, Thanksgiving); "rites of exchange and communion" (e.g., sacrifice, gift giving, prayer); "rites that address affliction" (e.g., exorcisms, healings, the Ghost Dance); rites of "feasting, fasting, and festival" (e.g., carnival, eucharist, family meals); and "political rites" (e.g., coronations, parades, the "pledge of allegiance").[28] Remarkably, John's Apocalypse includes elements that correspond with each of these ritual genres. In what follows I draw out the connections briefly for political rites; rites of "feasting, fasting, and festival"; and calendrical and commemorative rites, then a bit more elaborately for rites of affliction, rites of exchange and communion, and rites of passage.

While it mimics ceremonies associated with the Roman imperial cult,[29] as a whole the Apocalypse focuses on the coronation of Jesus/the Lamb/the divine warrior, and aims to associate divine power with the lordship of Jesus Christ, thereby serving the interests of "political ritual." An association with "feasting, fasting, and festival" is also clear: as already noted, there is wide agreement that Revelation was meant to be performed in the context of the eucharistic assemblies of the early Christians and includes among its culminating images the vision of the wedding feast of the Lamb (19:9). While Revelation does not so clearly manifest the characteristics of calendrical rites, which provide socially meaningful definitions of the passage of time and mark recurrent orders, it does impose a new order on time itself and commemorates the definitive rupture in human time that Christ's death and resurrection accomplish, while also "reminding" the hearers of what is to come.[30]

Rites of affliction often involve "elements of rebellion against social restraints" and "may even institutionalize methods of inverting, reversing, or undermining other dimensions of the religious and social order."[31] The Seer's burlesque of the powers of the empire—that is, the depiction of Roman grandeur as beasts, whore, and destroyed city—works toward a similar subversion of the dominant order. Revelation also seeks to use its visions of both the heavenly realm and the destruction of the earthly powers to redress the suffering of the saints. John Gager has argued that the Seer structures the visions in order to accomplish the "mythological enactment" of the future in the present, that is, not merely to console the afflicted but already to transform their perception of reality.[32] In short, Revelation embodies the functions of a ritual of affliction.

Rites of exchange and communion typically seek to mediate the complexity of divine/human relationships, often through offerings or sacrifices that anticipate something in return, such as health, long life, or good crops. John's visions in themselves already mediate between the human and divine realms, but rather than seeking to manipulate the divine by means of sacrifice, for example, Revelation persistently sets forth the image of Christ as the sacrificial victim who mediates divine power from heaven into the human realm. The whole performance, then, functions as rite of exchange and communion, initiated from the divine realm and embodied in the human realm through the eucharistic worship of the assembled community.

Finally, while Revelation does not celebrate a typical "rite of passage" moment, such as birth, death, or marriage, it nonetheless accomplishes passage from one world to another. Rites of passage move participants from one social group and identity into a stage with no identity and finally to a new social group that confers a new identity.[33] Revelation employs spatial and temporal dislocations,[34] structural disorientation,[35] visionary images, and the affectation of a "biblical" dialect[36] to move its audience from their roles and identities in the world of the Roman Empire to the revealed world that exists in the presence of God and the Lamb and finally to ongoing life of the worshiping community, which endures, resists, and gives witness to the lordship of Christ amidst empire.

The Apocalypse thus draws the worshiping community into temporal and spatial "betwixt- and between-ness," separated from the everyday world, wherein it is possible to nurture a critical perspective on that world.[37] But in this reflexive ritual state, where action and awareness may merge, the audiences may both identify with characters and experiences in the story and also begin to lend their voices to the chants of the worshipers in the narrative.[38] Because it involves participation in a performance, this reflexive ritual transformation entails becoming part of something larger than oneself as well as participation in the construction of a larger order of relationships.[39] And by joining in the performance, the audience-cum-performers indicate functional acceptance of the order of things encoded in the performance.[40] In this way the performance of Revelation also realizes three of the foundational functions of ritual:[41] (1) the fostering and maintenance of community, in which the participants become not merely an aggregate of individuals, but a real body; (2) the integration of thought and action, perception and practice, and emotion and reflection, which lends the experience a holistic power; and (3) the sacralization of the community's ordering of reality, confirmed, in this case, in the realization of communion with the Lamb and with God who dwells with the saints in the new Jerusalem.

It is these features that distinguish the performance of Revelation from mere readings of it. Just as reading a musical score is not the same as either hearing it performed or participating in its performance, so also reading Revelation, especially in a text-oriented world, is not the same as joining in its performance. Joining the performance produces a community of martyrs who join their stories and their lives with the story of the living Lamb, a community that witnesses and gives witness to the Lamb's redemptive power, and a community that joins its voice with the heavenly choirs giving praise to the Lamb who alone is worthy. In contrast, to read Revelation as we have learned to do in the modern West inevitably entails both "adding to" and "taking away from" the (performative) words of the book (22:18–19), regardless of the content of our interpretation. Our ways of reading have domesticated and marginalized the Apocalypse, wrought division and sacralized violence, and deprived the book of much of its power to challenge, to transform, and to generate communities of witness and resistance.

The Apocalypse begins with a blessing upon those who read aloud (perform) and who hear and keep what is written in it (1:3), and it ends with a severe warning to those who add to or take away from its words of prophecy (22:18–19). The history of the use and abuse of this book should lead us to take this blessing and this warning seriously. The words of the Apocalypse are alive in the world all around us, suspended—as are we in the church—between violence and peace, hope and despair, between the powers of this world and the reign of the Lamb, between blessing and curse. May we learn again what it means to read aloud, to hear, and to keep the words of this prophecy.

## NOTES

1. Among the many books that explore the relations between terror, violence, and religion, see especially Bruce Lincoln, *Holy Terrors: Thinking about Religion after September 11* (Chicago: University of Chicago Press, 2003); Lee Griffith, *The War on Terrorism and the Terror of God* (Grand Rapids: Wm. B. Eerdmans Publishing Co., 2002); Mark Juergensmeyer, *Terror in the Mind of God: The Global Rise of Religious Violence* (Berkeley: University of California Press, 2000); Marc Gopin, *Between Eden and Armageddon: The Future of World Religions, Violence, and Peacemaking* (Oxford and New York: Oxford University Press, 2000); Oliver McTernan, *Violence in God's Name: Religion in an Age of Conflict* (Maryknoll, N.Y.: Orbis Books, 2003).
2. David Gates, "Religion: The Pop Prophets," *Newsweek*, May 24, 2004. For a brief, accessible analysis of Revelation in popular culture, see Jon Paulien, "The Lion/Lamb King: Reading the Apocalypse from Popular Culture," in *Reading the Book of Revelation: A Resource for Students*, ed. David L. Barr (Atlanta: Society of Biblical Literature, 2003), 151–61.
3. Ron Powers, "The Apocalypse of Adolescence," *The Atlantic Monthly* 289, no. 3 (March 2002): 68–69. One educator describes the juvenile prisoners with whom he works within Vermont's Department of Corrections as follows: "They're a community of believers, in a way. They come from all kinds of backgrounds. But what unites them are these apocalyptic suspicions that they have. They think and act as though it's an extremely late hour in the day, and nothing much matters anymore. Most of them see themselves as frustrated travelers. Solitary wayfarers. They've done things that have broken them off from their past and set off on the open road. Eventually they got arrested. This may be hard for some people to swallow, I guess, but they talk about their crimes almost as if they were acts of faith. Maybe these kids themselves wouldn't use those words. But the things they've done, on some level, strike me as almost ecstatic attempts to vault over the shabby facts of their everyday lives. They haven't read much. But some of them, the more down-and-out ones especially, read the Book of Revelation a lot" (p. 69).
4. Griffith, *The War on Terrorism*, 205.
5. David E. Aune, *Revelation 1–5*, Word 52a (Dallas: Word, 1997), 9–10.
6. David L. Barr, *Tales of the End: A Narrative Commentary on the Book of Revelation* (Santa Rosa, Calif.: Polebridge, 1998), 3.
7. There remains no finer exposition of Paul' s understanding of the cross than Charles Cousar, *A Theology of the Cross: The Death of Jesus in the Pauline Letters*, OBT (Minneapolis: Fortress Press, 1990).
8. Griffith, *The War on Terrorism*, 211.
9. There is now virtual consensus among interpreters that the Apocalypse was created for oral performance in the worship settings of the early church. See especially David Barr, *Tales of the End*; Barr, "The Apocalypse of John as Oral Enactment," *Interpretation* 40 (1986): 252–56; Harry O. Maier, *Apocalypse Recalled: The Book of Revelation after Christendom* (Minneapolis: Fortress Press, 2002), 91–122.
10. Eugene H. Peterson, "Apocalypse: The Medium is the Message," *Theology Today* 26 (1969): 134–35.
11. Catherine Bell, *Ritual: Perspectives and Dimensions* (New York: Oxford University Press, 1997), 204.

12. For discussion of the oral dimensions of Scripture and their implications for interpretation see especially Walter J. Ong, *Orality and Literacy: The Technologizing of the Word* (London and New York: Methuen, 1982); William A. Graham, *Beyond the Written Word: Oral Aspects of Scripture in the History of Religion* (Cambridge: Cambridge University Press, 1987); Susan Niditch, *Oral World and Written Word: Ancient Israelite Literature* (Louisville, Ky.: Westminster John Knox Press, 1996).
13. Peterson, "Apocalypse," 134. Walter Ong (*Orality and Literacy*, 36–57) lists many features that distinguish primary oral cultures from text-based cultures, including strong communal, participatory, agonistic, and present-time orientations. Walter D. Mignolo, *The Darker Side of the Renaissance: Literacy, Territoriality, and Colonization* (Ann Arbor: University of Michigan Press, 1995) carefully and provocatively draws out the cultural and political differences associated with the shift to text-based culture.
14. These distinctions are drawn from Lucretia B. Yaghian, "Ancient Reading," in *The Social Sciences and New Testament Interpretation*, ed. Richard Rohrbaugh (Peabody, Mass.: Hendrickson, 1996), 206–30. See also William V. Harris, *Ancient Literacy* (Cambridge, Mass.: Harvard University Press, 1989); and P. J. J. Botha, "Greco-Roman Literacy as Setting for New Testament Writings," *Neotestamentica* 26, no. 1 (1992): 195–215.
15. Maier, *Apocalypse Recalled*, 91.
16. Ibid., 96.
17. Elizabeth Schüssler-Fiorenza, "Revelation," in *The New Testament and Its Modern Interpreters*, ed. Eldon Jay Epp and George W. MacRae, S. J. (Philadelphia: Fortress Press and Atlanta: Scholars Press, 1989), 417.
18. Allen Dwight Callahan, "The Language of Apocalypse," *Harvard Theological Review* 88, no. 4 (1995): 459.
19. Ong, *Orality and Literacy*, 75.
20. Hubert Cancik, "The End of the World, of History, and of the Individual in Greek and Roman Antiquity," in *The Encyclopedia of Apocalypticism*, vol. 1, *The Origins of Apocalypticism in Judaism and Christianity*, ed. John J. Collins (New York: Continuum, 1998), 99.
21. Virgil, *The Aeneid*, 1.265ff.: "To them [the Romans, the city Rome] no bounds of empire I assign, / Nor term of years to their immortal line" (1.268). For an accessible discussion of the imperial cult see Klaus Wengst, *Pax Romana and the Peace of Jesus Christ*, trans. John Bowden (Philadelphia: Fortress Press, 1987). The definitive treatment of the imperial cult in Asia Minor is S. R. F. Price, *Rituals and Power: The Roman Imperial Cult in Asia Minor* (Cambridge: Cambridge University Press, 1984). With regard to Revelation in particular, see Steven J. Friesen, *Imperial Cults and the Apocalypse of John: Reading Revelation in the Ruins* (Oxford: Oxford University Press, 2001).
22. Friesen, *Imperial Cults*, 126.
23. See, for example, Friesen, *Imperial Cults*, 167–79; Wes Howard-Brook and Anthony Gwyther, *Unveiling Empire: Reading Revelation Then and Now* (Maryknoll, N.Y.: Orbis Books, 1999), 223–35; Adela Yarbro Collins, *Crisis and Catharsis: The Power of the Apocalypse* (Philadelphia: Westminster Press, 1984).
24. Among many treatments of worship in the Apocalypse, see especially David E. Aune, "The Influence of the Roman Imperial Cult Ceremonial on the Apocalypse of John," *Papers of the Chicago Society of Biblical Research* 28 (1983): 5–26; Leonard Thompson, "Cult and Eschatology in the Apocalypse of John," *Jour-*

*nal of Religion* 49 (1969): 330–50; and Thompson, *The Book of Revelation: Apocalypse and Empire* (Oxford: Oxford University Press, 1990).

25. Wes Howard-Brook and Anthony Gwyther, *Unveiling Empire: Reading Revelation Then and Now* (Maryknoll, N.Y.: Orbis Books, 1999), 198.
26. Adela Yarbro Collins, *The Combat Myth and the Book of Revelation* (Missoula, Mont.: Scholars Press, 1976).
27. See especially Barr, *Tales of the End*, 171–75; and Friesen, *Imperial Cults*, 179.
28. Bell, *Ritual: Perspectives and Dimensions*, 93–137.
29. See Aune, "Roman Imperial Cult Ceremonial," 5–26.
30. See the insightful discussions of time in Revelation in Friesen, *Imperial Cults*, 157–61; Maier, *Apocalypse Recalled*, 123–63; and Howard-Brook and Gwyther, *Unveiling Empire*, 123–26.
31. Bell, *Ritual: Perspectives and Dimensions*, 117.
32. John Gager, "The Attainment of Millenial Bliss through Myth," in *Kingdom and Community: The Social World of Early Christianity* (Englewood Cliffs, N.J.: Prentice-Hall, 1975), 49–57.
33. Bell, *Ritual: Perspectives and Dimensions*, 95. Rites of passage were the focus of Arnold van Gennep's and Victor Turner's work as ritual theorists. Turner's work especially has enjoyed much attention among theologians and exegetes. See especially Victor Turner, *The Ritual Process: Structure and Antistructure* (Ithaca, N.Y.: Cornell University Press, 1969). Bobby Alexander offers a very good summary and development of Turner's theories in *Victor Turner Revisited: Ritual as Social Change* (Atlanta: Scholars Press, 1991).
34. See Howard-Brook and Gwyther, *Unveiling Empire*, 126–35; Friesen, *Imperial Cults*, 152–57.
35. See Stanley P. Saunders, "Revelation and Resistance: Narrative, Myth, and Worship in John's Apocalypse," in *Narrative Reading, Narrative Preaching*, 128–29.
36. Ibid., 130–31; also Allen Dwight Callahan, "The Language of Apocalypse," *Harvard Theological Review* 88 (1995): 464–70; Maier, *Apocalypse Recalled*, 108–16.
37. Jean-Pierre Ruiz, "Betwixt and Between on the Lord's Day: Liturgy and the Apocalypse," in *Society of Biblical Literature 1992 Seminar Papers*, ed. Eugene H. Lovering Jr. (Atlanta: Scholars Press, 1992), 665.
38. Maier, *Apocalypse Recalled*, 75–86, esp. 78.
39. Ruiz, "Betwixt and Between," 666; cf. Roy A. Rappaport, *Ritual and Religion in the Making of Humanity* (Cambridge: Cambridge University Press, 1999), 118–19.
40. Rappaport, *Ritual and Religion*, 119.
41. A wide range of diverse practices can be classified under the heading of ritual. Yet there is relative agreement on a basic list of characteristics and functions of rituals. See especially the surveys in Bell, *Ritual: Perspectives and Dimensions*, 138–69; and Rappaport, *Ritual and Religion*, 23–68.

# 13

# Concluding Reflections

*Walter Brueggemann*

I have been pondering the verb *shake*. Already in 1959, Brevard Childs showed that the Hebrew term for *shake* (*ra'aš*) was an apocalyptic term.[1] The term refers characteristically to deep world upheaval, articulated in poetry and wrought by God. Thus our topic is about the God-caused upheaval that is happening among us whereby a new creation is being wrought by God.

Thus the shaking is all God's work. I wish, however, to consider the derivative, subordinate, proximate "shaking" among us for which we have responsibility, a responsibility that concerns the *reception of God's shaking* through our own shaking. During these days, it has occurred to me that Scripture is a "shaker" as testimony to God when it is not domesticated by either historical criticism or doctrinal closure. I refer to Scripture à la Barth, "the Strange New World within the Bible," a strangeness that we are always wanting to make familiar and congenial. It follows, moreover, that those who interpret Scripture have a *shaking role* congruent with *God's shaking*, for it is the work of Scripture to deconstruct, destabilize, and subvert what is settled . . . in order that we may receive God's newness.

Charlie Cousar and I have been fortunate to be surrounded by colleagues who have been supportive conversation partners over time. I am glad to express thanks—for both Charlie and me—to those who have generously contributed to this volume.

I wish first to consider the contributions that were delivered as part of the Colloquium around the theme of Scripture as *proximate agent of shaking*.

David Petersen shows, I believe, that the good news of the Genesis ancestral narratives is that the "gospel beforehand" can be carried by a dysfunctional family. Because almost everyone lives in something of a dysfunctional family that is good news indeed. I propose that the way in which the ancestral narratives "shake" is to notice the profound tension between the plot line of real families engaged in all manner of typical disreputable behavior, on the one hand, and, on the other hand, the cleaned-up, canonical version of Father Abraham and Father Jacob who emerge in the sixth-century prophets and who eventually become one-dimensional figures "by faith" in Hebrews 11. (I note in passing that, in Hebrews 11:12, Abraham is said to be "him as good as dead." I heard a feminist interpreter say that that phrasing for Abraham must surely have been written by a woman.) The gap between *typical disreputable behavior* and *the canonical version* is unbridgeable in my judgment, even though so-called "canonical" reading proposes that good theological themes will completely trump the specificity of the text and the specificity of real life.

The church in its candor and attentiveness permits that deep tension to shake every family settlement, every sure conviction of providence, and every guarantee of the future. The outcome of such candor and attentiveness is to see that the newness from God is not flatly given but is always a vigorously disputatious negotiation through which new life comes. This is modest shaking in the midst of the great apocalyptic shaking of God, to be sure, but it is clearly shaking wherein the newness of God "invades" the dailyness of cunning and anxiety. The capacity to have these texts shake toward newness requires that we attend to their detail and nuance, which must not be swept away by large, theological generalizations.

Patrick Miller stands in a long line of "derivative Lutherans" from Martin himself who famously said of the first commandment, "That which the heart desires and relies upon, that properly is thy God." (I refer to "derivative Lutherans" because during the Colloquium Luther was called a "proto-Calvinist"; I believe that the equation can work in either direction. Surely Calvin is derivative in decisive ways from Luther.) Miller exposits the uncompromising command of obedience to God as pertains to the public spheres of economics and politics. It is clear, given our divided hearts, that the commands themselves are instruments of shaking, for they shake us away from our dividedness in an invitation to "will one thing." Miller rightly observes that the command is *gospel*, the declaration that the world is other than we had imagined.

The shaking quality of the commands, however, is even more destabilizing, as Miller well knows, when we remember that, in the early traditions, the Sinai Pericope of Exod. 19–24 is followed promptly by Exod. 32, the narrative of the golden calf. In that episode Aaron has systematically violated the first commandment in order to produce other gods. Not surprisingly, the God of the first commandment is properly enraged at this breach of obedience by Aaron and is prepared to act as a terminator.

But notice that YHWH will commit such an act only if YHWH can do so apart from Moses, for Moses is a check on YHWH's rage: "Now let me alone, that my wrath may burn" (Exod. 32:10). And then Moses speaks beginning in verse 11. He addresses YHWH and makes a powerful appeal to YHWH not to act in rage. Moses invokes the ancestors of Genesis and appeals to YHWH's vanity. For the moment, Moses' petition causes YHWH to pause and to defer the enactment of rage.

Now what interests us in this narrative is that Moses has enough freedom and *hutzpah* to be in the face of the God of the first commandment; Moses takes initiative to cause YHWH to act as YHWH had not intended. This is a staggering dialogic grid of faith, one that is characteristic of the Bible as with Abraham (Gen. 18), Jeremiah, and Job. The God of the first commandment is no absolute monarch who functions by flat fiat in one-way communication. Rather, this God who has immense freedom as sovereign, as Miller urges, is one who relates to a subject who also has freedom and who engages in free dialogue with the God of the first commandment. By and large, popular understandings of biblical monotheism know nothing of this; consequently, flights of shrill moralism from the right or the left depend on a distortion of this covenantal God. The first commandment is testimony to new creation in which *mutuality between incommensurate partners* is the nature of the case. Such a command—and such a commander—shake both *one-dimensional absolutism* and its counterpoint, *unfettered autonomy*. The shaking toward newness thus is a shaking toward *dialogic interaction* that does not mock sovereignty. This is, however, no generic notion of sovereignty—the kind many Calvinists often voice—but a sovereignty peculiar to the community of the Father, Son, and Spirit, a peculiar sovereignty that reimagines all forms of authority and power, political and economic, in terms of the new creation.

As Louis Stulman shows, with reference to Jer. 4:23–26, the book of Jeremiah shakes what is old and settled in Jerusalem—temple, king, city. Of course! What is remarkable, as Stulman also shows so well, is that it is not only "plucking up and tearing down" that shakes. It is even more poignant that hope—"building and planting"—shakes, subverts, and destabilizes, because the God who makes futures does not make them according to our hopes. So I offer three reflections on hope that shakes in Jeremiah:

1. The familiar text of the new covenant in 31:31–34 turns out to be a more quintessentially Jewish text than we had noticed. Our long misreading of the epistle to the Romans has led us to image a "gospel" that is beyond "law." New covenant hope, however, is *Torah hope*, the invitation to come under obedience to the detail of Sinai. This submission to Sinai is a point voiced by Jesus, of course, when he said, "You have heard it said of old but I say to you" (Matt. 5:21–48). Thus hope is constituted in a *recovery of discipline* so pervasive that all

will come under Torah "from youngest to oldest." The point of the recovery of discipline has enormous implications for baptism.

2. As Judaism came to understand, the future depends upon Cyrus the Gentile. In Jer. 50:9 it is promised that God will "stir up" Cyrus; this point is grasped in Isa. 45:1 wherein Cyrus is designated as "the Messiah" and, at the end of Chronicles, the last two verses of the Hebrew Bible in 2 Chr. 36:22–23. In the latter text, Cyrus is the gate of hope for all futures in Judaism. Hope's agent here is not one of "us" or one congenial to "us," but one alien to us, unwelcome, as unwelcome as was Jesus in Nazareth. And therefore we must watch for the strange bringers of hope whom God will yet designate.

3. I have come to think that the recovery of the Oracles Against the Nations is urgent in our ministerial task. The reason that I think these texts are crucial is that we in the United States do not read the biblical text "as Israel." Rather, we read the text "as Babylonians," as the last superpower that has been for a time blessed by God. In the tradition of Jeremiah, Babylon and Nebuchadnezzar are for a time "the servant of YHWH" but then that role is forfeited (see Jer. 25:9; 27:6). It is interesting to imagine the leader of the last standing superpower being for a time "the servant of YHWH," but only for a time. Toward the end of the book of Jeremiah in 51:59–64, it is imagined that the last superpower will sink like a rock sinks into the Euphrates . . . of all rivers, the one in Baghdad! "Blup, blup." Imagine how that text of hope is read in Cuba or Latvia or Tibet. And we of the United States read that the future depends upon the "blup, blup, blup" of world power.

On three counts and many more, hope in the tradition of Jeremiah "shakes":

1. restored Torah discipline;
2. rescue by a *goi* agent;
3. the sinking of superpower that opens a world of new possibility.

Along with these three presentations, Carol Newsom was invited to present a paper at the Colloquium but was unable to do so. I am delighted that she has contributed nevertheless to this collection. Newsom's imagined exchange between Eve and Enoch evidences the rich resources for fresh and faithful moral imagination. In our own anxious contexts of "monsters" and "giants," we do well to note from these materials that our contemporary issues are in fact very old and very deep. What we have called "fundamental myths" are, in fact, strategies for waiting and watching worlds end and new worlds emerge. Our current "shaking" invites us to reengage these testimonies on a very large screen of meaning and possibility.

I have been greatly privileged to have two colleagues in Old Testament studies at Columbia Seminary who are engaged powerfully with the texts. Beyond that, moreover, in our area of Old Testament studies we have been able